Optimizing Network Performance with Content Switching

Server, Firewall, and Cache Load Balancing

Prentice Hall PTR Series in
Computer Networking and Distributed Systems
Radia Perlman, Series Editor

Optimizing Network Performance with Content Switching

Server, Firewall, and Cache Load Balancing

Matthew Syme
Philip Goldie

PRENTICE
HALL
PTR

PRENTICE HALL
Professional Technical Reference
Upper Saddle River, New Jersey 07458
www.phptr.com

Library of Congress Cataloging-in-Publication Data

Syme, Matthew
    Optimizing network performance with content switching: server, firewall, and cache load
balancing / Matthew Syme, Philip Goldie.
        p. cm. -- (Prentice Hall series in computer networking and distributed systems)
    Includes index.
    ISBN 0-13-101468-4
    1. Network performance (Telecommunication) 2. Computer networks--Workload. 3.
Telecommunication--Switching systems. I. Goldie, Philip. II. Title. III. Series.
    TK5105.5.S955 2003
    004.6--dc21

                                                                  2003050878

Editorial/Production Supervision: *Techne Group*
Executive Editor: *Mary Franz*
Editorial Assistant: *Noreen Regina*
Development Editor: *Jennifer Blackwell*
Marketing Manager: *Dan DePasquale*
Manufacturing Buyer: *Maura Zaldivar*
Cover Design Director: *Jerry Votta*
Full-Service Production Manager: *Anne R. Garcia*

© 2004 Pearson Education, Inc.
Publishing as Prentice Hall Professional Technical Reference
Upper Saddle River, NJ 07458

Prentice Hall PTR offers excellent discounts on this book when ordered in quantity for bulk purchases or special sales. For more information, please contact: U.S. Corporate and Government Sales, 1-800-382-3419, corpsales@pearsontechgroup.com. For sales outside of the U.S., please contact: International Sales, 1-317-581-3793, international@pearsontechgroup.com.

Company and product names mentioned herein are the trademarks or registered trademarks of their respective owners.

Printed in the United States of America

First Printing

ISBN 0-13-101468-4

Pearson Education Ltd.
Pearson Education Australia PTY, Limited
Pearson Education Singapore, Pte. Ltd.
Pearson Education North Asia Ltd.
Pearson Education Canada, Ltd.
Pearson Educación de Mexico, S.A. de C.V.
Pearson Education—Japan
Pearson Education Malaysia, Pte. Ltd.

About Prentice Hall Professional Technical Reference

With origins reaching back to the industry's first computer science publishing program in the 1960s, and formally launched as its own imprint in 1986, Prentice Hall Professional Technical Reference (PH PTR) has developed into the leading provider of technical books in the world today. Our editors now publish over 200 books annually, authored by leaders in the fields of computing, engineering, and business.

Our roots are firmly planted in the soil that gave rise to the technical revolution. Our bookshelf contains many of the industry's computing and engineering classics: Kernighan and Ritchie's *C Programming Language*, Nemeth's *UNIX System Adminstration Handbook*, Horstmann's *Core Java*, and Johnson's *High-Speed Digital Design*.

PH PTR acknowledges its auspicious beginnings while it looks to the future for inspiration. We continue to evolve and break new ground in publishing by providing today's professionals with tomorrow's solutions.

PRENTICE
HALL
PTR

Contents

Chapter 2

Understanding Layer 2, 3, and 4 Protocols   13

Chapter 3

Chapter 6

Content-Aware Server Load Balancing   109

Chapter 9

Firewall and VPN Load Balancing   213

Chapter 10

The Architecture of a Content Switch   247

Preface

There are not many books written about content switching and all the associated applications that make up this exciting technology. The reason for this we believe is twofold. First, content networking is a huge discipline with many different areas ranging from switching to caching and content routing, and this can often be seen as confusing. Second, there is a perceived shortage of skills in the marketplace.

While content networking does cover many areas, they are all still inextricably linked with the existing technologies of today. They might have dedicated hardware, more feature-rich software, and allow for unconventional configurations, but ultimately they come back to existing technology with which we are all familiar.

On the skills and understanding front there is no shortage or lack of knowledge. Content networking is merely an extension to those existing skills we have developed. Taking the time to dig deeper into the workings of a content switch and understanding how the applications work provides the foundation on which we can build our knowledge. Using our existing knowledge, however, is key to content networking.

This book does not try to explain every aspect associated with content networking as a whole, but rather it covers what is called *content switching* and discusses the associated applications.

The Audience and Purpose of This Book

The purpose of this book is to eliminate the confusion and conflicting views about this expanding topic and ensure that the fundamental theory and technologies are presented in a clear and concise manner. This is done in a two-tier approach.

Managers, sales personnel, and executive-level individuals who require an overall understanding of this new breed of networking will be able to get an introductory overview of the topics involved. This will provide them with insight into the benefits and pitfalls of each application; why the need for such things as Secure Sockets Layer (SSL) offload, firewall load balancing, Web cache redirection, and so forth is a definite requirement for technology scaling; and the ability to understand the concepts of a technology that is continually changing. In short, this book will provide the individual with the basics of content switching, allowing them to make informed decisions in their day-to-day tasks and allow the sales and marketing personnel the ability to better position and sell these products.

For the engineering force, this book will provide a comprehensive explanation of the inner workings of content switching, allowing them to build on their Layer 2 and Layer 3 skills. A good understanding of Layer 2 and Layer 3 functionality will ensure that the individual benefits from the advanced topics in this book. These include TCP/IP flows and sessions, delayed binding, URL/URI parsing, cookie persistence, server health checking, and load-balancing metrics, among others. Any engineers exposed to these technologies will find that the material allows them to fully understand the core concepts and functionality behind the applications discussed, giving them a better understanding of what is happening "under the hood."

Case Studies

As we progress through this book we will discuss fictitious case studies that revolve around a company called Foocorp, Inc. Foocorp, Inc. is a typical large company. They have thousands of employees, located in the head office and also in remote branches. The employees need access to internal applications and systems. Foocorp has also extended its network to include access from its partners and customers over an extranet. Foocorp also has an online presence for e-commerce.

We will explain the benefits, the design, and the issues faced by Foocorp Inc. associated with each of the major chapters.

Explanation of Artwork

To clarify what the artwork represents, we now describe in a little more detail what each is capable of. This can be used as a reference when reading the chapters.

User

This is a computer of some sort. It is not specific to any operating system and can represent a single user or many thousands. It will typically have a TCP/IP address.

R (Router)

A Layer 3 router from any vendor running routing code of some sort. This can be any routing protocol and would typically have connectivity to the Internet.

Internet (Internet Cloud)

This symbol is used to represent a public or private network that could include an intranet or an extranet. Typically, routers, switches, and any other connectivity equipment, such as Frame Relay, ATM, and so forth, may be present here.

Layer 2 Switch

This represents any Layer 2 switch and could have many 10/100/1000 Ethernet ports. This switch is vendor independent and provides cost-effective connectivity.

Cache

While there are dedicated caching appliances, this could be caching software running on a PC platform.

Firewall

Again, this could be a dedicated firewall that is part of a large security deployment, or, could be a router with access control lists (ACLs) for security. Typically, it will be a Layer 3 device although Layer 2 (bridging) firewalls are not uncommon.

SSL (SSL Offload Device)

A device dedicated to handling SSL traffic.

CS (Content Switch)

This represents a Layer 4 to 7 switch. All of the functionality and features discussed in this book will be available within this device.

Server

This could be a single server or many hundreds of servers. These servers are not operating-system specific. If it can be connected to an IP-based network, it will typically be able to be load balanced.

About the Technical Reviewers

Ray d'Urso has over 25 years of experience in the voice and data networking industry. During this time he has worked on many major projects in London where he has leveraged his experience to ensure their success. He is currently Head of Technical Services for a large multi national financial organization.

Dave Weal has been working in Data Networks for 15 years. During that time, he has designed, implemented, and troubleshot networks involving technologies as diverse as X.25, ATM, Frame Relay, Token Ring, and, of course, Ethernet and TCP/IP.

Most recently, his role has been that of a solutions consultant at Nortel Networks, advising major Enterprise customers on both technology issues and product solutions to mission-critical network requirements.

Scott Reeves has been working in data networks since 1989, across a broad spectrum of WAN and LAN technologies, working for system integrators and Ethernet, Token Ring, and ATM vendors.

More recently, his role has been that of European Development Prime for content networking products, joining Nortel Networks through the acquisition of Alteon WebSystems, a pioneer in the content switching arena.

Acknowledgments

Writing your first book is a daunting and challenging experience, and now is the time to recognize that we did not do this alone. We would like to thank the technical reviewers—Ray d'Urso, David Weal, and Scott Reeves—for their invaluable technical and literary input. Thanks also to Mary Franz and her team at Prentice Hall for their interest, encouragement, and guidance over the past 12 months. While we have kept this book as an independent view of the content switching space, we are also both indebted to the efforts of those people behind the scenes at Alteon WebSystems and Nortel Networks who create the tools we use.

I would like to thank my family and friends, all of whom have offered love and encouragement not only during the task of writing this book, but in everything I do. This is my time to say thank you for all your love and support. All my love to Fleur, who put up with many long weeks and months of tapping keys and a furrowed brow—thanks.

Philip Goldie, December 2002

During my career I have come across many individuals who have assisted and helped me learn and better myself—to those people I say thank you. I hope I have been able to provide something back to others who have worked with me over the years. I would like to thank Ray d'Urso who has had significant influence in my learning and made me look at problems from outside the square. It has been a privilege to have him review this book. Also to my family for their love and support over the years, and in particular, Debra, Jessica, and Cameron for hanging in there during those long evenings. To all, I say thank you.

Matthew Syme, December 2002

Summary

While writing a book on a topic that is new and exciting and one that allows even the most seasoned professional to experience some sort of satisfaction after completing a difficult configuration or finally solving an impossible problem, we have tried to ensure that we have covered the technical aspects, including the advantages and disadvantages of content switching, without discussing vendor-specific configurations and CLI commands, and so forth. Our aim throughout has been to discuss the power and benefits of this technology. While this is a technology with which we are proud to be associated, it does not solve all problems and has many areas that need attention and better design and planning. Regardless, content switching opens a whole new area that allows us to extend our knowledge, enhance our skills, and, hopefully, in the process have some fun. We hope that you find this book a useful addition to your reference library.

1

Introduction to Content Switching

Content switching, server load balancing, intelligent switching, Layer 4 switching, session switching, application switching. Like any maturing technology, no one name has been accepted to encompass all that content switching covers. We will use the term *content switching* throughout this book, as it appears to be the most commonly used method by which to express this technology. However, please understand that even this might change depending on what your requirements are.

Therefore, before we begin our journey through the workings and terminology of content switching, we should first pause and understand where and how this technology evolved.

Without a doubt, the roots of content switching can be tied directly to the growth of the Internet in the late 1990s, where Ethernet and TCP/IP became the king of the corporate networks. Suddenly, network manufacturers were not focusing their research and development staff on Token Ring, ATM, or FDDI, or protocols such as IPX, SNA, or NetBIOS, but rather on how to leverage this new and growing phenomenon that was being driven by the unilateral acceptance of TCP/IP and Ethernet across the globe.

The Evolution of Layer 2 and Layer 3 Networks

Networking had come a long way by the mid to late 1990s, and routing at Layer 3 was beginning to become an application that could be moved to the edge of the network or to the wiring closet, enabling networks to be more easily managed by grouping smaller quantities of devices together in a single subnet. Companies, such as Wellfleet and Cisco Systems were the key players in the routing arena and had been able to leverage the development of Layer 2 switches, which in turn allowed the amalgamation of Layer 2, and Layer 3 functionality on the same device. The use of virtual LAN (VLAN) technology made it even easier for network administrators to deploy networks around their campuses with relative ease. Users within a department could be grouped together in one subnet allowing everyone local access. Security rules and policies could be implemented on a VLAN basis if required. By using VLANs, no longer were users forced to change IP address based on location but could remain within their relevant departments regardless of physical location. This type of flexibility coupled with the likes of automatic IP address allocation ensured that users had the ease and freedom to connect to the network and still retain access to their applications.

By enabling many users to connect to the network and access corporate information, new applications evolved that improved productivity and increased profitability. Then came the killer application—the Internet. This has changed the way we do business, and was the key driver behind many new technologies, including content switching.

The Bigger, Faster Internet

The Internet has enabled anyone to have access to any information. Information about obscure and unknown facts is available to anyone who wants it. In addition, countries that have tried to control the media have found that the Internet does not discriminate; it allows anyone access to any information, anytime, anywhere. This is its biggest advantage but also can be its biggest downside, as with no regulation, it can be a mechanism that promotes and assists antisocial behavior and radical views. Be that as it may, the Internet is the most powerful tool the average person in the street has today, and we should embrace its potential.

Most importantly, however, the Internet has changed the way we look and do business today. Suddenly, companies and their products and services were accessible to billions of people 365 days a year. At first, this was seen as a surefire method to increase revenues. Creating and offering any Internet-based product or service seemed destined to make those involved millions of dollars. This, like any shaky business plan, has not been the case for some organizations. Using the

Internet as an extension to your existing business, or creating a viable business plan with sound research has enabled companies to leverage the reach and ubiquitous nature of the Internet. There are many success stories of companies that have done just that, and by maintaining cautious investment, were able to grow while offering quality products and services. The road to success, however, is also littered with those companies that blindly saw the Internet as an easy way to create business opportunities and provide obscure services and products. Those are unfortunately not with us today.

One of the other key things spawned by the Internet explosion is the use of the Web browser. Almost every computer in the world today is running a browser, typically from either Microsoft or Netscape. Most people know how to use a Web browser, and it is this that has ensured that companies are starting to use browsers as the front end to all their applications, thus minimizing training for the front-end software. Web enabling of legacy applications is happening across the globe. No more do companies have to buy, install, and maintain client software. The Web browser is now the default client software of choice. So now the Internet has penetrated internal organizations, and names such as *intranets* and *extranets* are widely used. While we often think of Web-based applications as being for online trading and surfing, we now see them being used for internal access within organizations. In most large enterprises today, the intranet is the single most important place where employees gain their information. From booking meeting rooms, to checking pay slips, filling in leave forms, getting the latest company news, downloading product or sales information, completing and submitting expenses, the possibilities to drive productivity and increase employee satisfaction are endless. And all of this is done using a Web browser.

The Drive for Richer Content

As the Internet has evolved, PCs have increased in speed and processing power. Bandwidth to the average user has increased significantly and the ability to provide new and exciting services over the Internet has been enabled. Aside from the services mentioned in the previous paragraph, new and emerging technologies such as e-learning, e-conferencing, streaming media and Voice over IP (VoIP) will and are being delivered over the Internet. No longer do we want text-based Web sites; interactive games and multimedia applications are the requirement of today. Digital TV, downloadable music in whatever form will be the norm. Most radio stations are available over the Internet, and one could argue that it will be only a matter of time before free-to-air television becomes available. With the public hooked on the Digital Age, we will require richer, more powerful content, not less.

Companies are starting to exploit and leverage the Multimedia Age by broadcasting company updates and product launches over the Internet. All of this has led to dependence on the infrastructure similar to the way we are dependent on the mature voice networks of today. While convergence is happening between voice, data, and video, we will need to see a huge increase in the quality of service over the Internet before we can effectively use its reach for business-critical voice traffic as well.

As we travel through the 21st century, we can only assume that the Internet will bring more content, more information, more applications, and above all, more fun to us, the users.

Solving the Problems with Content Switching

Nearly every company in business today has some form of online presence, be it internal, external, or both. Regardless of how a company does business, having information available to its customers, partners, and employees is crucial to its success. The issue facing these organizations is that the infrastructure underpinning this requirement has often been deployed with little thought to the growth and the success of online commerce. The server, switching, and routing infrastructure is not geared for content networking as a whole. We need to move away from the traditional Layer 2 and Layer 3 deployments and increase network and server performance, and manage and control content much more effectively in order to provide the business performance required by today's competitive organizations. Content switching is the technology that enables this.

Overview of Content Switching

In the old days, bandwidth was king—performance issues were solved by increasing bandwidth. However, as more information is flowing at faster speeds, servers are swamped with data and are not able to respond with critical information in a timely fashion.

The problem in the data arena is, how do we differentiate between "Spam" and valuable content, critical applications and noncritical, faster and slower servers, and local or remote sites? The archetypal Layer 2 and Layer 3 approach has no concept of content, merely an address to send the data. For example, consider your postal address. Imagine if you could get the mail sorted before it arrived in your post box—no junk mail, no offers for unlimited credit, or health care, or "you have won $100,000—all you need to do is return this within 7 days and you will be eligible for a free pencil holder" mail—only mail you truly need.

Unfortunately, there is minimal intelligence in a Layer 2 and Layer 3 switch but plenty of processing power, so throughput of a 100 million packets per second is great but this would fill your post box faster than you could open the letters. Enter content switching.

"For checking accounts please key 1, for savings accounts please key 2, for all other services please key 3…"

This is basic content switching—streamlining requests matching what is needed to the correct destination. The ability to make intelligent decisions based on traditional Layer 2 and Layer 3 criteria as well as looking deeper into the packet to determine what the user is actually trying to access. To achieve this, the switch needs to inspect the packet in real time and determine what is being requested. The level of inspection varies depending on configuration and application requirement.

In most cases, this would be application specific based on TCP/UDP port such as FTP, HTTP, SMTP, and so forth. This allows content for those specific applications to be sent to the correct server or group of servers. This has the benefit of matching content or applications to specific servers and eradicates the need to have all content for a specific site mirrored across all servers. Security can be better managed on a per-service or per-application basis rather than a per-server basis.

In addition to looking at the Layer 4 information, content switching allows for more granular inspection at Layer 7. Instead of sending all HTTP traffic to a set of servers, requests sent to *www.abc.com* can get sent to a designated set of servers, while those being sent to *www.xyz.com* can be sent to a different set. This provides more specific load balancing than just a TCP/UDP port and allows for virtual hosting. Content switching also has the ability to send specific Uniform Resource Locators (URLs), file types, Uniform Resource Indicators

(URIs), cookies, and so forth to a certain set of servers. A request to *www.abc.com/products* could be sent to the Products servers, while *www.abc.com/technical* could be sent to those specific servers handling Technical content. This provides customers the ability to steer traffic to where they need it sent based on processing required to perform the request, or availability of content or even site availability. Without doubt, it enhances the user experience by increasing throughput and response times as servers are able to handle what they are designed for and what the network and server administrators have configured.

The Virtual World

The basics behind content switching revolve around the ability to provide a single point to which a session is established. By using the concept of a virtual IP address (VIP) that is configured on the content switch, the user can connect to this single point and it is the content switch that determines or load balances the request to the appropriate server. Content switches are able to support hundreds of servers behind a single VIP. Figure 1–1 illustrates this concept.

This concept allows businesses to create a single entry point to their site because the VIP is associated with the domain name. It also allows the backend servers to be in a secure, nonaccessible zone from external devices. The reason

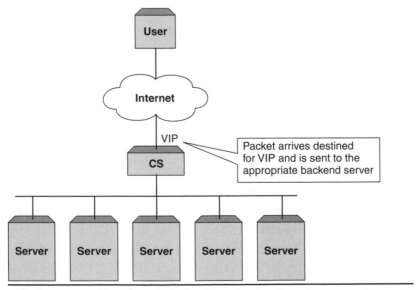

Figure 1–1   A content switch with a single VIP and many real servers that can be used for load balancing.

why this is possible is that the content switch is the device to which the user connects, and it is the content switch that then forwards the session on to the selected server. For the duration of the session, all traffic to and from the user will traverse the content switch, and because the content switch is intelligent, the data can be manipulated. This is discussed in more detail in Chapter 5, *Basic Server Load Balancing*. It is important to understand that content switches need to sit in the data path in order to have visibility of the user sessions. They also need to have powerful processors as they need to manipulate every packet within a session that passes through the switch. With these thoughts in mind, we will now discuss the content switching market from a technical viewpoint. We should also remember that as with any technology, the goal posts shift daily, new companies emerge, existing ones disappear or are swallowed by large competitors, and market requirements constantly change. We will attempt to cover the history of content switching, the milestones, and major current and, potentially, future trends that will drive this technology forward.

The Pioneers

The content switching market started to gain acceptance in 1997 after a relatively slow start in late 1995 and 1996. Without a doubt, 1998 and 1999 turned out to be the two years that enabled this technology to grow, and saw real players emerge and begin to take ownership of the market. All of the players were startups or new kids on the block, with no proven track record and were not associated with the giants of the networking space at the time—Cisco Systems, 3Com, Bay Networks, and Cabletron. All had seen this as a niche technology and had attempted to get a share of the market before the incumbent providers could get a foothold. No one really predicted the massive growth that took place through the late 1990s in the content switching arena, and few would have predicated the crazy days of the year 2000 when the dot.com era boomed.

It was this that allowed content networking to forge ahead and generate large amounts of revenue through sales of new technology and hugely successful Initial Public Offerings (IPOs) that enabled these new companies to challenge the incumbent networking manufacturers. We will look at the major influencers in this arena, remembering that in today's current market, mergers and acquisitions happen that change the landscape as we know it. Before we do, we should understand that the content switching market was traditionally made up of three areas:

- Software
- Appliances
- Layer 7 switches

Software was deployed on any device, and it was up to the device to load balance and redirect traffic just as another service or thread within the operating system. Appliances, on the other hand, were devices that had been optimized to run the content switching software and had been tested and bedded in by the manufacturer. They were often seen as cheaper or lower end options, with good features but performance limitations due to their PC-like nature. Layer 7 switches, however, were designed from the ground up and had silicon and dedicated processors for specific tasks. These devices were and still are seen as the top tier of the products, but do command a higher price tag as would be expected.

Nortel Networks (Alteon WebSystems)

In July 2000, Nortel Networks acquired a company called Alteon WebSystems for $7.8 billion. This company, which had 650 employees, had been founded in 1996 and was based in San Jose in Silicon Valley, California. Alteon WebSystems had been one of the first companies to market with the gigabit network interface card (NIC), and from that success started to create dedicated Layer 7 switches, or content switches as they are now known, using their expertise gained in ASIC design for the gigabit NIC.

Alteon WebSystems has continued to lead the content switching market in features, performance, and reliability, and has added additional security, caching, and content routing products to their portfolio. Nortel Networks has managed to ensure that the products are integrated with the existing product range and continue to build on the success of this early pioneer.

Cisco Systems (ArrowPoint)

With Cisco losing market share to the startups in this area through 1998, 1999, and 2000, it was inevitable that an acquisition would take place. In May 2000, Cisco acquired ArrowPoint, one of the main players in this arena, for $5.8 billion. Based in Boston, Massachusetts, ArrowPoint had developed a chassis-based solution to enhance their existing Layer 7 content switches that allowed them to penetrate large ISP and hosting environments. ArrowPoint was seen as one of the visionaries of this area with features such as flash crowd and hot content support.

Prior to this, however, Cisco had a product called Local Director, which had also been obtained through an acquisition. Since then, Cisco has acquired another content switching company, Netiverse, and OEM security products to ensure that they offer an end-to-end solution in content switching products. As we write this book, Cisco is bringing all their content networking products to a common operating system, or at least a common look and feel.

F5 Networks

Established in 1996, F5 managed to catch the market at the right time and, with good marketing has been able to not only survive, but also side step the acquisition trend. Having been an appliance-based company, they have managed to form relationships with some of the larger companies, and it is this that has probably kept them as a major player in content networking. Development of a new switching platform has seen them embrace the Layer 7 switching market, and they now offer an appliance and dedicated switch in their portfolio. Investment from Nokia has ensured that F5 will be able to compete effectively for some time to come.

Foundry Networks

Founded in 1996, Foundry Networks' major success has been in the high-end Layer 2 and Layer 3 space competing with core routing technology. By using this as a base, Foundry has been able to offer comprehensive content switching. Their products are true Layer 7 switches and make use of the powerful Layer 2 and Layer 3 design. These products might not be as feature rich as some of the competitive offerings, but content switching is not their core business; it is one of their businesses, and development time needs to be centered on routing and content switching. Like F5, Foundry has also managed to side step the acquisition trend.

As can be seen, these companies are fairly young in networking terms, most having started in 1996, but have made huge advancements in cementing this technology into today's communications infrastructure. There are many players in the content switching market offering software, appliances, and Layer 7 switches, and all have added and contributed to this exciting marketplace. However, it would be almost impossible to cover each in this chapter, so we have only focused on these four manufacturers who are typically seen as the early pioneers in content switching and are still regarded as market leaders today.

Current Market Landscape

We feel it is important to discuss the current market and the history, but as we write this book, the technology market is changing due to many influences, from economic to behavioral to technology and consumer demands. It is important to understand that this can and will influence the way in which content networking is deployed, developed, and accepted, and going into great depth would be a task that could and probably would be superceded very quickly. We would rather discuss the underlying concepts and issues that will not change due to the fact that they are directly associated with protocols and communications in general. However, we have dedicated a few lines on market trends.

Market Trends

With high-speed network access being easily available and affordable to the average person and to small business, content and online communications will continue to grow. It is this growth, coupled with the changes in the wireless world, that will ensure that content is king. Users demand quality, and they also change their habits, likes, and dislikes quickly; therefore, being able to provide the latest, feature-rich content to the consumer will be key. The major issue to the content providers is how to deliver this content quickly and intelligently. Content switching will become an integral player in allowing this to happen. In addition, companies are moving to unified messaging where voice, data, and video merge. Ensuring quality of service across the Internet and intranet will be a massive task that will require the intelligence of content switching to differentiate the traffic streams and sessions. Regardless of the application, content switching will play a key role in the networks of the future.

Summary

Content networking is a technology that is here to stay. It will slowly become ingrained into networking products just like spanning tree and routing protocols have in Layer 2 and Layer 3 devices. While skills are not as widespread as needed, education and a desire by the content manufacturers to simplify and automate these processes will ensure that penetration into the marketplace is a given. With the early pioneers and the new players all still competing for market and mind share, we will not see a slowdown in this area for some time to come. We believe that content networking is an exciting technology to work with, and hope that this book goes some way to not only educating you but also providing you with the ability to enhance the way you and your company do business.

2

Understanding Layer 2, 3, and 4 Protocols

While many of the concepts well known to traditional Layer 2 and Layer 3 networking still hold true in content switching applications, the area introduces new and more complex themes that need to be well understood for any successful implementation. Within the discussion of content networking, we will replace terms such as *packets* and *frames* with *sessions* and *transactions* as we move our attention further up the OSI Seven Layer Model. Before we move into these new terms, however, let's look at some standard Layer 2, 3, and 4 networking concepts.

The OSI Seven Layer Model—What *Is* a Layer?

Established in 1947, the International Organization for Standardization (ISO) was formed to bring together the standards bodies from countries around the world. Their definition of the model for Open Systems Interconnection, or OSI, is used to define modes of interconnection between different components in a networking system. This means that the physical method of transport can be designed independently of the protocols and applications running over it. For example, TCP/IP can be run over both Ethernet and FDDI networks, and Novell's IPX and Apple's AppleTalk protocols can both be run over Token Ring networks. These are examples of having independence between the physical network type and the upper layer protocols running across them. Consider also, two TCP/IP-enabled end systems communicating across a multitude of different network types, such as Ethernet, Frame Relay, and ATM. Figure 2–1 shows the OSI Seven Layer Model.

When we talk about Layer 2 and Layer 3 networking, it is these layers that we're referring to, and logically the further up the OSI model we move, the greater intelligence we can use in networking decisions.
Each layer plays its part in moving data from one device to another across a network infrastructure by providing a standard interface to the surrounding layers.

The Application Layer (Layer 7)

The top layer in the stack, the Application layer is where the end-user application resides. Think of the Application layer as the browser application or email client for a user surfing the Web or sending email. Many protocols are defined for use at the Application layer, such as HTTP, FTP, SMTP, and Telnet.

In content switching terms, Layer 7 refers to the ability to parse information directly generated by the user or application in decision making, such as the URL typed by the user in the Web browser. For example, *http://www.foocorp.com* is an example of Application layer data.

The Presentation Layer (Layer 6)

The Presentation layer is used to provide a common way for applications (residing at the Application layer) to translate between data formats or perform encryption and decryption. Mechanisms to convert between text formats such as ASCII and Unicode may be considered part of the Presentation layer, along with compression techniques for image files such as GIF and JPEG.

7	Application Layer
6	Presentation Layer
5	Session Layer
4	Transport Layer
3	Network Layer
2	Data Link Layer
1	Physical Layer

Figure 2–1   The OSI Seven Layer Model.

The Session Layer (Layer 5)

The Session layer coordinates multiple Presentation layer processes communicating between end devices. The Session layer is used by applications at either end of the communication between end devices to tie together multiple Transport layer sessions and provide synchronization between them.

The HTTP protocol can use multiple TCP connections to retrieve objects that make up a single Web page. The Session layer provides application coordination between these separate TCP connections.

The Transport Layer (Layer 4)

The Transport layer is responsible for providing an identifiable and sometimes reliable transport mechanism between two communicating devices. User or application data, having passed through the Presentation and Session layers, will typically be sequenced and checked before being passed down to the Network layer for addressing.

The Transport layer is the first at which we see the concept of packets or datagrams of information that will be transported across the network. TCP, UDP, and ICMP are examples of Layer 4 protocols used to provide a delivery mechanism between end stations. It is also at this layer in the model that applications will be distinguished by information in the Layer 4 headers within the packets. Content switching operates most commonly at this layer by using this information to distinguish between different applications and different users using the same application.

The Network Layer (Layer 3)

Whereas Layer 4 is concerned with *transport* of the packets within a communication channel, the Network layer is concerned with the *delivery* of the packets. This layer defines the addressing structure of the internetwork and how packets should be routed between end systems. The Network layer typically provides information about which Transport layer protocol is being used, as well as local checksums to ensure data integrity. Internet Protocol (IP) and Internet Packet Exchange (IPX) are examples of Network layer protocols.

Traditional Internet routers operate at the Network layer by examining Layer 3 addressing information before making a decision on where a packet should be forwarded. Hardware-based Layer 3 switches also use Layer 3 information in forwarding decisions. Layer 3 routers and switches are not concerned whether the packets contain HTTP, FTP, or SMTP data, but simply where the packet is flowing to and from.

The Data Link Layer (Layer 2)

The Data Link layer also defines a lower level addressing structure to be used between end systems as well as the lower level framing and checksums being used to transmit onto the physical medium. Ethernet, Token Ring, and Frame Relay are all examples of Data Link layer or Layer 2 protocols.

Traditional Ethernet switches operate at the Data Link layer and are concerned with forwarding packets based on the Layer 2 addressing scheme. Layer 2 Ethernet switches are not concerned with whether the packet contains IP, IPX, or AppleTalk, but only with where the MAC address of the recipient end system resides.

The Physical Layer (Layer 1)

As with all computer systems, networking is ultimately about making, moving, and storing 1s and 0s. In networking terms, the Physical layer defines how the user's browser application data is turned into 1s and 0s to be transmitted onto the physical medium. The Physical layer defines the physical medium such as cabling and interface specifications. AUI, 10Base-T, and RJ45 are all examples of Layer 1 specifications.

Putting All the Layers Together

Let's take an example of a Web user visiting the Web site of Foocorp, Inc. Within the browser application, at the Application layer, the user will type in the URL, typically something like *http://www.foocorp.com/*. While this is the only input the *user* will provide the application, there is much more information generated by the browser application itself, including:

- The type of browser being used (e.g., Microsoft Internet Explorer, Netscape)
- The operating system running on the user's machine

- The version of the HTTP protocol being used by the browser
- The language, or languages, supported by the browser (e.g., English, Japanese, etc.)
- Any Presentation layer standards that are supported by the browser, such as compression types, text formats, and file types

In terms of HTTP-based Web browser traffic, these pieces of information can be thought of as the Application, Presentation, and Session layers of the OSI model. They provide not only the raw data input by the user in the application, but also information needed by the application to ensure successful communication with the end system; in this case, a Web server at Foocorp. HTTP information for the Web user would look something like:

```
Hypertext Transfer Protocol

GET / HTTP/1.0\r\n
Accept: image/gif, image/x-xbitmap, image/jpeg, image/pjpeg\r\n
Accept-Language: en-gb\r\n
User-Agent: Mozilla/4.0 (compatible; MSIE 5.01; Windows NT 5.0)\r\n
Host: www.foocorp.com\r\n
Connection: Keep-Alive\r\n
\r\n
```

Once this application information has been generated, it can be packaged and passed on to the next layer for transport. HTTP requires a connection-oriented Transport layer protocol to guarantee the delivery of each packet in the session. Transmission Control Protocol (TCP) is used in HTTP applications to ensure this successful packet delivery. Other applications will make use of different Transport layer protocols. TFTP, for example, uses the User Datagram Protocol (UDP) as its Layer 4 transport because it does not require the guaranteed delivery provided by TCP. Routing updates sent between Layer 3 devices can use OSPF, RIP, or BGP as their Layer 4 transport.

At the Transport layer, information about the port numbers, sequence numbers, and checksums are included to provide reliable transport. The Layer 4 headers in our example would look something like:

```
Transmission Control Protocol
    Source port: 3347 (3347)
    Destination port: http (80)
    Sequence number: 52818332
    Next sequence number: 52818709
    Acknowledgement number: 3364222344
```

```
Header length: 20 bytes
Flags: 0x0018 (PSH, ACK)
        0... .... = Congestion Window Reduced (CWR): Not set
        .0.. .... = ECN-Echo: Not set
        ..0. .... = Urgent: Not set
        ...1 .... = Acknowledgment: Set
        .... 1... = Push: Set
        .... .0.. = Reset: Not set
        .... ..0. = Syn: Not set
        .... ...0 = Fin: Not set
Window size: 17520
Checksum: 0xb043 (correct)
```

Once the Transport layer information has been added to the head of the packet, it is passed to the Network layer for the Layer 3 headers to be appended. The Network layer will include information on the IP addresses of both the client and the end system, and a reference to which Transport layer protocol has been used. The Network layer information is used to ensure the correct delivery path from the client to the end system and the ability for the receiver to identify which Transport layer process the frames should be forwarded to once they arrive. For the Web user example, the Network layer information would look as follows:

```
Internet Protocol
    Version: 4
    Header length: 20 bytes
    Time to live: 128
    Protocol: TCP
    Header checksum: 0x2df9 (correct)
    Source: 192.168.254.201 (192.168.254.201)
        Destination: 216.239.51.101 (216.239.51.101)
```

For transmission across the local, physical network, the frame is then passed to the Data Link layer for the addition of the local physical addresses. In terms of Ethernet, this would be the Ethernet Media Access Control (MAC) address of the user machine and the MAC address of the default gateway router on the Ethernet network. The Layer 2 protocol, such as Ethernet, will also include a reference to which Layer 3 protocol has been used and a checksum to ensure data integrity. For our example, the Layer 2 information might look something like:

```
Ethernet II
    Destination: 00:20:6f:14:58:2f (00:20:6f:14:58:2f)
```

```
Source: 00:30:ab:17:0d:1a (00:30:ab:17:0d:1a)
Type: IP (0x0800)
```

Figure 2–2 depicts this process of repackaging each layer with new header information at the layer below.

Switching at Different Layers

Now that we've seen examples of different information available within different layers of the OSI model, let's look at how this information can be used to make intelligent traffic forwarding decisions. Before the development of switching, Ethernet relied on broadcast or flooding of packets to all end stations within a network to forward traffic. Ethernet is effectively a shared medium with only one Ethernet end station able to transmit at any time. Combine this with early implementation techniques relying on every end station in an Ethernet network seeing every packet, even if it was not addressed to it, and issues of scalability quickly surface.

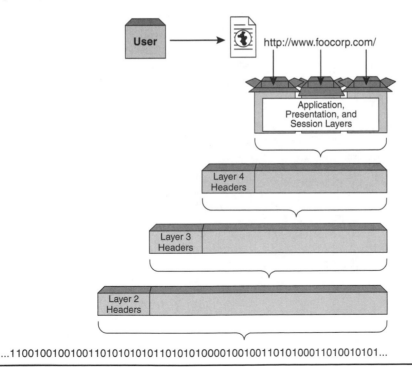

Figure 2–2   Passing data through the seven OSI layers.

Layer 2 Switching

The first implementation of Ethernet or Layer 2 switching uses information in the Ethernet headers to make traffic forwarding decisions. Intelligent switches learn which ports have which end stations attached by recording the Ethernet MAC addresses of packets ingressing the switch. Using this information along with the ability to parse the Layer 2 headers of all packets means that a Layer 2 switch need only forward frames out of ports where it knows the end station to be. For end station addresses that have not yet been learned, frames with unknown destination MAC addresses are flooded out of every port in the switch to force the recipient to reply. This will allow the switch to learn the relevant MAC address, as it will be the *source* address on the reply frame.

Layer 2 switching is implemented along side Layer 3 routing for local area networks to facilitate communication between devices in a common IP subnet. As the information at this layer is relatively limited, the opportunity to configure Layer 2 switches to interpret address information and act upon it in any way other than described previously is generally not required. Many Layer 2 switches will offer the ability to configure intelligent services such as Quality of Service (QoS), bandwidth shaping, or VLAN membership based on the Layer 2 information. Figure 2–3 shows a simplified Layer 2 frame with examples of information that might be used to make switching decisions.

Layer 3 Switching and Routing

Traditional protocol routers work by using information in the Layer 3 headers of Ethernet frames. While routing platforms exist for many different protocols (e.g., IPX, AppleTalk, and DECNet), in TCP/IP terms a router or routing device will typically use the destination IP address in the Layer 3 header to make a forwarding decision. The main advantage of Layer 3 routing in its earliest guises was that it gave the network designer the ability to segregate the network into distinct IP networks and carefully control the traffic and reachability between each.

Figure 2–3   Example Layer 2 headers for switching.

Many of the early implementers and pioneers of Layer 3 routing devices used software-based devices as platforms that, while offering a flexible platform for development of the technology, often provided limitations in terms of performance. As Layer 2 switching became more commonplace and the price per port of Ethernet switching systems dropped, manufacturers looked to combine the performance of ASIC-based Layer 2 switching with the functionality and flexibility of Layer 3 routing. Step forward the Layer 3 switch. Layer 3 switches work by examining the destination IP address and making a forwarding decision based on the routing configuration implemented. The destination subnet might be learned via a connected interface, a static route, or a dynamic routing protocol such as RIP, OSPF, or BGP. In all instances, once the Layer 3 switch has examined the frame and compared the destination IP address against the information in its routing database, the destination MAC address is changed and the frame is forwarded through the relevant egress port. For IP frames traversing a Layer 3 device, such as a router or Layer 3 switch, the TTL field in the IP header is also decremented to indicate to end stations and intermediaries that a routing hop has occurred.

It is once we reach the Layer 3 switching environment that configuration for devices become inherently more complex. The administrator must configure the correct routing information to enable basic traffic flow along with the interface IP addresses in each of the subnets to which the Layer 3 switch is attached.

Figure 2–4 shows the typical information used by a Layer 3 switch in making a forwarding decision.

Understanding Layer 4 Protocols

To appreciate the part that a content switch plays in the lifecycle of a user session, it is important to understand the component parts that make up such a session. Many protocols can be considered as Layer 4. Routing protocols such as OSPF, proprietary ones such as EIGRP, redundancy protocols such as the Virtual Router Redundancy Protocol (VRRP), and a host of others such as ICMP,

L2 Headers	Src: 192.168.254.201	Dst: 216.239.51.101	IP Proto	Payload

Figure 2–4   Example Layer 3 headers for switching and routing.

IGMP, and IP itself can all be identified by a unique protocol number in the IP header (see Figure 2–5).

The list of IP protocol numbers is administered and controlled by the Internet Assigned Numbers Authority (IANA), and a comprehensive list can be found at *www.iana.org/*. Table 2–1 lists some of the more common IP protocol numbers.

Table 2–1   Some Examples of Common IP Protocol Numbers

IP PROTOCOL NUMBER	LAYER 4 PROTOCOL
1	ICMP—Internet Control Message Protocol
6	TCP—Transmission Control Protocol
17	UDP—User Datagram Protocol
112	VRRP—Virtual Router Redundancy Protocol

Some Layer 4 protocols effectively operate at this layer alone. VRRP, for example, uses Layer 4 headers to transport all information between a series of participating routers in an IP subnet and consequently has no need for upper layer protocol information. Its payload is simply the information contained at Layer 4. Other routing protocols, such as the Border Gateway Protocol (BGP), will use the reliable Layer 4 Transport layer protocol with the BGP routing information and updates carried in the upper layer payloads.

In terms of content switching, the two most commonly understood Layer 4 protocols are TCP and UDP. The majority of the standard Application layer protocols are carried either within TCP or UDP depending on whether there is a requirement for a reliable end-to-end connection. Taking a Web user example, the browser application needs to ensure that all packets are successfully delivered when presenting the user with the desired Web page. The HTTP protocol will

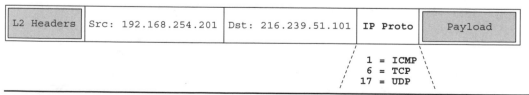

Figure 2–5   Different IP protocol numbers identify which Layer 4 protocol is being used.

therefore rely on TCP as its Transport layer protocol, to guarantee delivery, which in turn will use IP as its delivery mechanism.

Transport Control Protocol (TCP)

As the Layer 3 IP protocol is principally a connectionless and best-efforts delivery mechanism, there is a requirement for many applications to ensure the correctly sequenced delivery of *all* packets within a conversation. Consequently, many applications will use Transport Control Protocol (TCP) at Layer 4 to guarantee successful delivery. TCP has several characteristics built in to ensure this delivery:

- **Checksum**: The TCP header contains a 16-bit data checksum that is computed from all other data elements in the TCP header. The receiving end station uses this checksum to ensure that the packet arrived without corruption.
- **Sequence and acknowledgment numbers**: Each octet of data sent and received by end stations has an associated sequence number associated with it. These sequence numbers are cumulative, whereby a certain sequence number inside the TCP header will be used to indicate that all data up to and including *X* should have been received. Sequence and acknowledgment numbering is used to bring the concept of order to packet delivery over IP.
- **Windowing**: The TCP windowing technique allows two communicating end stations to build on the sequencing and acknowledgments above by removing the need for each sequence of data to be individually acknowledged. In LANs where packet loss is usually minimal, it is far more efficient to allow the sender to transmit several frames of data before an acknowledgment is sent.

Along with these mechanisms, TCP must also be able to uniquely identify each conversation within an internetwork. We've already seen the idea of a TCP port number that is used, among other things, to identify the application process to the high OSI layers during the conversation. Within a TCP conversation, there are in fact two port numbers used: one to identify the sender's listening port and the other to identify the receiver's listening port. Depending on the direction of each individual frame in the conversation, these ports become either the source port or the destination port within the Layer 4 headers.

This combination of source and destination ports, along with the Layer 3 IP addressing, gives TCP the ability to uniquely identify each conversation or session within an internetwork, even in the case of the Internet itself.

The Lifecycle of a TCP Session

Let's put these concepts of addresses, ports, and sequencing numbers together and look at how a conversation between two end stations is initiated, sustained, and terminated. Throughout the following example, we will assume that the client is a PC (10.10.10.10) initiating a connection to a Web server (20.20.20.20).

1. Initiating a Session

Before initiating the session, there are two pieces of information upon which the client must decide. First, in order to identify the session uniquely between itself and the server, it selects a TCP port number to represent the session. This port will be the source port for packets from the client to the server and the destination port for packets from the server to the client. The client will select the source port sequentially on a connection-by-connection basis starting from a value greater than 1024. Port numbers below 1024 are typically referred to as well-known ports and are used to identify well-known applications. Table 2–2 shows some well-known reserved ports as defined by IANA.

Table 2–2   Some Well-Known TCP Port Number Assignments

TCP PORT NUMBER	APPLICATION
20 and 21	File Transfer Protocol (FTP)
25	Simple Mail Transfer Protocol (SMTP)
23	Telnet
80	HyperText Transfer Protocol (HTTP)

The second element that needs to be decided by the client is the starting sequence number. This will be selected based on an internal 32-bit clock that ensures both randomness and that sequence numbers will not overlap should a lost packet reappear some time after its original transmission. Just as with the

TCP ports used by both the client and server, each side also uses its own sequence numbering to identify where within the session each frame fits.

Once the client has determined these two variables, it is ready to send the first packet of the session and initiate the connection to the server. Using TCP flags, the client will indicate to the server that it wants to initiate a connection by setting the SYN or synchronize flag showing that this is the first pack in the session. In TCP terms, this element is the first packet in what is commonly referred to as the "three-way handshake." This is simply because three packets are exchanged between the client and server to bring the TCP state into that which can transport data. Consequently, no Application layer data is transmitted until at least the fourth packet in the session, a concept which we will see has an important consequence when applied to content switching. Figure 2–6 shows a simplified representation of the three-way handshake to illustrate which side sends which of the packets when a new connection is initiated.

Taking this sequence packet by packet, we can see the importance of the port and sequence numbers in ensuring the reliable transport between the client and server. The first frame from the client to the server initiates the connection by setting the client side port and sequence numbers as shown in Figure 2–7. As we can see, the client chooses a random source port that will be used by the client to identify this session uniquely in cases where it has concurrent sessions to the same server.

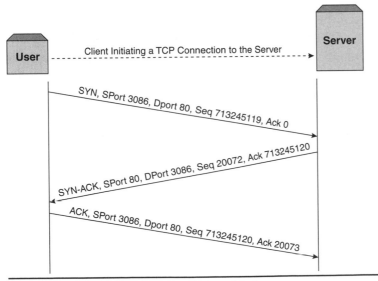

Figure 2–6   The TCP three-way handshake.

```
Internet Protocol Headers
    Version: 4
    Time to live: 128
    Protocol: TCP (0x06)
    Header checksum: 0xb926 (correct)
    Source: 10.10.10.10
    Destination: 20.20.20.20
Transmission Control Protocol Headers

    Source port: 3086 (3086)
    Destination port: http (80)
    Sequence number: 713245119

    Header length: 28 bytes
    Flags: 0x0002 (SYN)
        0... .... = Congestion Window Reduced (CWR): Not set
        .0.. .... = ECN-Echo: Not set
        ..0. .... = Urgent: Not set
        ...0 .... = Acknowledgment: Not set
        .... 0... = Push: Not set
        .... .0.. = Reset: Not set
        .... ..1. = Syn: Set
        .... ...0 = Fin: Not set
```

Figure 2–7   The SYN packet sent by the client.

When the server replies, both the SYN and ACK flags are set in the TCP headers to indicate that the server acknowledges the client's connection request. To ensure that each packet can be accounted for, the server will set an acknowledgment number that is equal to the last byte received from the client, relative to the starting sequence number, plus one. In our example, the client started with a sequence number of 713245119 and transmitted no user data, meaning that the server will use an acknowledgment of 713245120.

It is also important to notice the change in source and destination ports depending on which way a particular packet is directed. In our example, the client sends on port 80 and listens on port 3086, whereas the server sends on port 3086 and listens on port 80. Figure 2–8 shows the return packet from the server to the client.

The final packet exchanged during this handshake period is an acknowledgment from the client to the server. This allows the client to correctly acknowledge the sequence numbering used by the server in the previous packet and remove the SYN flag being used to show the start of the session. Once this final

```
Internet Protocol Headers
    Version: 4
    Time to live: 114
    Protocol: TCP (0x06)
    Header checksum: 0x9889 (correct)
    Source: 20.20.20.20
    Destination: 10.10.10.10
Transmission Control Protocol Headers

    Source port: http (80)
    Destination port: 3086 (3086)
    Sequence number: 20072
    Acknowledgement number: 713245120

    Header length: 28 bytes
    Flags: 0x0012 (SYN, ACK)
        0... .... = Congestion Window Reduced (CWR): Not set
        .0.. .... = ECN-Echo: Not set
        ..0. .... = Urgent: Not set
        ...1 .... = Acknowledgment: Set
        .... 0... = Push: Not set
        .... .0.. = Reset: Not set
        .... ..1. = Syn: Set
        .... ...0 = Fin: Not set
```

Figure 2–8   The SYN-ACK packet sent by the server.

packet of the handshake has been received, both sides of the connection can move into the *established* state, indicating that the transfer of user or application data can now commence. Figure 2–9 shows this final packet of the handshake. Note that in our example, the client has changed the acknowledgment numbering to match that initiated by the server and has also removed the SYN flag in the TCP header.

2. Data Transfer

Once the connection has moved into the *established* state, data transmission can begin between the two end points. During this state, the ACK flag is always set and the two end stations use the sequence and acknowledgment numbering to track the successful delivery of each segment of data. TCP also employs a number of windowing and buffering techniques to ensure the optimal delivery, retransmission, and buffering of data during this state. The discussions of such techniques are outside of the scope of this book.

```
Internet Protocol Headers
     Version: 4
     Time to live: 128
     Protocol: TCP (0x06)
     Header checksum: 0xb92c (correct)
     Source: 192.168.254.201 (192.168.254.201)
     Destination: 212.58.226.40 (212.58.226.40)
Transmission Control Protocol Headers
     Source port: 3086 (3086)
     Destination port: http (80)
     Sequence number: 713245120
     Acknowledgement number: 20073

     Header length: 20 bytes
     Flags: 0x0010 (ACK)
          0... .... = Congestion Window Reduced (CWR): Not set
          .0.. .... = ECN-Echo: Not set
          ..0. .... = Urgent: Not set
          ...1 .... = Acknowledgment: Set
          .... 0... = Push: Not set
          .... .0.. = Reset: Not set
          .... ..0. = Syn: Set
          .... ...0 = Fin: Not set
```

Figure 2–9   The final ACK packet of the handshake.

3. Terminating a Session

Unlike the session initiation, the termination of a TCP connection can be initiated from either side. Once one side of the connection decides that it has no more data to transmit, it will set the FIN flag in the TCP header to indicate to the other side that it is ready to terminate the connection. In simple terms, the receiving station will then acknowledge the FIN, by setting the ACK flag, and set its own FIN flag to show that it too is ready to terminate the connection. This series of exchanges results in both sides moving through the *TIME WAIT* state to the *CLOSED* state and the connection is closed.

In some instances, when the client receives the FIN it might still have data to send, in which case it will issue only an ACK back to the closing station. This allows the client to continue sending data until it is complete and then issue a FIN to show that the termination of the session can commence. During this period, the initiator and recipient of the initial FIN are referred to as being in the *FIN WAIT 2* and *CLOSE WAIT* states, respectively. Some applications, such as Web browsers, will often use this type of exchange to leave the connection in a type of half-closed state, thereby allowing the connection to be brought back into use when needed without having to reinitiate the entire connection (see Figure 2–10).

A more detailed description of TCP can be found in RFC 793.

User Datagram Protocol (UDP)

The User Datagram Protocol, or UDP, is the other most commonly used Transport layer protocol found within the Internet. While TCP is designed to provide *connection-oriented* delivery of packets, UDP implements a *connectionless* or *unguaranteed* delivery mechanism that is suitable for a number of upper layer applications. For some applications, the overhead of TCP, such as handshaking, is not required and for these, UDP is best suited.

A comparison between TCP and UDP can be drawn from the world of cellular phones. TCP is similar in nature to a full telephone conversation, whereby you establish a connection to the receiving station by dialing their number, hold a conversation with them using verbal interaction and acknowledgments, and finally terminate the call. UDP is much more akin to SMS or text messaging,

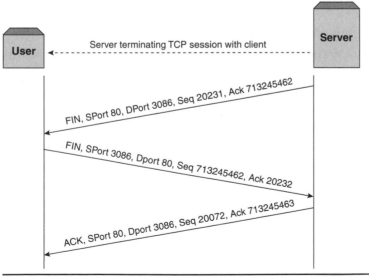

Figure 2–10   Closing a TCP session.

whereby you write a message and send it without receiving any acknowledgment of its delivery from anything other than a local call access point.

UDP does share some common characteristics with TCP, as it does implement source and destination ports, to identify application sockets, and a checksum to verify the correct delivery of the layer 4 datagram.

A Simple UDP Data Flow

Let's consider our two example machines again, but this time interacting using UDP rather than TCP. The Domain Name System, or DNS, is one of the most commonly implemented UDP-based applications—our example will consider a client (10.10.10.10) requesting a name resolution from a DNS server (20.20.20.20).

It is important to note that UDP traffic can be both bidirectional, such as the request-response nature of DNS queries, and unidirectional, such as alerts raised through the Simple Network Management Protocol (SNMP). In both instances, the nature of the application determines whether a response is required; UDP simply provides a datagram format for the data between the two end points.

The Request

The first thing you will notice in Figure 2–11 is that the structure of the UDP header is far simpler than that used by TCP. There are only four fields used within the UDP header, to indicate the source and destination ports, the header length, and the checksum. It is clear from this that many of the techniques used by TCP are simply not present in UDP, such as sequencing, handshaking, and flow control.

The Response

As DNS is a bidirectional, request-response application, the frame shown in Figure 2–11 will yield an answer from the DNS server, also carried using UDP. Figure 2–12 shows the response. Note that the source and destination ports are reversed as with TCP, as the client sending the request will be listening and expecting an answer on port 1763.

```
Internet Protocol Headers
    Version: 4
    Time to live: 249
    Protocol: UDP (0x11)
    Header checksum: 0xc8de (correct)
    Source: 20.20.20.20
    Destination: 10.10.10.10
Transmission Control Protocol Headers

    Source port: domain (53)
    Destination port: 1763 (1763)
    Length: 276
    Checksum: 0x04bc (correct)

Domain Name System (response)
    Answers
        www.foo.com: type A, class inet, addr 1.2.3.4
            Name: www.foo.com
            Type: Host address
            Class: inet
            Time to live: 10 minutes
            Data length: 4
            Addr: 1.2.3.4
```

Figure 2–11   A UDP-based DNS query.

This is again a very brief overview of the UDP protocol. A more detailed description is available in RFC 768, available on the IETF Web site.

Virtual Router Redundancy Protocol (VRRP)

The Virtual Router Redundancy Protocol, or VRRP, is inextricably linked with the implementation of content switching, not because it is used by user applications, but because it provides a mechanism to eliminate single points of failure within content switching topologies. VRRP provides a mechanism to group two or more IP addresses, typically representing a routed interface, and make them appear to all surrounding devices as a single logical IP address.

Many of the topologies described later in this book will show how multiple content switches, and other routers, can be deployed to ensure a resilient and fault-tolerant implementation. For this reason, we need to examine the concepts and theory of VRRP in some more detail.

```
Internet Protocol Headers
     Version: 4
     Time to live: 249
     Protocol: UDP (0x11)
     Header checksum: 0xc8de (correct)
     Source: 20.20.20.20
     Destination: 10.10.10.10
Transmission Control Protocol Headers

     Source port: domain (53)
     Destination port: 1763 (1763)
     Length: 276
     Checksum: 0x04bc (correct)

Domain Name System (response)
     Answers
         www.foo.com: type A, class inet, addr 1.2.3.4
             Name: www.foo.com
             Type: Host address
             Class: inet
             Time to live: 10 minutes
             Data length: 4
             Addr: 1.2.3.4
```

Figure 2–12   The UDP-based DNS response.

Layer 2 and 3 Redundancy

Let's consider a network as shown in Figure 2–13. To eliminate a single point of failure for clients on the network accessing the Internet, the network administrator might consider deploying two Internet facing routers, R1 and R2. The client PC on the network will have been configured with a default route; for example, 10.10.10.2 pointing to router R1.

This "hard-coding" of the default gateway IP address into the client's TCP/IP settings presents the network administrator with two challenges when considering resilience:

- Router R1 might fail, leaving the client with a default gateway of an unreachable IP address.
- The client PC will resolve the IP address of the default gateway to the Ethernet address of router R1. This means that even if we replace the hardware of router R1, the client will still not have access to the Internet until its ARP cache has timed out or has been cleared.

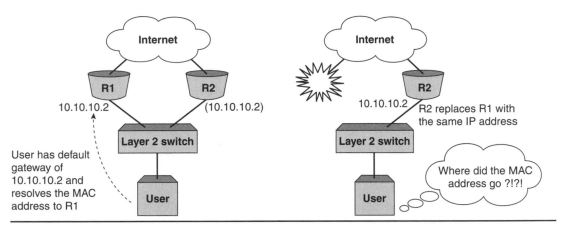

Figure 2–13   Example network without VRRP.

It is for these reasons that we need VRRP to provide resilience at both Layer 2, by providing a virtual MAC address, and at Layer 3, by providing a virtual IP address. This virtualization of addresses amongst two or more physical units means that the client or client router will always have a default gateway both in terms of MAC address and IP address.

The Components of VRRP

RFC 2338 defines the following component parts in a network running VRRP:

- **VRRP router**: A router running VRRP. It can participate in one or more virtual routers.
- **Virtual router**: An abstract object managed by VRRP that acts as a default router for hosts on a shared LAN. It consists of a virtual router identifier (VRID) and a set of associated IP address(es) across a common LAN. A VRRP router can back up one or more virtual routers.
- **IP address owner**: The VRRP router that has the virtual router's IP address(es) as real interface address(es). This is the router that, when up, will respond to packets addressed to one of these IP addresses for ICMP pings, TCP connections, and so forth. Other routers that do not have an IP interface equal to the virtual IP address are commonly referred to as an *IP address renter*.
- **Primary IP address**: An IP address selected from the set of real interface addresses. One possible selection algorithm is to always select the first

address. VRRP advertisements are always sent using the primary IP address as the source of the IP packet.

- **Virtual router master**: The VRRP router that is assuming the responsibility of forwarding packets sent to the IP address(es) associated with the virtual router, and answering ARP requests for these IP addresses. Note that if the IP address owner is available, it will always become the master.

- **Virtual router backup**: The set of VRRP routers available to assume forwarding responsibility for a virtual router should the current master fail.

- **VRID**: Configured item in the range 1–255 (decimal). There is no default.

- **Priority**: Priority value to be used by this VRRP router in master election for this virtual router. The value of 255 (decimal) is reserved for the router that owns the IP addresses associated with the virtual router. The value of 0 (zero) is reserved for the master router to indicate that it is releasing responsibility for the virtual router. The range 1–254 (decimal) is available for VRRP routers backing up the virtual router. The default value is 100 (decimal).

VRRP Addressing

Let's take our previous example and expand it now to include VRRP on the two routers, R1 and R2. Assuming that router R1 is configured with the IP address that matches the proposed VRRP address, it will become the *VRRP master* and *VRRP owner*. Router R2 will become the *VRRP backup*.

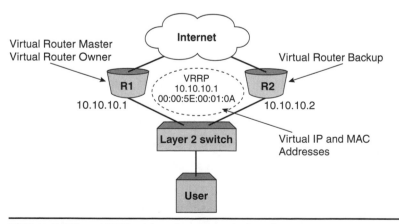

Figure 2–14   VRRP addressing example topology.

The IP address of router 1, 10.10.10.1, is also configured to be the VRRP router address, and this will be used by all clients on the network as a default route to the Internet. If router R1 was to fail, router R2 would take over while preserving the IP address to the clients. To manufacture a resilient Layer 2 MAC address, the following standard is used:

```
00:00:5E:00:01:[VRID]
```

where the virtual router ID is used to make the last byte of the MAC address. In our example, let's assume that a VRID of 10 has been used, giving us the VRRP MAC address of 00:00:5E:00:01:0A. Figure 2–14 shows our implementation with the new VRRP addressing.

VRRP Operation

Now that we have all of the component parts in place, let's look at how the routers operate together to provide a resilient pair. VRRP uses advertisement messages between all participating routers to indicate the health and availability of the current virtual router master. These messages are exchanged using a common multicast destination address of 224.0.0.18, and it is to this address that the current master router will continually advertise to indicate that it is still operational on the network.

In our example topology, during normal operation, router R1 will continually advertise the virtual router ID, the virtual router address, and its priority inside the multicast frame. The source IP address on these advertisements will be the interface on router R1 along with a source MAC address of the virtual MAC address we calculated earlier. The use of this virtual MAC address in these advertisements allows any Layer 2 infrastructure surrounding the VRRP routers—typically Layer 2 switches—to source learn where the common MAC address is currently located.

Now for the interesting part, a router failure. Let's imagine that router R1 experiences a power failure and effectively disappears from the network. In this instance, the following series of events would occur:

1. The master router, R1, would cease sending multicast packets advertising the virtual router.

2. After several missed packets, the standby router, R2, will acknowledge this occurrence by commencing with its own multicast advertisements.

When it does, it will use a source MAC address of the VRRP virtual MAC address, thus informing the attached Layer 2 switch that the MAC address has moved ports.

3. Since the virtual IP address and associated virtual MAC address have now survived the failure of router R1, the client will notice only minimal disruption during the re-election. This period is dependent on the configurable parameters associated with the advertisement intervals, but should typically be no more than 2 to 3 seconds.

VRRP, or variations on it, is commonly implemented in many content switching platforms, and as such it forms an important part of any implementation. More information about VRRP can be found in RFC 2338.

Summary

Many books have been written on the TCP/IP protocol stack and the higher layer applications such as HTTP and FTP that it supports. While it is outside the scope of this book to cover all the details and caveats, this chapter provided sufficient overview of the workings most relevant to content switching. Understanding the concept of a user session—being the total user experience of interacting over a period of time with a resource—and how that maps down the OSI seven-layer model and into the frames, packets, and TCP sessions below is key to understanding and successfully deploying content switching. In Chapter 3, *Understanding Application Layer Protocols*, we'll look at some of the Application layer protocols common to content switching.

3

Understanding Application Layer Protocols

In this chapter, we'll move further up the OSI Seven Layer Model and take an in-depth look at the workings of some of the Application layer protocols that are most commonly used in content switching. These include TCP-based services such as HTTP, UDP services like DNS, and applications that use a combination of TCP and UDP, such as the Real Time Streaming Protocol (RTSP). Finally, we'll look at how these types of applications can be secured using Secure Sockets Layer (SSL).

HyperText Transfer Protocol (HTTP)

The HyperText Transfer Protocol, or HTTP, must be the most widely used Application layer protocol in the world today. It forms the basis of what most people understand the Internet to be—the World Wide Web. Its purpose is to provide a lightweight protocol for the retrieval of HyperText Markup Language (HTML) and other documents from Web sites throughout the Internet. Each time you open a Web browser to surf the Internet, you are using HTTP over TCP/IP.

HTTP was first ratified in the early 1990s and has been through three main iterations:

- **HTTP/0.9**: A simplistic first implementation of the protocol that only supported the option to get a Web page.
- **HTTP/1.0**: Ratified by the IETF as RFC 1945 in 1996. This version added many supplemental data fields, known as *headers* to the specification.

This allowed for other information passing between the client and server, alongside the request and consequent page.

- **HTTP/1.1**: Defined in RFC 2068 by the IETF, version 1.1 implemented a number of improvements over and above the 1.0 specification. One of the main improvements of 1.1 over 1.0 was the implementation of techniques such as persistent TCP connections, pipelining, and cache control to improve performance within HTTP-based applications.

Most browsers these days offer support for both 1.0 and 1.1 implementations, with new browsers using 1.1 as a default but supporting the ability to fall back to earlier versions if required. One thing the RFC definitions are clear to point out is that all implementations of the HTTP protocol should be backward compatible. That is to say that a browser implementing the HTTP/1.1 specification should be capable of receiving a 1.0 response from a server. Conversely, a 1.1 implementation on the server side should also be capable of responding to requests from a 1.0 browser.

It is well outside the bounds of this book to cover the HTTP protocols in huge detail, so let's concentrate on those elements most relevant to content switching.

Basic HTTP Page Retrieval

Let's start at the beginning and see how a basic browser retrieves a Web page from a Web server. The first important point to note is that a Web page is typically made up of many dozens of objects, ranging from the HTML base through to the images that are present on the page. The HTML can be thought of as the template for the page overall, instructing the browser on the layout of the text, font sizes and colors, background color of the page, and which other images need to be retrieved to make up the page.

Think of the process, taking place in the following order:

1. Client sends a request for the required page to the Web server.
2. The server analyzes the request and sends back an acknowledgment to the client along with the HTML code required to make the page.
3. The client will begin interpreting the HTML and building the page.
4. The client, in subsequent requests, will retrieve any embedded objects, such as images or other multimedia sources.

Once all elements of the page have been retrieved, the client browser will display the completed Web page. The order and timing of the process described previously depends largely on which implementation of HTTP is used—1.0 or 1.1—although all browsers work in this way of request and response.

HTTP Methods

HTTP does not only offer a mechanism for the client to receive data from the server, but also other communication types such as the passing of data from the client to the server. Such mechanisms are known within the HTTP specifications as a *method*. Table 3–1 shows the supported method types in HTTP/1.0 and 1.1.

Table 3–1   The HTTP Method Headers in HTTP/1.0 and HTTP/1.1

METHOD	DESCRIPTION	HTTP/1.0	HTTP/1.1
GET	Retrieve the information specified.	✔	✔
HEAD	Identical to the GET request, but the server must not return any page content other than the HTTP headers.	✔	✔
POST	Allows the client to submit information to the server, used for submitting information from a form, etc.	✔	✔
PUT	Allows the client to place an item on the server in the location specified.		✔
DELETE	Allows the client to delete the item specified in the request.		✔
TRACE	Allows the client to see the request it made to the server. This acts as a loopback in effect.		✔
OPTIONS	Allows the client to determine the communications options available on the server.		✔

In terms of general Web browsing, the GET and POST methods are by far the most commonly used. For a browser to build a standard Web page, the GET method is used to retrieve each object individually, whereas for transactional Web sites implementing shopping cart style applications, the POST method will also be used.

The HTTP URL

The URL is the most important piece of information that the client browser includes in any GET request. The URL is defined as being a combination of the host where the site is located, the scheme used to retrieve the page, and the full path and filename. Optionally, the URL may include information such as the TCP port number to be used or a unique reference point within a larger page. Figure 3–1 shows the breakdown of an example URL.

The URI is also commonly used when referencing the location of documents within HTTP. The formal definition of the difference between a URL and a URI is simple: A URI is a URL without the scheme defined.

Persistent Connections in HTTP

One of the other major differences in operation between HTTP/1.0 and HTTP/1.1 is the handling of TCP connections required to retrieve a full Web page. Given that a client will typically have to retrieve multiple objects to make up a single Web page, it is often inefficient to open and close TCP sessions repeatedly when retrieving objects from the same server. To improve the overall performance of HTTP in this instance, the protocol defines the `Connection:` header that communicates to the server whether the TCP session should be

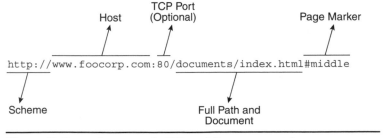

Figure 3–1   An example URL and its components.

closed or remain open once the object has been retrieved. The `Connection:` header has two options:

- **Connection: Closed**: The default for HTTP/1.0
- **Connection: Keep-Alive**: The default for HTTP/1.1

The `Closed` state indicates that the server should close the TCP connection once the request has been fulfilled. The `Keep-Alive` state indicates that the server should keep the TCP connection open after the request has been fulfilled. Along with an obvious performance increase from removing the need to open and close TCP connections, the `Keep-Alive` state also allows the implementation of *pipelining*. Pipelining allows a client to send multiple HTTP GET requests over the same TCP connection without needing to wait for individual responses after each. Figure 3–2 shows the difference in these connection types.

The final piece in the puzzle of interaction between client and server is in opening multiple TCP connections. We've already seen that a client can open a persistent TCP connection to the server and pipeline HTTP requests. To further improve performance of the HTTP operation, many browsers will open several simultaneous connections. Figure 3–3 gives examples of pipelining and multiple connections.

Other HTTP Headers

The HTTP protocol includes definitions for dozens of headers that can be included in the client-to-server and server-to-client requests and responses. We will not attempt to list and describe all those available here; for a full description, the RFC for HTTP/1.0 and HTTP/1.1 offers a better source. The RFCs define a series of standard headers, which can be complemented by adding user-defined headers from either the client or server side.

As headers are ASCII readable text in every HTTP request and response pair, they can prove very useful in the implementation of content switching. Let's look at some of the HTTP headers most commonly used in content switching.

The "`Accept:`" Header

The client browser uses the "`Accept:`" header to indicate to the server which content and media types can be accepted. Examples of the "`Accept:`" header include:

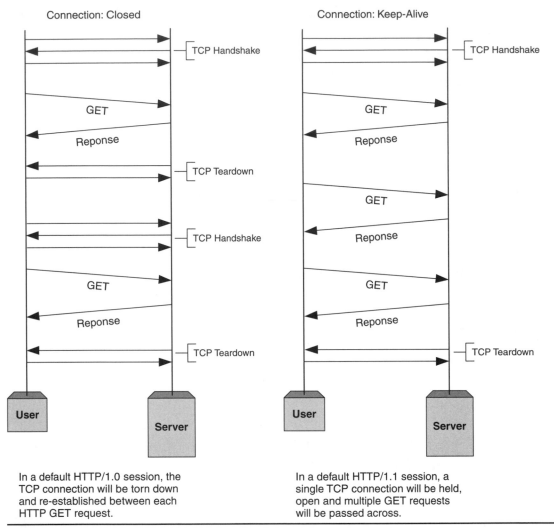

Connection: Closed

TCP Handshake

GET

Reponse

TCP Teardown

TCP Handshake

GET

Reponse

TCP Teardown

User

Server

In a default HTTP/1.0 session, the TCP connection will be torn down and re-established between each HTTP GET request.

Connection: Keep-Alive

TCP Handshake

GET

Reponse

GET

Reponse

GET

Reponse

TCP Teardown

User

Server

In a default HTTP/1.1 session, a single TCP connection will be held, open and multiple GET requests will be passed across.

Figure 3–2   The difference in TCP handling between HTTP/1.0 and HTTP/1.1.

`Accept: */*`	Accept anything
`Accept: text/plain; text/html`	Accept plain text and HTML
`Accept: text/html; image/jpeg; image/bmp`	Accept HTML and JPEG and bitmap images

The `"Accept:"` header is useful in the context of content switching to be able to determine the capabilities of a particular client. If the client browser cannot accept images, for example, the request can be directed to a server optimized to deliver text-only versions of the Web pages.

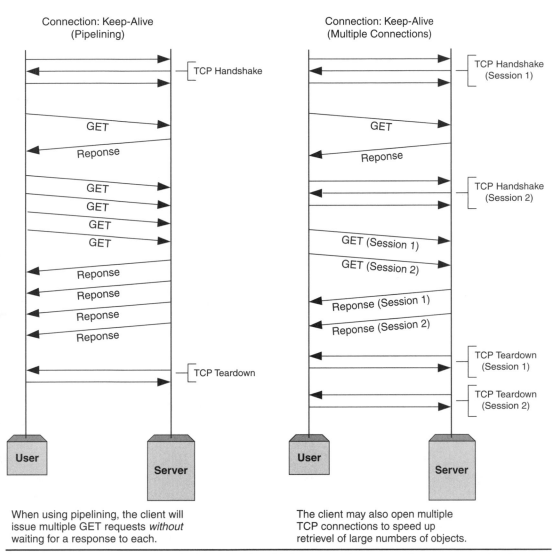

Figure 3–3   Implementing pipelining and multiple connections as performance mechanisms.

The "Host:" Header

One of the main problems in the original HTTP/1.0 specification was that a user's request as typed into the browser (e.g., *http://www.foocorp.com/index.html*) would not contain the host (*www.foocorp.com*) element in the GET request sent to the server. This represents a problem if virtual hosting is used within a Web server farm, where the server is potentially hosting multiple Web sites and needs to use this host information to determine which path and page the user is requesting.

Within the HTTP/1.1 specification, and subsequently in many new HTTP/ 1.0 browsers, support was added for the `"Host:"` header. This allows the user's requested URL, typed into the browser, to be converted into a GET request containing the full path and filename along with the host from which the content is being fetched. The following is an example of translating a full URL into its component parts.

```
URL : http://www.foocorp.com/directory/somewhere/page.html

GET /directory/somewhere/page.html HTTP/1.0\r\n
Host: www.foocorp.com
```

The `"Host:"` header has many uses within content switching, examples of which are shown in Chapter 6, *Content-Aware Server Load Balancing*.

The `"User-Agent:"` Header

The `"User-Agent:"` header indicates to the server the type of browser being used by the client. The `"User-Agent:"` header is useful in the context of content switching as it can be used to determine the browser type used by the client and direct the request to a resource offering content optimized for such a browser. The following is an example of the `"User-Agent:"`.

```
User-Agent: Mozilla/4.0(Compatible; MSIE 6.0; Windows NT 5.0)
```

Cookies—The HTTP State Management Mechanism

As we'll see in later chapters, one of the biggest challenges in HTTP environments, whether content switched or not, is maintaining some form of client-side state that enables Web servers and intermediary devices to recognize the client session and understand the current status of the user session. This issue was tackled in RFC 2109, which defined the use of the `Set-Cookie` and `Cookie` HTTP headers used to set and use the cookies, respectively. In HTTP, cookies take the form of a small piece of text information that is implanted into the user's browser either permanently or temporarily. The term *cookie* is commonly used in computing to describe an opaque piece of information held during a session and, unfortunately, seems to have no more interesting origin than that. Once the backend server has implanted the cookie into the user's browser, the information can be used for a number of different applications ranging from content personalization, user session persistence for online shopping, and the collection of demographic and statistical information on Web site usage.

The server issuing a `Set-Cookie` header in any HTTP response can post a cookie to the client at any time during an HTTP session. This `Set-Cookie` header has the following syntax:

```
Set-Cookie: <name>=<value>; expires=<date>; path=<path>;
domain=<domain>; secure
```

The `name` and `value` fields are the only ones that are mandatory when issuing a cookie. As the name suggests, these define the name of the cookie and its value, such as `UserID=Phil`, for example. The `expires` field identifies, down to the second, the date and time on which a cookie will expire and be deleted from the client computer. The `path` and `domain` fields indicate the domain, such as *www.foocorp.com*, and the URL, such as /home/brochures/, for which the cookie should be used. Both of these options can effectively be wild-carded by specifying foocorp.com to match *www.foocorp.com* and *intranet.foocorp.com*, for example. Finally, the `secure` field indicates to the client that the cookie should only be used when a secure connection (SSL secured HTTP or HTTPS) is used between the client and server. Figure 3–4 shows the interaction between a client and server as two different cookies are inserted and used.

The following code shows the HTTP responses from the server in more detail. Note that the second cookie includes the `Path` field, which will limit the use of the cookie to URLs requested by the user that include the string /docs.

```
Hypertext Transfer Protocol
    HTTP/1.1 200 OK\r\n
    Set-Cookie: UserID=Phil
    Connection: Keep-Alive\r\n
    Content-Type: text/html\r\n
    \r\n

Hypertext Transfer Protocol
    HTTP/1.1 200 OK\r\n
    Set-Cookie: UserType=Gold; Path=/docs
    Connection: Keep-Alive\r\n
    Content-Type: text/html\r\n
    \r\n
```

The mechanism that governs whether a cookie is permanent (i.e., stored on the hard disk of the user's machine) or temporary (i.e., removed once the user closes the browser application) is the `Expires` field in the `Set-Cookie`

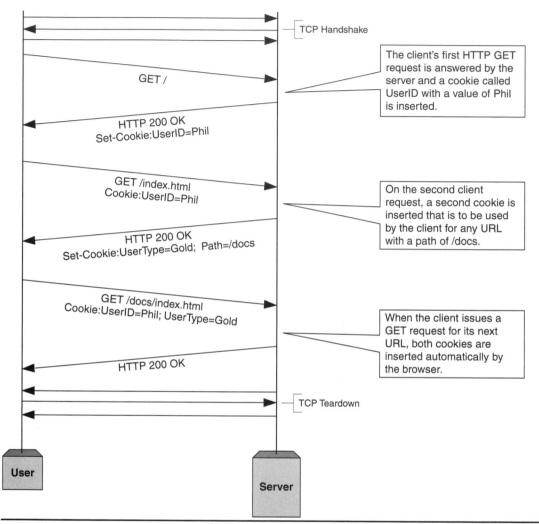

Figure 3–4   The interaction between a client and a server when two different cookies are implanted and used.

header. If the server does not issue an Expires directive when implanting the cookie, it is considered temporary, whereas if the Expires directive is used, then the cookie will be stored on the client machine until the expiry date has passed.

Cookies are by far one of the most useful additions made to the HTTP specifications, and as we'll see in later chapters can be used in conjunction with content switching to enable a whole host of new experience-enhancing services.

HTTP—Further Reading

It is outside the scope of this book to cover the HTTP protocol in its entirety;. the RFC for HTTP/1.1 alone is over 160 pages. For more in-depth detail on the protocol, it's worth looking at the following RFCs:

- RCF 1945 Hypertext Transfer Protocol—HTTP/1.0
- RFC 2068 Hypertext Transfer Protocol—HTTP/1.1
- RFC 2109 HTTP State Management Mechanism

File Transfer Protocol (FTP)

In Internet terms, The File Transfer Protocol, or FTP, has been around for a long time. First defined in RFC 172 written in June 1971, the protocol has been through several changes through to the current specification, which is defined in RFC 959. Again, while it's not the purpose of this book to describe every detail about FTP, it's worth looking at its basic operation to get a better understanding of how content switching can improve performance and reliability in FTP environments.

FTP Basics

FTP exists primarily for the transfer of data between two end points. The RFC itself actually states that two of the objectives of the protocol are to "promote the sharing of files" and "transfer data reliably and efficiently." FTP differs from HTTP fundamentally as it is an application made up of two distinct TCP connections:

- **Control connection**: This TCP-based connection is used to provide a communications channel for the delivery of commands and replies. This is effectively the mechanism that enables the user to tell the server which file is being requested, which directory it is in, and so forth.
- **Data connection**: The second TCP-based connection is used for the actual transfer of user data. Once the Control connection has been used to exchange information on which file is required, the Data connection is used to transfer the file between the client and server.

Using these two communication connections, two distinct modes of operation determine in which direction the connections are established: Active mode and Passive mode.

Active Mode FTP

Within an Active FTP session, the Control connection is established from the client to the server, with the Data connection established back from the server to the client. In order to do this, the client issues a PORT command to the server that contains the IP address and source and destination TCP ports that should be used during the Data connection. Figure 3–5 shows the lifecycle of an Active FTP session.

As we can see from Figure 3–5, once the user has logged on with a valid username and password, the very first "data" that is passed—in this case, a directory listing—is carried using a separate data channel. The format for communicating the IP and TCP information of the data channel is as follows:

```
PORT [Octet 1],[Octet 2],[Octet 3],[Octet 4], [TCP Port 8 Bytes],[TCP
Port 8 Bytes]
```

Therfore, in the preceding example, the PORT command of PORT 10,10,10,10,15,199 equates to IP address 10.10.10.10 and TCP port 4039 [15×256 + 199×1].

In some instances, Active FTP can be considered a security risk mainly because there is often little control over the contents of the PORT command. Under normal usage, this information *should* be the IP address and listening TCP port of the client waiting for the Data connection. When used maliciously, however, the client could issue PORT commands with IP addresses and TCP ports of other machines either within the same network as the server or remotely. Many Application layer firewalls and proxies, or firewalls with support for FTP command parsing can be used to reduce the effectiveness of such attacks. One alternative is to implement the second method of FTP—Passive mode FTP.

Passive Mode FTP

Passive mode FTP works similarly to Active mode FTP with one major exception: both the Control and Data connections within a Passive mode FTP session are established from the client to the server. To implement this, rather than use the PORT command, Passive mode FTP implements the PASV command, which instructs the server that *it* should listen for the incoming Data connection. Figure 3–6 shows the Passive mode FTP in more detail.

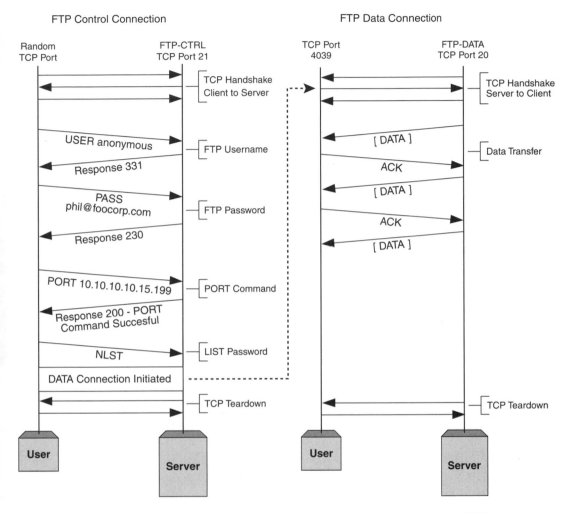

FTP Control Connection

FTP Data Connection

In an active FTP connection, the client will use the Control connection to tell the server, via a PORT command, which IP address and TCP port it should establish the Data connection to. The server then opens a Data connection to that IP address and port using the well-known Port 20 as the source.

Figure 3–5   An active FTP session example.

In Figure 3–6, we can see that rather than the client dictating the parameters of the Data connection, it simply requests this information from the server. Similarly to the PORT command in Active mode, the server's RESPONSE to the PASV request from the client can be interpreted as follows:

```
RESPONSE 227 (10,10,10,10,41,38)
```

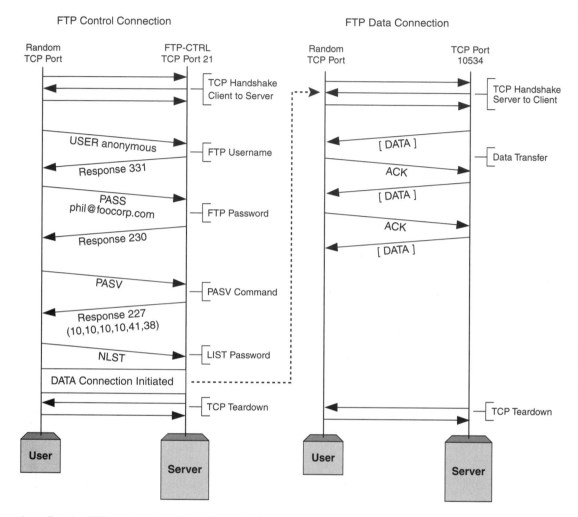

In an Passive FTP session, the client will use the Control connection to request from the server, via a PASV command, which IP address and TCP port it should establish the Data connection to. The client then opens a Data connection to that IP address and port using a random TCP port as the source.

Figure 3–6   A Passive FTP session example.

which means open from client to server on IP address 10.10.10.10 and TCP port 10534 [41×256 + 38×1].

FTP—Further Reading

For further information on the detailed workings of FTP, it's worth looking at RFC 959.

Real Time Streaming Protocol (RTSP)

In the modern Internet, applications are required to deliver value. One of the biggest conundrums in recent years has been the battle to actually make the Internet a viable platform for making money. As we'll see throughout the course of this book, one of the biggest drivers for delivering on the "Gold Rush" promise of Internet technologies is *content*. Making content attractive to end consumers to the point where they are willing to pay is a big challenge and one that has been aided by the delivery of Application layer protocols such as RTSP, which enables the delivery of real-time video and audio in variable qualities. The other Application layer protocols we've looked at so far in this chapter work in a request/response manner, whereby the client asks for some piece of content, the content is delivered using TCP or UDP, and then the client application can display the content to the user. While these mechanisms are suitable for a large number of applications in the Internet, there also exists a requirement to deliver content, be it images, audio, video, or a combination of all three, in real time. Imagine if a user were to try to watch a full-screen video file of a one-hour movie using HTTP or FTP as the Application layer protocol. The movie file might be several hundred megabytes, if not several gigabytes, in size. Even with modern broadband services deliverable to the home, this type of large file size does not fit well in the "download then play" model we saw previously.

RTSP uses a combination of reliable transmission over TCP (used for control) and best-efforts delivery over UDP (used for content) to stream content to users. By this, we mean that the file delivery can start and the client-side application can begin displaying the audio and video content before the complete file has arrived. In terms of our one-hour movie example, this means that the client can request a movie file and watch a "live" feed similar to how one would watch a TV. Along with this "on demand" type service, RTSP also enables the delivery of live broadcast content that would not be possible with traditional download and play type mechanisms.

The Components of RTSP Delivery

During our look at RTSP, we'll use the term to describe a number of protocols that work together in delivering content to the user.

RTSP

RTSP is the control protocol for the delivery of multimedia content across IP networks. It is based typically on TCP for reliable delivery and has a very similar operation and syntax to HTTP. RTSP is used by the client application to communicate to the server information such as the media file being requested, the type of application the client is using, the mechanism of delivery of the file (unicast or multicast, UDP or TCP), and other important control information commands such as DESCRIBE, SETUP, and PLAY. The actual multimedia content is not typically delivered over the RTSP connection(s), although it can be interleaved if required. RTSP is analogous to the remote control of the streaming protocols.

Real Time Transport Protocol (RTP)

RTP is the protocol used for the actual transport and delivery of the real-time audio and video data. As the delivery of the actual data for audio and video is typically delay sensitive, the lighter weight UDP protocol is used as the Layer 4 delivery mechanism, although TCP might also be used in environments that suffer higher packet loss. The RTP flow when delivering the content is unidirectional from the server to the client. One interesting part of the RTP operation is that the source port used by the server when sending the UDP data is *always* even—although it is dynamically assigned. The destination port (i.e., the UDP port on which the client is listening) is chosen by the client and communicated over the RTSP control connection.

Real Time Control Protocol (RTCP)

RTCP is a complimentary protocol to RTP and is a bidirectional UDP-based mechanism to allow the client to communicate stream-quality information back to the object server. The RTCP UDP communication *always* uses the next UDP source port up from that used by the RTP stream, and consequently is *always* odd. Figure 3–7 shows how the three protocols work together.

RTSP Operation

The RTSP protocol is very similar in structure and specifically syntax to HTTP. Both use the same URL structure to describe an object, with RTSP using the

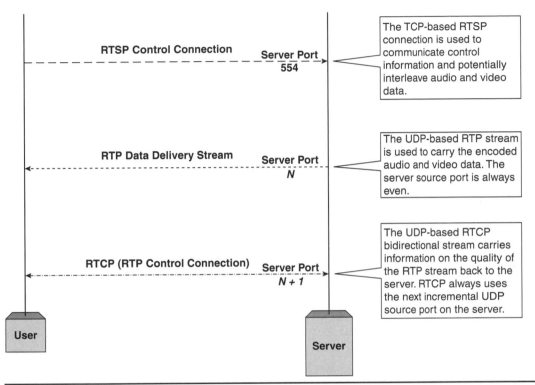

Figure 3–7   The three main application protocols used in real-time streaming.

rtsp:// scheme rather than the http://. RTSP, however, introduces a number of additional headers (such as DESCRIBE, SETUP, and PLAY) and also allows data transport out-of-band and over a different protocol, such as RTP described earlier. The best way to understand how the components described previously work together to deliver an audio/video stream is to look at an example. The basic steps involved in the process are as follows:

1. The client establishes a TCP connection to the servers, typically on TCP port 554, the well-known port for RTSP.

2. The client will then commence issuing a series of RTSP header commands that have a similar format to HTTP, each of which is acknowledged by the server. Within these RTSP commands, the client will describe to the server details of the session requirements, such as the version of RTSP it supports, the transport to be used for the data flow, and any associated UDP or TCP port information. This information is

passed using the DESCRIBE and SETUP headers and is augmented on the server response with a Session ID that the client, and any transitory proxy devices, can use to identify the stream in further exchanges.

3. Once the negotiation of transport parameters has been completed, the client will issue a PLAY command to instruct the server to commence delivery of the RTP data stream.

4. Once the client decides to close the stream, a TEARDOWN command is issued along with the Session ID instructing the server to cease the RTP delivery associated with that ID.

Example—RTSP with UDP-Based RTP Delivery

Let's consider an example interaction where the client and server will use a combination of TCP-based RTSP and UDP-based RTP and RTCP to deliver and view a video stream. In the first step, the client will establish a TCP connection to port 554 on the server and issue an OPTIONS command showing the protocol version used for the session. The server acknowledges this with a 200 OK message, similar to HTTP.

```
C->S  OPTIONS rtsp://video.foocorp.com:554 RTSP/1.0
Cseq: 1

S->C  RTSP/1.0 200 OK
      Cseq: 1
```

Next, the client issues a DESCRIBE command that indicates to the server the URL of the media file being requested. The server responds with another 200 OK acknowledgment and includes a full media description of the content, which is presented in either Session Description Protocol (SDP) or Multimedia and Hypermedia Experts Group (MHEG) format.

```
C->S  DESCRIBE rtsp://video.foocorp.com:554/streams/example.rm RTSP/1.0
      Cseq:2

S->C  RTSP/1.0 200 OK
      Cseq: 2
      Content-Type: application/sdp
Content-Length: 210
      <SDP Data...>
```

In the third stage of the RTSP negotiation, the client issues a SETUP command that identifies to the server the transport mechanisms, in order of preference, the client wants to use. We won't list all of the available transport options here (the RFC obviously contains an exhaustive list), but we'll see the client request RTP over UDP on ports 5067 and 5068 for the data transport. The server responds with confirmation of the RTP over UDP transport mechanism and the client-side ports and includes the unique Session ID and server port information.

```
C->S  SETUP rtsp://video.foocorp.com:554/streams/example.rm RTSP/1.0
      Cseq: 3
      Transport: rtp/udp;unicast;client_port=5067-5068

S->C  RTSP/1.0 200 OK
      Cseq: 3
      Session: 12345678
      Transport: rtp/udp;client_port=5067-5068;server_port=6023-6024
```

Finally, the client is now ready to commence the receipt of the data stream and issues a PLAY command. This simply contains the URL and Session ID previously provided by the server. The server acknowledges this PLAY command, and the RTP stream from the server to client will begin.

```
C->S  PLAY rtsp://video.foocorp.com:554/streams/example.rm RTSP/1.0
      Cseq: 4
      Session: 12345678

S->C  RTSP/1.0 200 OK
      Cseq: 4
```

Once the client decides that the stream can be stopped, a TEARDOWN command is issued over the RTSP connection referenced only by the Session ID. The server again acknowledges this and the RTP delivery will cease.

```
C->S  TEARDOWN rtsp://video.foocorp.com:554/streams/example.rm RTSP/1.0
      Cseq: 5
      Session: 12345678

S->C  RTSP/1.0 200 OK
      Cseq: 5
```

Figure 3–8 shows this example in a simplified graphic form.

Other Options for Data Delivery

In certain scenarios, the best-effort, dynamic port methods of UDP-based RTP, as described previously, are not suitable. Some environments might consider the

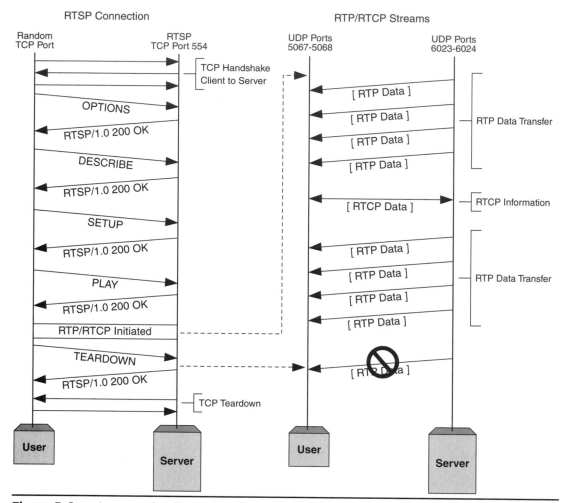

Figure 3–8   An example of RTSP in action with the video and audio data being delivered over a separate UDP-based RTP stream.

allocation of dynamic source and destination UDP ports through firewalls to be something they can live happily without. Moreover, just the nature of the Layer 1 and Layer 2 transport mechanisms underlying the data delivery might not be suited to nonguaranteed UDP traffic. In either instance, RTSP allows for the negotiation of the RTP delivery of the media data to be interleaved into the existing TCP connection.

When interleaving, the client-to-server SETUP command has the following format:

```
C->S   SETUP rtsp://video.foocorp.com:554/streams/example.rm RTSP/1.0
         Cseq: 3
         Transport: rtp/avp/tcp; interleaved=0-1
```

The changeover in the preceding example is in the transport description. First, the transport mechanisms have changed to show that the RTP delivery must be over TCP rather than UDP. Second, the addition of the `interleaved` option shows that the RTP data should be interleaved and use channel identifiers 0 and 1—0 will be used for the RTP data and 1 will be used for the RTCP messages. To confirm the transport setup, the server will respond with confirmation and a Session ID as before:

```
S->C   RTSP/1.0 200 OK
         Cseq: 3
         Session: 12345678
         Transport: rtp/ avp/tcp; interleaved=0-1
```

The RTP and RTCP data can now be transmitted over the existing RTSP TCP connection with the server using the 0 and 1 identifiers to represent the relevant channel.

One further delivery option for RTP and RTCP under RTSP is to wrap the delivery of all media streaming components inside traditional HTTP frame formats. This removes most barriers presented when using streaming media through firewalled environments, as even the most stringent administrator will typically allow HTTP traffic to traverse perimeter security. While HTTP and RTSP interleaved delivery of the streamed media data will make the content available to the widest possible audience, when you consider the overhead of wrapping all RTP data inside either an existing TCP stream or, worse still, inside HTTP, it is the least efficient method for delivery. To enable the streaming media client browser to cope with the different options described previously, most offer the client users the ability to configure their preferred delivery mechanism or mechanisms, and the timeout that should be imposed in failing between them. What you will see from a client perspective is that the client application will first request that the stream be delivered using RTP in UDP, and if the stream does not arrive within x seconds (as it is potentially being blocked by an intermediate firewall), it will fail back to using RTP interleaved in the existing RTSP connection.

RTSP and RTP—Further Reading

For further information on the RTSP and RTP protocols, RFCs 2326 and 1889, respectively, are a good source.

Secure Sockets Layer (SSL)

The final protocol we'll look at in this chapter is neither a Layer 4 transport protocol nor an Application layer protocol, but one that sits between these layers to provide security services to many modern Internet applications. Secure Sockets Layer, or SSL, has been one of the major forces in Internet security technology since its inception by Netscape Communications, and continues to be included in all major browsers. This has enabled Web application developers to deliver secure content and services using traditional HTTP servers with few changes required in terms of the setup of the basic server or restructuring of the HTML content. The other major advantage of the integration of SSL into all major browsers is its transparency to the user. SSL typically gets used without the knowledge of the client, other than the appearance of a small padlock in the corner of the browser window, thus meaning that no additional level of expertise is required to use Internet applications with this security. Figure 3–9 shows a browser that is currently using SSL.

While the most common implementation of SSL is within Web browsers, creating the application protocol hybrid known as HTTPS, it should be remembered that it is a transparent protocol available to any TCP/IP-based application. Along with HTTPS, other common SSL secured protocols include SMTPS and Telnet-S.

The Need for Application Security

The need for security within Internet applications is clear—the Internet is still a public network with little or no security infrastructure designed to protect *all* users. Imagine using the online services of your favorite bank. Passing important data such as your bank account number, password, and balance across the Internet using only HTTP represents a huge personal security risk, as the data is potentially visible to any device sitting between your browser and the bank's Web site. SSL can be used very effectively to hide all of all the application data

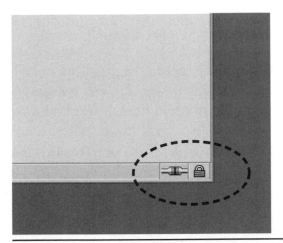

Figure 3–9   A Web browser will typically use SSL when instructed by the Web site with little or no input required by the user. The use of SSL can be seen by the inclusion of a small padlock in the browser.

as it traverses the Internet to prevent anybody snooping the connection from reading personal data—a process referred to as *encryption*.

The second important feature provided by SSL for Internet applications is authentication; in other words, the ability for the client to be able to distinguish the Web site as valid. Imagine in our previous bank example if another rogue site were to masquerade as the bank's Web site. This might allow the rogue site to intercept the personal and banking details of thousands of customers, not a welcome situation. SSL provides mechanisms to implement *authentication* as a way for each side to identify itself to the other.

The final security element that is provided by SSL is *tamper detection*. Imagine finally that someone were to sit between the client and the bank's Web site and change certain pieces of data as they pass back and forth. This would give the opportunity to alter key personal and banking data and potentially set up fraudulent transactions. SSL provides mechanisms for each side to ensure that the Application layer data being sent and received has not changed in any way as it traverses the Internet.

For the Internet to continue to grow, not only in size, but also as a credible medium for business and commerce, it must be able to provide mechanisms such as SSL as a way to guarantee security.

Fitting SSL into the Seven Layer Model

In the concepts of the OSI Seven Layer Model as we saw in Chapter 2, *Understanding Layer 2, 3, and 4 Protocols*, SSL sits between the Application layer and the Transport layer, traditionally seen as part of the Presentation layer. This means that the use of SSL is selectively performed by each application rather than as a whole with encryption based in IPSec. This gives the client machine the ability to run secure services for certain applications only, while remaining impartial to the underlying Layer 3 and 4 services below. In comparison, IPSec, for example, can operate in a tunneling mode, which means that all traffic flowing to or from a particular address or range of addresses is encrypted right down to the IP layer. Within SSL, only the Application layer data is encrypted. Figure 3–10 shows the presence of SSL in the OSI model.

Encryption and Cryptography

The process of encryption and decryption fundamentally means to take some source data, transform it to a state where it cannot be read by anyone else, and then transform it back to its original state, thus rendering it readable once more. This approach requires the use of two important elements: the *Cryptographic Algorithm*, or *cipher*, and a *key*. A cipher is a mathematical formula or function that is applied either to the original data (to encrypt) or to the transformed data (to decrypt). One thing always remains true, however—the cipher used to encrypt the data must also be used to decrypt at the other end. To enable this commonality in a network such as the Internet where there are enormous numbers of potential client-server connection combinations, a series of standard ciphers have been developed over time such as Data Encryption Standard (DES) and RC4.

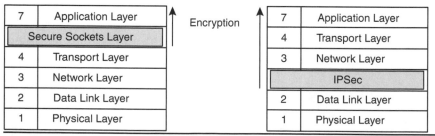

Figure 3–10   Where SSL sits in the OSI model in comparison to IPSec.

As these ciphers are well known, they rely on the second element to introduce some form of random factor to the process, known as a key. The use of a key, or series of keys, gives the cipher the ability to encrypt the data in such a way so as not to be decrypted easily. If you were to encrypt a simple sentence using an algorithm that is widely known, it would be a relatively simple task to run the data through the same algorithm and arrive at the answer. The use of a key means that in order to decrypt the data, the recipient must know both the appropriate cipher to use and the key used to encrypt the data originally.

This combination of cipher and key forms the basic premise of modern cryptography: Decryption with the known key is simple, but decryption without the key is extremely difficult and in most cases computationally impossible. SSL uses a combination of two basic encryption techniques, *symmetric-key encryption* and *public-key encryption*.

Symmetric-Key Encryption

With symmetric-key encryption, both sides use the same key value to perform both the encryption and decryption. Figure 3–11 shows a simple graphical representation of symmetric-key encryption.

Symmetric-key encryption has a number of advantages and disadvantages. First, performing this type of encryption and decryption is computationally inexpensive, which means that the performance of applications using symmetric keys is generally better. On the downside, if the shared key is compromised on either side, the security of the encryption between the parties is broken. Moreover,

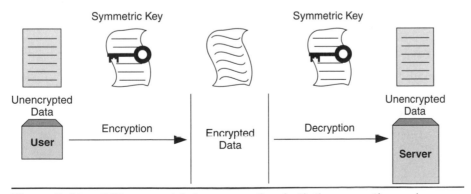

Figure 3–11   With symmetric-key encryption, both the encryption and decryption use the same key.

the process of sharing a single shared key between two sides wanting to use symmetric-key encryption can be cumbersome. Imagine two Internet-based users wishing to communicate—they must first share a key to use before they can encrypt and transmit data. This in itself is a major headache, as the key cannot just be simply sent in clear text over the Internet for fear of being captured. SSL uses symmetric-key encryption for bulk encryption—that is, the encryption of all Application layer data—but it employs a very clever technique to arrive at a common shared key—*public-key* or *asymmetric-key encryption*.

Public-Key or Asymmetric-Key Encryption

As its name suggests, public-key or asymmetric-key encryption uses two different keys to perform encryption and decryption, respectively. These keys are known as the *public* and *private* keys and are mathematically linked to security. The mathematics of public-key encryption are different from those in symmetric-key encryption, as any data encrypted using the public key cannot be easily decrypted using the public key, and similarly with the private key. For public-key encryption to work correctly, the client must encrypt using the public key and the server must decrypt using the private key. As a result, the security of the public key is largely irrelevant and it is commonly available. In SSL terms, the public key is carried in a certificate—more on that later. The security of the private key, however, is of utmost importance, and typically, the private key will never leave the server for which it was generated for fear of compromising the security of the key pair. Therefore, in summary, if you encrypt with the widely available public key, the resulting data can only be decrypted using the corresponding private key. Figure 3–12 shows a simple representation of public-key encryption.

This approach affords private-key encryption a couple of key advantages. First, the combination of corresponding, mathematically linked keys means that once the data has been encrypted, it can only be decrypted by the holder of the private key. Second, as the public key can be transmitted in clear text to the intended receiver, it is well suited to large-scale, public networks such as the Internet. The main downside of public-key encryption is that it is computationally expensive, thus rendering it unsuitable for situations in which large volumes are required. Above all, the security of the private key is paramount; if it is lost or compromised, the entire premise on which the process is built is broken.

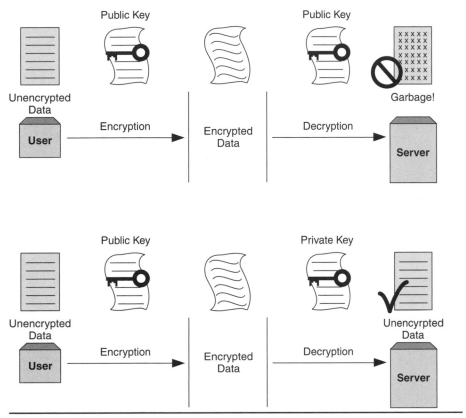

Figure 3–12   In asymmetric-key or public-key encryption, any data encrypted using the easily available public key can only be decrypted using the corresponding private key.

SSL—Combining Symmetric and Asymmetric Encryption

Therefore, on the one hand we have a symmetric encryption mechanism that is computationally cheap but does not scale well to large numbers of users, and on the other, we have a computationally expensive algorithm which *does* scale well due to its concept of public keys. The answer in terms of SSL is to use a combination of both of these mechanisms to achieve the result we're looking for. The aim of combining the two methods is to allow for encrypted access from anywhere by anyone. The process uses asymmetric encryption to initialize the connection, and then uses symmetric encryption to provide a secure communication channel for the duration of the conversation.

When communications begin, the client creates a random number whose length is determined by the encryption strength required. This large random number will effectively form the shared private key for the symmetric encryption that will be used to exchange application data. The client encrypts this random number with the public key and sends the encrypted version of this to the server. The asymmetric encryption at this stage ensures that only the private key can decrypt the data. Once decrypted, this random number is now used as the symmetric key for the duration of the conversation, as each party has successfully shared a common key. The beauty of this process is that the actual private keys (random numbers) never actually traverse the connection in clear form, thus minimizing the chance of being intercepted. Figure 3–13 shows this combination of symmetric and public-key encryption as used by SSL.

Encryption Algorithms

There are many encryption algorithms used, and each provides different levels of encryption, depending on the degree of security required. Earlier algorithms were 40 bits in length, but with today's computing power can typically be cracked within a few hours. The longer the encryption length, the harder they are to crack. All algorithms work in conjunction with a secret key to create the encryption. In the case of SSL, this secret key is the randomly generated number. Common encryption algorithms used today are DES, 3DES, and AES.

Certificates

Now that we've seen the importance of passing the public key within SSL, let's look at the mechanism used to undertake this. Certificates are used in SSL to perform two key functions: first, they provide a level of authentication, potentially for both sides, and second, they provide a standard format in which to pass the public key to the requester. Certificates are like digital passports that can authenticate an organization to a user on connection to its site. Two types of certificates can be used: a *server* certificate and a *client* certificate. In a typical SSL environment, only the server certificate is used. This is so that the server (or site) can authenticate who they are on the initial client request and pass the public key. Remember, it is the client that initiates the connection and asks for the certificate to be sent. This allows an organization to publish its services, and even though the users cannot see where they are going (e.g., there is no storefront, or actual physical structure), they know they have connected to the site based on the server certificate issued. While we agree that this could be spoofed

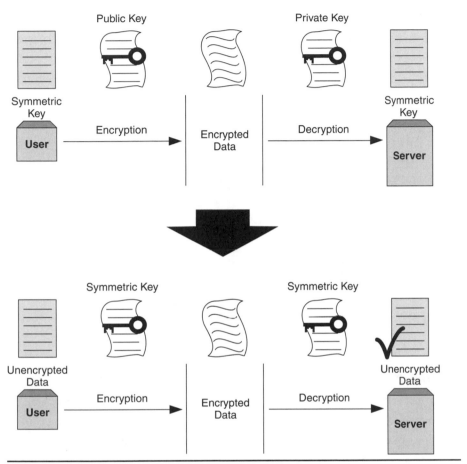

Figure 3–13   SSL uses a combination of public-key encryption to exchange the symmetric-key and symmetric encryption to encrypt the bulk application data.

in theory, one has to question the rationality of this. It requires that the private key be retrieved, DNS entries to that site be hijacked, or updated to the new address, and all of this needs to happen without the existing site becoming aware of it. This is highly unlikely in an age where security is a number-one agenda item, and a highly active site would be immediately aware of a site failure or attack. In addition, a user must actually make a credit card payment to this fraudulent site. If this did happen, it would have to be to a site that is not well monitored and actively trading, and therefore very rarely visited, which in turn makes the exercise superfluous as no huge revenue or loss of reputation would be achieved by the hacker. Typically, the receipt of a server certificate is all that is required to begin a secure connection with a site. In some cases, the site also wants to ensure that the users are who they say they are. This is certainly a requirement in business-to-business transactions where companies want to be able to control access to their site, especially when access to sensitive information or large sums of money are involved.

Client certificates are used to provide client-side authentication. These certificates, normally derived from the server certificate, are loaded on to the user's machine, and on connection, the server will request the certificate to be sent to it to authenticate the user. As each certificate will have a unique identifier, this can be used to track access. Should connectivity no longer be permitted or required, then this unique identifier can also be used to revoke access to the specific site.

Having the ability to provide client and server authentication builds a very compelling case for SSL deployment. Figure 3–14 is an example of what a certificate looks like followed by the associated private key:

Certificates such as these can be easily copied and pasted into a security appliance.

Certificate Authorities

Certificate authorities (CAs) are like the passport control of the SSL world. They confirm that a site is what it says it is, as they have signed the certificate. Many organizations act as CAs and sign certificates on behalf of sites. These organizations are often seen as respected businesses or in some cases quasi-government type departments such as a post office or telecommunications provider. The largest ones around today are dedicated to providing a certificate signing function, such as Verisign, Entrust, and Thawte. By default, Web browsers have a list of accepted CAs, which is checked when a site is accessed. If the CA is not present, the browser will display a message asking if this certificate should be accepted. Adding or deleting CAs can be done by users within their favorite browser. Certificates have the ability to be chained. This means that a certificate can be trusted if it has a link or chain back to the original issuer whom you trust. This method is transparent to the user and is handled by the SSL protocol.

-----BEGIN CERTIFICATE-----
IFtTCCBR6gAwIBAgIEN0sJFTANBgkqhkiG9w0BAQQFADCBwzELMAkGA1UEB
VVMxFDASBgNVBAoTC0VudHJ1c3QubmV0MTswOQYDVQQLEzJ3d3cuZW50cnV
ZXQvQ1BTIGluY29ycC4gYnkgcmVmLiAobGltaXRzIGxpYWIuKTE1MCMGA1U
LmVudHJ1c3QubmV0L0NQUyBpbmNvcnAuIGJ5IHJlZi4gKGxpbWl0cyBsaWF
THChjKSAxOTk5IEVudHJ1c3QubmV0IExpbWl0ZWQxOjA4BgNVBAMTVudHJ1c3QubmV0IFNlY3Vy
ZSBTZXJ2ZXIgQ2VydGlmaWNhdGlvbiBBdXRob3JpdHkxDjAMBgNVBAMTBUNSTDEyMCygKqAohiZ
odHR3QubmV0
L0NSTC9zZXJ2ZXIxLmNybDAfBgNVHSMEGDAWgBTwF2ITVT2z/woAa/tQhJfz7WLQGjAdBgNVHQ4
EFgQU3Rc4WmXyFuApzKBZCUyzwqoO6jkwCQYDVR0TBAgkqhkiG9n0HQQAEDDAKGwRWNC4wAwIDq
DANBgkqhkiG9w0BAQQFAAOBgQBbSMGk6BtJ7g6UzC4hL1nJZYQldua3ot6K7EstAu6pBiE0DhAG
JKm0tCrS16h
KGMpIDE5OTkgRW50cnVzdC5uZXQffffltaXRlZDE6MDgGA1UEAxMxRW50cn
ZXQgU2VjdXJlIFNlcnZlciBDZXJ0aWZpY2F0aW9uIEF1dGhvcml0eTAeFw0
MDgxNjA4MjdaFw0wMjAxMDgxNjM4MjdaMH4xCzAJBgNVBAYTAlNFMRIwEAY
EwlTdG9ja2hvbG0xEjAQBgNVBAcTCVN0b2NraG9sbTEUMBIGA1UEChMLQmx
aWwgQUIxFDASBgNVBAsTC0RldmVsb3BtZW50MRswGQYDVQQDExJ2aXXAyYS5
dGFpbC5jb20wgZ8wDQYJKoZIhvcNAQEBBQADgY0AMIGJAoGBALctVjRkmPJ
FsI/oo1Xh0yJqyC/Vl2tWS3ujM8lSqCA9afq8cqfcRN5cWcelix5oEbaz5e
GdtLVWqBHw09As3w1AyZsdiSUpdOFNdjPhv9IC9S13y7zCzr0SyS/u7l1c4
c3QubmV0L2NwczCBwAYIKwYBBQUHAgIwgbMwEhYLRW50cnVzdC5uZXQwAwI
9TsMAFHBudxPK58IPkKUSpdxZvg7AgMBAAGjggL4MIIC9DCCAQcGA1UdIAS
/DCB+QYJKoZIhvcZ9B0sCMIHrMCYGCCsGAQUFBwIBFhpodHRwOi8vd3d3LnEudHJ1c3QubmV0IE
NQUyBpbmNvcnBvcmF0ZWQgYnkgcmVmZXJlbmNlIiBUayBjb250YWludcyBsaW1pdGF0aW9ucyBvb
iB3YXJyYW50aWVzIGFuZCBsaWFi
aWxpdGllcy4gIENvcHlyaWdodCAoYykgMTk5OSBFbnRyydXN0Lm5ldCAgd3d
dHJ1c3QubmV0L2NwczALBgNVHQ8EBAMCBaAwKwYDVR0QBCQwIoAPMjAwMTA
NjM4MjdagQ8yMDAxMDkyMTA0MzgyN1owEQYJYIZIAYb4QgEBBAQDAgZAMBM
JQQMMAoGCCsGAQUFBwMBMIIBHQYDVR0fBIIBFDCCARAwgd+ggdyggdmkgdY
CzAJBgNVBAYTAlVTMRQwEgYDVQQKEwtFbnRy5ldDE7MDkGA1UECxMyd3d3
/wWqspaKSNsWfqc0AWFfgKznJJmnxsyThudodg5iTM1Nfr93aD2P/3qPMxSSEm/T/
uOKBaLPLVd3dmjPc/0v1AU48dc0hgx6VhqX98poLiHJAHg==
-----END CERTIFICATE-----

-----BEGIN RSA PRIVATE KEY-----
Proc-Type: 4,ENCRYPTED
DEK-Info: DES-EDE3-CBC,9BCDFA41DAC78C8D

+AsRro1zm2vlV0deB0kw9geWpMJoLOz67sdb8+8E2Pal5hZC1asZapwHGXOAgqeQfUb6VZKy+2H
zjz8Nw6I3xcAyi7xnF1YYRJxlz7sA+5ACBSAYvZGZRXF7jyTXomIITrwPt40V9uGldjFmwAd6e1
k1qxKi2T6qtzdVeYZhz27+njtMkDa1PVdJWbcLFyLMRZAUp5Ubu8mIUgkReyMSPMdn6bjmf7hKE
3jbT/REnICiDcLe3SZzXes8mckUOOV++dBD+orBxeU8dkB59ivWE/WlAP4cf1wOPS/
B1yzFsHqlbyqlvtfxjF472vU4V0JLOe0RQ5NyVqw09N/NHrgBHce6JgwEHfmgfRr/
P2RFYvwhs1wUvKVgOOK8KxHdRgNMGshFWMOGmrWV82dO0pywC25Xlq1GiC6vqlwHxvzfSr4pnYv
5VcgDzfkvsYJCVpTiWYiS522Svb0Ln3Gyx55JgIdlaMVhZUCmdbRqH6KFoWyr0Ud+++6PbI+HWb
VPBpifrqyj3LDnuPTRTDkwy7WlzggXXY1TbdO8XY7KrhgpcBpN4amILANhcZG/
-----END RSA PRIVATE KEY-----

Figure 3–14   Sample of a public certificate and private key. As you can see, it is merely clear text and can be easily copied.

SSL in Action

Let's see the combination of cipher suites, keys, algorithms. and certificates in action as we run through an example SSL session.

When enabling SSL on services on your server, you will first need to create a private and public key pair and corresponding certificate. This process is automatically initiated on most Web servers and will result in the creation of what is known as a certificate signing request, or CSR. This CSR, containing the public key, should be forwarded to the chosen CA for signing, and once completed imported back into the Web server. A point to note here is that the private key must stay private; if it were available, someone could easily masquerade as your site because the public key is just that, public. With the private and public key pair, all encrypted traffic can be decrypted. But let's get back to the CSR. The CSR needs to be sent to a CA, who will sign it and return it to you for you to validate your domain name. We must point out here that a certificate is tied to a domain name and not an IP address. This domain name needs to be resolved to the address of the server in order to work. Once complete, the Web site can be ready for use, and all that is required is that the servers have the SSL service running.

Now we are ready to begin the actual SSL setup as illustrated in Figure 3–15. Let's look at the steps in more detail, remembering that certain message types within the SSL protocol are used to determine specific requests:

1. Once the client has established a TCP session on port 443 with the server, the client sends a client hello message. This client hello includes information such as the cipher suites that it supports.

2. The server selects the cipher suite from the list presented and responds with a server hello indicating to the client the ciphers it deems suitable. The client and the server have now agreed on a cipher suite to use.

3. The server then issues the client a copy of its certificate (remember that this certificate also contains the public key). Optionally, the server may request a copy of the client's certificate if client-side authentication is required.

4. Next, the server sends a server hello done message to tell the client it has completed the first phase of the session setup. As there is no key yet, this process is carried out in clear text.

5. The client now generates a random number, encrypts it with its public key, and sends the server the client key. This process is known as the *client key exchange*. This is the symmetric key that will be used for the duration of the symmetric encryption session. Communication from here on is encrypted.

6. The client now sends a change cipher spec message to the server to say it will now begin using the negotiated cipher suite (determined in step 2) for the duration of the session.

7. Once this is done, the client sends a finished message to the server to say that it is ready.

8. The server, in turn, sends a change cipher spec message to the client using the agreed information. The server also sends out a finished message on completion.

9. A secure encrypted tunnel is now set up, and communication can begin using the symmetric encryption details negotiated.

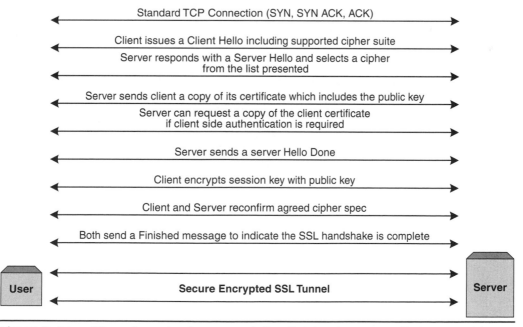

Figure 3–15 SSL session setup is a computationally intensive process that we need to offload to increase network performance.

One key piece of information in this exchange, which we will see has relevance in content switching in later chapters, is the SSL Session ID. This is a random identifier agreed by both sides when first initiating the SSL session to the server and is used to uniquely identify the tunnel they have established. One option that is held by the client during the negotiation process described previously is to reuse a set of agreed ciphers and keys by including the Session ID in the client hello it sends to the server. Provided that the server is configured to allow this type of session reuse, it will skip the need to swap the symmetric key and thus bypass the big number arithmetic needed, in turn speeding up the process. The SSL Session ID can be read in clear text, as it is not passed encrypted between client and server.

SSL Summary

SSL is a standards-based encryption and authentication mechanism widely used within the Internet today. While by far the most common implementations use HTTP as the Application layer protocol, SSL can be used to secure other applications. As we'll see in later chapters, the inclusion of SSL as a security mechanism for modern Web sites creates yet another part of the puzzle of content switching.

Summary

As with our coverage of Layer 2, 3, and 4 protocols, there are many other more detailed books covering the Application layer protocols we saw in this chapter. Hopefully, however, this chapter has served to give a better understanding of the ways in which TCP, UDP, and IP can be combined to provide application services, all optionally wrapped in SSL for greater security. Equipped with this understanding, we can begin to understand the concepts of content switching and put the techniques to use to solve many of the scalability problems of modern IP networks.

4

The Concepts of Content Switching

Before we look at the applications of content switching, such as server and firewall load balancing, it's important to understand some of the underlying terms and concepts we'll use freely in later chapters. As with all modern networking disciplines, content switching has its own vocabulary. We'll use terms like *virtual servers*, *application redirection*, and *deep packet inspection* to describe the applications, so a good grounding now will aid our understanding later. This chapter will look at each of these terms and concepts in turn as a precursor to more in-depth discussion in later chapters.

Virtual Services and Application Redirection

One of the most fundamental concepts in content switching is the difference between virtual services and application redirection. The simplest way to understand this difference is to consider two applications that best describe their operation—server load balancing and Web cache redirection. First, in server load balancing, the client will be directing traffic toward an end point of the content switch. That is to say that the content switch "owns" a virtual IP address to which the client will attach. When we refer to these services and IP addresses being virtual, we mean that they are used to represent a series of hidden resources such as Web servers—in every other way these virtual services are real in that they are normal, routable IP addresses accessible across the public or private network. Server load balancing is an example of an application that uses

71

virtual services, and the destination address of the client's requests are owned by the content switch.

In Web cache redirection, the client will typically be directing its requests to a service that sits away from the content switch. The natural direction of the traffic flow is such that the request will pass transparently through the content switch, giving it access to manipulate the traffic as it passes. Think of Web cache redirection as an application that intercepts or hijacks the application data as it passes through, offering the network designer or administrator the ability to manipulate the traffic flow. Web cache redirection is an example of an application redirection service where the client's requests are passing through the content switch on their way to the destination.

Virtual Services and Virtual IP Addresses

Let's look in a little more detail at the concept of a virtual service. For virtual services, the content switch will own an address that is used to represent a pool of resources, typically servers, residing behind it. The virtual service will be represented by an IP address, commonly referred to as the VIP, to which the client will attach. While the resources to which the client's requests will eventually be directed may be either directly attached to, or some way from, the content switch, all requests from the client's perspective will appear to terminate there. Figure 4–1 shows a logical representation of virtual services.

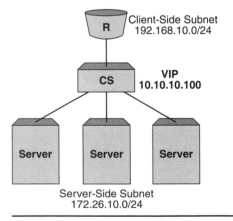

Figure 4–1   Virtual IP address used for standard load balancing.

In Figure 4–1 we can see that the switch owns the IP address 10.10.10.100 that has TCP service attached to it for HTTP traffic. The content switch can be referred to as listening on TCP port 80 at address 10.10.10.100. Behind the content switch are the resources to which connections will be distributed. In server load balancing, as with most virtual service applications, the destination IP address and destination MAC address are translated by the content switch as the mechanism to allocate the required resources. It is important that the response packets return back through the content switch so that the necessary translations are done, ensuring that the clients receive a response from the device to which they are connected; in other words, the content switch VIP.

Application Redirection

Figure 4–2 shows an example of an application redirection service. In this example, the client is requesting a Web page from the Web site of *www.foocorp.com*, which is hosted in a data center many Internet "hops" away. As we see the request in this example, the session is passing through the infrastructure of an ISP looking to reduce demand on their transatlantic Internet connections by implementing caching in their POP. The content switch does not have a virtual service or IP address created, but instead is monitoring the traffic flows for certain matches, typically by things such as destination TCP ports to identify the application being used by particular clients. If the switch sees HTTP traffic

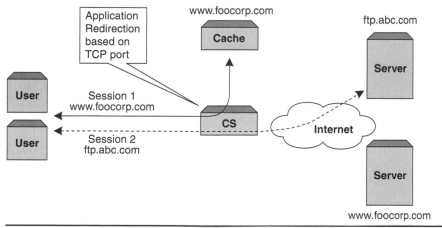

Figure 4–2   Application redirection based on TCP port.

flowing, identified by a destination TCP port of 80, it will redirect the traffic to the one of the caches in the POP rather than consume unnecessary Internet bandwidth sending the requests to the Foocorp Web site.

Web cache redirection, as with most applications implemented using application redirection, works by changing only the destination MAC address rather than both the MAC address and IP address. As we will see in later chapters, this is an important concept when the traffic is only part way to its end destination and there are further network hops remaining.

Resources and Real Servers

The concept of a real server in content switching is very important. While the name might give the impression that the definition must be a traditional server of some flavor, this is not necessarily always the case. In the instances of server load balancing as an application, the real server definitions *are* typically normal Web or application servers. In the instance of cache redirection, the real servers will be the caches rather than a Web server, and in firewall load balancing the real servers merely represent the path through the firewalled network. From this, it's easy to see that a real server is merely the definition of a resource, typically identified by a unique real server IP address, or RIP.

In server load balancing terms, an RIP is the actual IP address the content switch will use when performing the translation required to send a client request to an object server. In application redirection, the real server enables the content switch to resolve a MAC address that must be used when the translation takes place at Layer 2 only.

Real servers are traditionally associated to a group. This means that load balancing is typically done to a group of real servers rather than an individual server. This allows administrators to bring servers into and out of a group without impacting the application. The more servers in a group, the more the load will be distributed. Load distribution is dependent on load balancing metrics discussed in Chapter 5, *Basic Server Load Balancing*.

Frames, Packets, and Sessions

Throughout this book, we will talk about frames, packets, and sessions. In a very basic way, a frame is what is used to communicate at Layer 2 and holds the

MAC address and protocol type information, among others. Packets are traditionally used for layer 3 communications and have the source and destination IP address within the header. A packet is inserted into a frame for communication across a network. A session is made up of a series of packets transporting user requests to a server. Today, most traffic sent across content switches is HTTP. Each object retrieved for a Web page or similar is seen as a single TCP session. When a user requests a page, some having up to 80 or more objects, a session needs to be set up for each object. All of these sessions are "collated" and referred to as a user session.

Determining switch performance, however, relies on session setup. The quicker we can set up a session and tear it down, the quicker we can complete the user session and ultimately display the content requested. Having a low session setup rate can impact the performance of a network and severely delay user response times. Some content switch manufacturers promote simultaneous session support as the key area in order to mask their inefficiencies in the session setup arena.

Lets look at an example. In Table 4–1, we can see that while content switch manufacturer A only supports 500,000 simultaneous sessions, it can set up and tear down 300,000 per second. Content switch manufacturer B can support 2,000,000 simultaneous sessions, but can only set up 10,000 per second.

Table 4–1   Session Per Second vs. Simultaneous Sessions

	MANUFACTURER A	MANUFACTURER B
Maximum simultaneous sessions supported	500,000	2,000,000
Maximum sessions setups per second	300,000	10,000
Time taken to setup 300,000 sessions	1 second	30 seconds

As you can see, the ability to set up and tear down sessions is far more important than maximum simultaneous sessions.

Deep Packet Inspection

This is where content networking really comes into its own. Content switches can typically function extremely well when using Layer 4 information in order to make load balancing decisions. The reason for this is that the Layer 4 information is at a known point within the data packet and will never change. The source IP address, destination IP address, and source and destination TCP ports will always be x bits from the front of the Ethernet packet as they are resident in the IP and TCP headers and will never move—just the values will be different. It is therefore easy to develop ASICs to inspect those headers by counting x bits and scanning 4 bytes, in the case of an IP address. Once the necessary information is found, the switch can then make a load balancing decision. This is why Layer 4 switching is becoming readily available, as this functionality can be done in hardware because the data that is required is constant.

As networks move more into application awareness, the need to look past the TCP port becomes a requirement. Deep packet inspection allows this to happen. By being able to look at varying values within the content of the request, switches can make decisions based on the application type, user request, unique user ID such as cookie, and so forth. One major issue here is that this information might not live within the first frame inspected; it might traverse multiple frames. How content switches handle this is unique to each manufacturer, but essentially, it is this ability that differentiates one content switch from another.

Some manufacturers will use software to perform this function, while others will use ASIC-based hardware with software assist for deep packet inspection.

Summary

While brief, this chapter covers some of the main topics and terms used during this book. Each chapter contains a more in-depth description of these terms while discussing the specific content switching applications.

5

Basic Server Load Balancing

Determining where to begin when discussing the applications of content switching isn't easy. If one thing comes across from the reading of this book, it should be the breadth of applications possible with this technology and how it can be put to use to solve many issues in IP networking. That aside, by far the most well known and commonly implemented applications of content switching is server load balancing. Before any form of naming commonality existed, content switching was most often referred to as server load balancing.

Why Load Balance Servers?

There are often many reasons for using content switching to implement server load balancing solutions, and it's not our intention to cover all of those reasons here. The main contributing factor over the past few years has been the explosion in Internet use and the consequent need for bigger, faster, and more reliable Web sites. While many of the examples given in this book refer to protocols and applications that have their roots in the Internet such as HTTP, HTTPS, and SMTP, it is not true that implementations of server load balancing are limited to these areas. Indeed, anywhere servers exist, it's increasingly likely that there is also a requirement for some form of server load balancing.

While early users of the Internet came to often expect a slow and frustrating experience when browsing the Web, today's user is blessed with ever-increasing access speeds and technologies that in turn drive their expectations of how a Web site should perform. Modern networking has often become a battle of moving the bottleneck around the network with increasing speeds and feeds available to address the issues at all points. While historically server administrators might not have concerned themselves with performance and scalability beyond the bounds of a single box, the ever-increasing performance of networking technology means that the bottleneck can quickly end up being the application or server.

One other key driver of the Internet Age is the globalization of customer base. With a Web presence, an organization need never close its shop doors to customers and can operate 24 hours a day, 7 days a week. This again introduces an interesting challenge to the server administrator in terms of maintenance and availability.

To this end, the implementation of server load balancing can provide advantages such as:

- **Scalability**: An application need no longer be bound by the performance of being hosted on a single server. The ability to organically grow the resources of an application N fold with the implementation of further servers means that server administrators need not be faced with justifying the expense of implementing large scale servers, but can provide a plug-and-play structure potentially using smaller physical servers with better economies of scale.

- **Reliability/redundancy**: The action of putting all your eggs into one proverbial basket comes with inherent risk. No matter how reliable a single server is made to be, a failure in one server will effectively bring down the entire application. Spreading the load over a number of physical servers reduces this exposure enormously.

- **Operability and maintenance**: With a 24 × 7 availability expectation, implementations of server load balancing can help with providing an environment in which servers can be removed from operation for scheduled maintenance such as operating system upgrades, hardware upgrades, and so forth. The ability to roll out new versions and builds of applications while retaining control of when the switch-over occurs can be a powerful use of server load balancing.

The Alternatives to Server Load Balancing

Prior to hardware- or network-based server load balancing technologies, multi-server implementations have used other approaches to increase the availability and scalability of server farms. Typically, such implementations would take the form of server clustering for server load balancing. Such clustering technologies often rely on technologies such as multicast to achieve similar results if somewhat less reliable and, as we've seen in other content switching applications, scalable.

Topologies of Server Load Balancing

The science of implementing networks, whether based on Layers 2, 3, 4, or 7, is never exact. There are many ways to skin the proverbial cat, and while the topology examples shown here are designed to convey some of the common approaches and best practices, they are merely that: examples. Every network, application, and implementation is different, and finding the approach best suited is a skill that comes only from experience.

Most server load balancing topologies can be broadly grouped into one of the following three types:

- **Layer 2 or Bridging SLB**, where the client (or client router) and servers exist in the same Layer 2 VLAN and Layer 3 subnet.
- **Single Arm SLB**, where the content switch is attached via a single logical interface to a Layer 2 or Layer 3 switch.
- **Layer 3 or Routing SLB**, where the client (or client router) and servers exist in different Layer 2 VLANs or Layer 3 subnets.

Layer 2 (Bridging) Server Load Balancing

The most simplistic implementation of server load balancing is using the Layer 2 or bridging model. In this instance, all interfaces on the content switch are in the same VLAN and IP subnet as both the client-side router and the object servers. The content switch presents a VIP in this subnet, which represents the object servers below. Figure 5–1 shows a simplistic representation of a Layer 2 or bridging implementation.

The primary advantage of deploying a solution based on Layer 2 server load balancing is simplicity. The content switch can be placed into the network without any topology alteration other than the introduction of another bridge hop between the client-side router and the object servers. No restructuring of the IP addressing is required to implement the content switch in this instance, thus

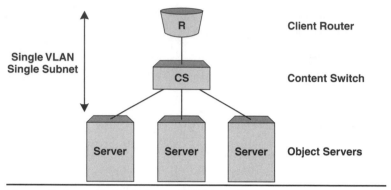

Figure 5–1   Example Layer 2 SLB topology.

eliminating changes to routing tables on the client-side router and default gateways on the object servers.

Traffic flow in Layer 2 server load balancing

Let's walk through an example TCP session using Layer 2 server load balancing for HTTP to see what's involved for all components in the network. Figure 5–2 shows an example Layer 2 server load balancing infrastructure and client. Let's assume that the client is establishing an HTTP connection to the Web site housed in the 10.10.10.0 network that is being server load balanced by the content switch with VIP 10.10.10.100.

The flow from client toward the server looks like:

1. The client issues a DNS lookup to its local DNS server that is resolved to the VIP on the content switch and establishes a TCP session to the VIP by sending a TCP SYN packet.

2. The TCP SYN packet is routed to the client-side router. The client-side router will send a broadcast ARP into the 10.10.10.0 network to resolve the MAC address for 10.10.10.100. The content switch will reply to the router's ARP broadcast with a MAC address it owns and uses to represent the VIP.

3. The client-side router will forward the frame to the MAC address of the content switch. At this point, the content switch will make a load balancing decision and translate the destination MAC and destination IP addresses, altering the checksum information at each layer.

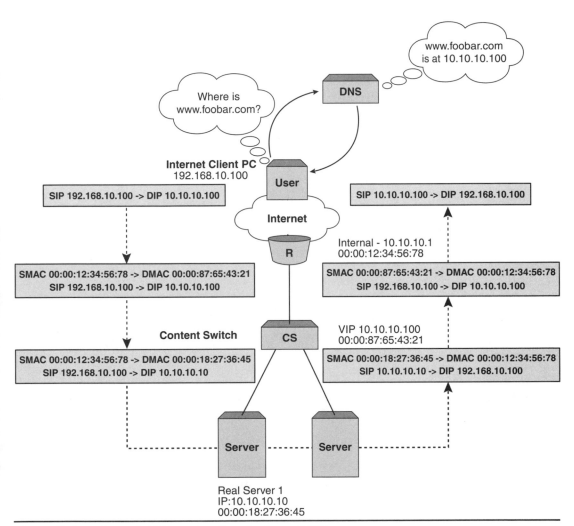

Figure 5–2   Example TCP session flow for Layer 2 SLB.

It's important to note that when the TCP SYN frame, along with all subsequent frames in the TCP session, arrives, the server has no evidence of the involvement of the content switch. That is to say that the Layer 2 and 3 source address information is identical to that which would have been received if the client was talking directly to the object server.

For the flow from the server to the client, the reverse is true:

4. The server replies to the TCP SYN-ACK by sending the frame to its default gateway 10.10.10.1.

5. As the frame has to pass through the Content Switch to get to the default gateway on the Client side Router, the reverse translations are performed with the Source MAC and Source IP addresses translated.

6. Finally, the content switch forwards the frame to the MAC address of the client-side router, which routes the return packet back to the client.

An important point to note during this process is that neither the client nor the object server has visibility of the load balancing that is taking place. The client sees a continuous connection between itself and the VIP owned by the content switch, while the server sees the client connection without evidence of the content switch being involved.

Layer 3 (Routing) Server Load Balancing

Probably the most common implementation of server load balancing is Layer 3 or routing SLB. This is conceptually similar to Layer 2 SLB, but with the distinction that the client router and object servers exist in different Layer 2 VLANs and IP subnets. The content switch can present a VIP in either of these subnets, or in a subnet without a physical interface in certain instances. Figure 5–3 shows a simplistic representation of a Layer 3 or routing implementation

There are two primary advantages of deploying Layer 3 server load balancing:

- **Conservation of address space**. As the object servers are attached into a different subnet to the client router, the opportunity exists to address them using RFC 1918 compliant address space. In many hosting environments and commonly in general ISP connectivity terms, a premium is charged for the use of fully registered IP address space. Deployments of Layer 3 server load balancing present the opportunity to reduce the number of registered IP addresses required.

- **Simplicity**. Logically, the content switch acts as both a Layer 4 (or 7) load balancer and a standard Layer 3 router, which can make the topology easier for standard Layer 2 and 3 network engineers to understand.

So, where does the VIP live in this type of Layer 3 SLB topology? Well, there are basically three options. First, and most commonly, the VIP can be a member

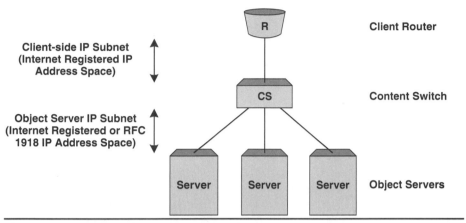

Figure 5–3   Example Layer 3 SLB topology.

of the client-side IP subnet. In this instance, the router does not need to be concerned with the remote subnet housing the object servers, and this allows the deployment to preserve the use of the costly registered Internet addresses. Second, the VIP can be a member of the same subnet as the object server. In this instance, the object server subnet must be publicly routable or translated by a NAT device further upstream. Finally, the VIP may be a member of a subnet not directly attached to the content switch. In this instance, the client router needs to be configured with a static route pointing to the interface of the content switch for the "virtual subnet" housing the VIP. Another alternative to the use of static routes is the use of a dynamic routing protocol. Many content switch vendors allow the configuration of dynamic routing protocols such as OSPF, RIP v2, and BGP with the added option of advertising a specific 32-bit host route corresponding to the VIP depending on its availability. Figure 5–4 shows the options of which subnet the VIP may belong to.

Traffic Flow in Layer 3 Server Load Balancing

Fundamentally, the traffic flow in Layer 3 SLB is the same as with Layer 2, but with two subtle differences. First, as the content switch is now routing rather than switching the frames between the client and server, the source MAC address is changed to that of the server-side router interface on the content switch. As with any switching and routing infrastructure, this fundamental difference remains with content switching.

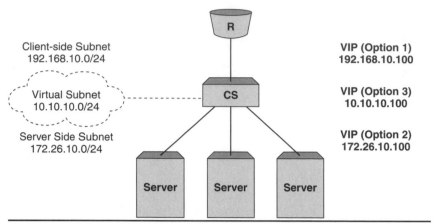

Figure 5–4   Where does the VIP live in Layer 3 SLB?

If we look at the example frame flow from the Layer 2 SLB implementation shown earlier, the steps are very similar and are shown in Figure 5–5:

1. The client resolves the Web site hostname via DNS and establishes a TCP session to the VIP by sending a TCP SYN packet.

2. The TCP SYN packet is routed to the client-side router. The client-side router will send a broadcast ARP into the 10.10.10.0 network to resolve the MAC address for 10.10.10.100. The content switch will reply to the router's ARP broadcast with a MAC address it owns and uses to represent the VIP.

3. The client-side router will forward the frame to the MAC address of the content switch. At this point, the content switch will make a load balancing decision and translate the source MAC, destination MAC, and destination IP addresses, altering the checksum information at each layer.

4. The server replies to the TCP SYN-ACK by sending the frame to its default gateway of 172.26.10.1, MAC address 00:00:89:ab:cd:ef.

5. With Layer 3 SLB, the server will forward the frame directly to the MAC address of the content switch, and the reverse translations are performed with the source MAC and source IP addresses translated. The content switch will also fulfill its role as the inter-subnet router and forward the frame to its default gateway, 10.10.10.1, and change the destination MAC address.

6. Finally, the client-side router routes the return packet back to the client.

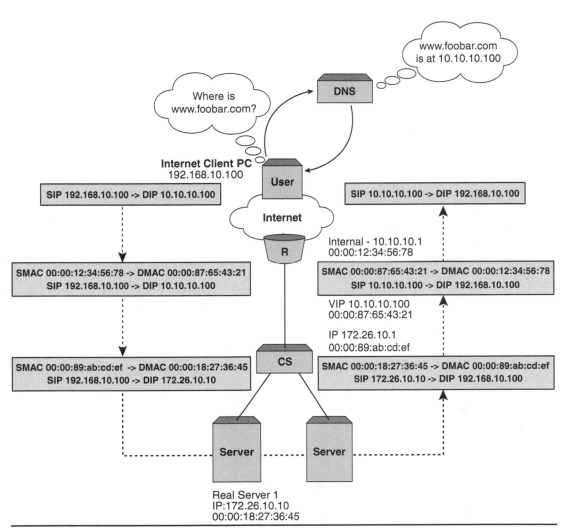

Figure 5–5   Example TCP session flow for Layer 3 SLB.

Single Arm Server Load Balancing

The final topology implementation option we will look at is commonly known as single arm server load balancing. For this implementation, the content switch sits logically to the side of the Layer 2 or 3 infrastructure and consequently out of the data path. While the general principles are similar to those seen in Layer 2 and 3 SLB, the traffic flow can be somewhat different. The main issue when implementing single arm SLB is how to deal with return path traffic from the object servers to the client. In the Layer 2 and 3 topology examples we saw earlier, the return traffic from the object server to the client is forced to pass back through the content switch by virtue of the fact that it is always directly in the data path. When implementing single arm SLB, without considering return traffic, we will end up with a broken TCP or UDP session, as the reverse address translations will not take place and the client will see the object server's IP address respond to a request that was originally sent to the VIP. Figure 5–6 illustrates this problem.

There are two options to deal with return traffic when implementing single arm SLB or any other topology instance where the traffic flow from server to client might bypass the content switch: proxy addresses or direct server return.

Proxy Addresses

The first solution to this issue is the use of proxy addresses. In this instance, when the content switch translates the frames and forwards them to the server, the source IP address will be translated to one owned by the content switch. This will have the effect of forcing traffic back to the content switch before returning to the client, as the object server will believe that the connection originated there.

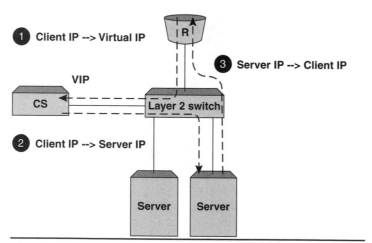

Figure 5–6   Problems with return traffic in single arm SLB can mean that the client ends up with a broken TCP or UDP session.

The main disadvantage of using proxy addresses is that the client IP address details will no longer be preserved through to the object servers; therefore, some of the elegance in the transparency of standard Layer 2 and 3 topologies is lost. The most notable example of this as an issue is the logging of IP address details within Web and application servers, specifically where such information is required as a mechanism for nonrepudiation. Figure 5–7 shows an example traffic flow when a proxy IP address is used for single arm SLB.

Direct Server Return

Direct Server Return (DSR) is useful in managing the issue of implementing single arm SLB, but also provides an advantage in environments where the majority of the data flow is from the server to the client. HTTP and FTP are examples of protocols where a large proportion of the data transfer takes place from the object server to the client, with the client sending only the initial GET request and TCP ACK messages.

In DSR mode, the content switch will NAT only the destination MAC address to that of the object server before forwarding the frame on. For this to work correctly, the object server also needs to be configured to respond to IP

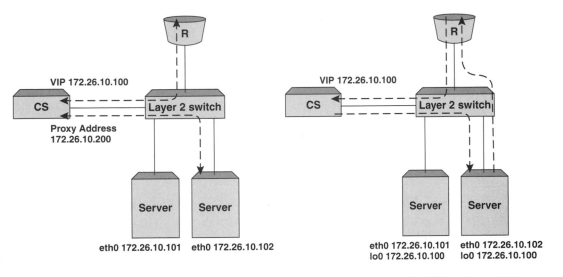

Single Arm SLB Using Proxy Addresses   **Single Arm SLB Using Direct Server Return**

Figure 5–7   The difference in traffic flow for single arm SLB implementations.

connections that are destined for the VIP, which is typically implemented using a loopback address or subinterface; for example, in Linux terms:

```
eth0      Link encap:Ethernet  HWaddr 00:A0:CC:33:74:EB
          inet addr:172.26.10.101  Mask:255.255.255.0
          UP BROADCAST RUNNING MULTICAST  MTU:1500  Metric:1
          RX packets:297581 errors:0 dropped:0 overruns:0 frame:0
          TX packets:266104 errors:1 dropped:0 overruns:0 carrier:2
          collisions:79 txqueuelen:100
          Interrupt:10 Base address:0x1300

lo        Link encap:Local Loopback
          inet addr:172.26.10.100  Mask:255.255.255.0
          UP LOOPBACK RUNNING  MTU:3924  Metric:1
          RX packets:1855 errors:0 dropped:0 overruns:0 frame:0
          TX packets:1855 errors:0 dropped:0 overruns:0 carrier:0
          collisions:0 txqueuelen:0
```

Implementing this loopback interface will allow the IP stack on the server to respond to requests for the VIP, but also use this address on return packets for the client.

Implementing High Availability for SLB

The implementations we've considered so far are simplistic, single component examples. While for some real-world situations this may prove suitable, commonly in today's 24×7 Internet, the requirement for "five nines" availability means that most implementations will need to avoid a single component failure causing a service disruption of any notable length.

Any high availability (HA) implementation will require the addition of more components and the use of resiliency protocols such as VRRP, HSRP, and the Spanning Tree Protocol (STP) to guarantee correct operation. HSRP stands for Hot Standby Router Protocol and is a common virtual router protocol implemented by Cisco Systems. For the purposes of this discussion, we will use the term *VRRP* to refer to both VRRP and HSRP as redundancy protocols. Another option that might be considered is multihoming the object servers to remove the risk of a NIC card failure taking a server out of operation.

Multiple Content Switches and Routers

The most obvious first step in developing an HA design is to add resilient content switches and routers. In the simple examples we've considered so far, we've seen a single Internet feed provided by a single router. Most Internet hosting environments now provide multiline feeds as standard, and many large enterprises are becoming so reliant on the Internet as a service that they are opting for multiple Internet feeds typically provided by different ISPs.

When using a simple HA setup with two routers and two content switches, VRRP instances must be implemented on the single subnet for Layer 2 SLB and on both subnets for Layer 3 SLB. This can be coupled with VRRP running on the upstream routers to provide resilient Layer 2 and 3 paths throughout the network.

Figure 5–8 shows a resilient Layer SLB infrastructure utilizing VRRP instances on both the content switches representing the VIP and the Internet routers. By setting the VRRP priorities to ensure that the left side of each redundant pair is master, a clean data path can be ensured. Client traffic will be naturally drawn in through the left-hand, master router and forwarded to the VIP instance on the left-hand content switch. For return traffic, the object server will forward traffic toward its default gateway, the VRRP instance in subnet 2 on the content switches, which will in turn forward back to the VRRP instance in subnet 1 on the routers. In this instance, the standby content switch on the right-hand side is used only to forward traffic at Layer 2 to the object servers attached directly to it and is performing no server load balancing.

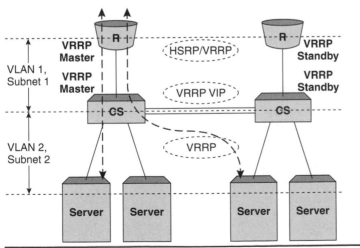

Figure 5–8   Layer 3 SLB implementation with VRRP for resilience.

Figure 5–9 shows the basic traffic flow for this HA implementation. In this instance, the content switch has two cross connects, one in the VLAN connecting the client-side routers and the other in the VLAN containing the servers. This dual cross connect could be replaced by an 802.1q VLAN tagged link comprising both VLANs on a single physical link. In the example shown, traffic entering from the primary router and being processed by the primary content switch may be forwarded across the server VLAN cross connect and to an object server directly attached to the backup content switch. It is important to note that in this instance the session processing and consequent session entry are held in the primary content switch.

Let's consider two possible failure scenarios for this topology. A failure on the primary router would have the following effects:

- The link status on the primary content switch port connecting to the primary router would change to down.

- The standby router would assume VRRP master status after seeing a number of missing multicast advertisements.

- The primary content switch would cease all VRRP multicast advertisements for both subnets (assuming the content switch supports VRRP

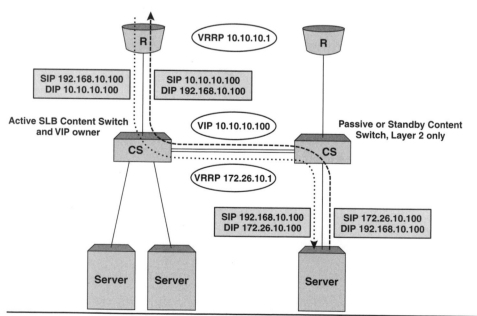

Figure 5–9   Traffic flow in a resilient Layer 3 SLB topology.

port tracking or hot standby functionality), and the standby content switch would assume master status for all VRRP instances.

- All traffic will resume through the stand-by router and content switch using all available server resources.

In this instance, a component failure will cause a minor service interruption while the VRRP statuses on each subnet stabilize. The second possible failure scenario is a failure on the primary content switch, which would have the following effects:

- The link status on the primary router changes to down.
- The standby router would assume VRRP master status after seeing a number of missing multicast advertisements.
- The standby content switch would assume VRRP master status for all instances after seeing a number of missing multicast advertisements.
- The two server resources attached to the primary content switch would become unavailable.
- All traffic would resume through the standby router and content switch using the two remaining server resources.

Figure 5–10 shows these two failure scenarios in more detail.

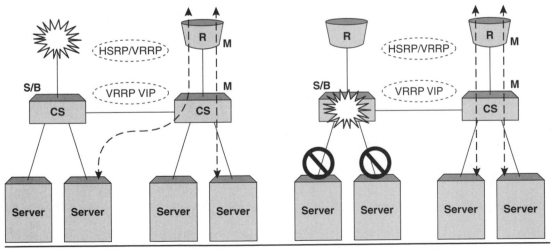

Figure 5–10   Two failure scenarios in a VRRP implementation. On the left, a failed router would result in the primary content switch changing, whereas on the right, a failure of the primary content switch would result in all servers directly attached becoming unavailable.

Adding Port Density and Resilience with Layer 2 Switches

The second consideration in adding greater resilience to a topology is increasing the server availability using Layer 2 switching. Commonly, additional Layer 2 switches are used to increase port density when using content switches, as the price per port cost of a standard Layer 2 switch is considerably lower. In Chapter 4, *The Concepts of Content Switching*, we saw that the processing power of a content switch is measured chiefly in terms of sessions rather than packets, which means that using a Layer 2 switch to provide greater port density does not mean a reduction in the overall capacity of the network.

Importantly, the addition of Layer 2 switches will not only increase the port density but also the resilience of the network. First, the object servers effectively become multihomed even with a single NIC implementation, as each Layer 2 switch attaches to both content switches. Second, the failure of a content switch, as seen in Figure 5–10, will no longer result in the loss of operation of the servers attached directly to it. Later we will see how the addition of multihoming techniques for the objects servers combined with additional Layer 2 switch implementation can increase this resilience further.

Figure 5–11 shows the first option for implementing Layer 2 switches for increased port density *without* the need to use STP to avoid Layer 2 bridging loops.

Using the Layer 2 switches in this configuration without a Layer 2 bridging loop can still provide better server resilience as shown. In this example, the failure of a content switch does not result in the removal from service of servers as a Layer 2 path is preserved. The use and operation of VRRP remains identical to that described previously with a failure on the primary content switch resulting in the fail-over of all VRRP instances in the topology to the standby devices and the traffic flow recovering within two to three seconds. One disadvantage of the topology described previously is that the failure of the cross-connect between the two Layer 2 switches still results in a loss of service of the servers attached to the right-hand switch.

An alternative to this topology is to create a fully meshed topology between the Layer 2 switches and content switches and use the STP to block the desired ports during normal operation. Here, the topology is less prone to cable (or port) failures, as alternate paths exist between each switch. Figure 5–12 shows an implementation using STP to block redundant links. It is advantageous to alter the STP priorities within the mesh topology to ensure that the correct link

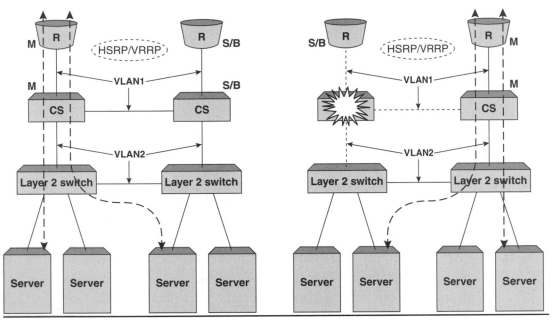

Figure 5–11   Using Layer 2 switches without STP.

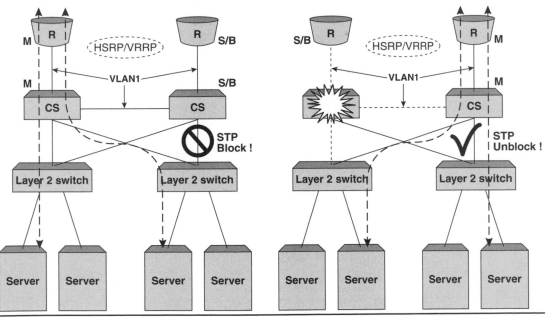

Figure 5–12   Using Layer 2 switches and STP for greater resilience to link or Ethernet port failures.

blocks as shown. In this instance, a failure on the primary content switch would result in the blocked link changing to a forwarding state and traffic recovering within the bounds of normal STP convergence. If anything, the primary disadvantage of implementations using STP is slower convergence times. In modern switches, this failure time can be greatly reduced with the implementation of fast-altering port states using "Port Fast" and other settings.

Increasing Server Resilience with Multihoming

The final alternative for increasing resilience and availability in the network design is the implementation of multihoming or dual homing. Multihoming refers to the ability to attach the object servers to the network using two NICs. In content switching topologies, there are two ways to achieve this effect. First, as shown in Figure 5–13, the interfaces can be given unique IP addresses in the same subnet (or different subnets). In this instance, each interfaces acts independently and will respond to traffic only targeted directly at its IP address. One common way to implement this approach when using content switches as load balancers is to define the secondary interfaces (in this example shown as eth1) as backup real servers in the configuration. The failure of the primary interface on any object server will result in the server being marked down and the backup server being brought into operation. As only the NIC has failed, the server is still capable of processing traffic and the content switch can begin assigning new

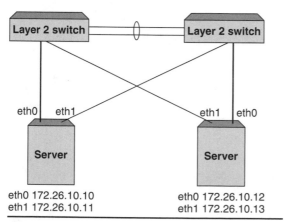

Figure 5–13   Multihoming servers using secondary IP addresses.

user sessions to the server through the secondary interface card. In practice this mechanism is not useful when used for load sharing among multiple interfaces, as in many operating systems even though traffic may enter through both interfaces, return traffic from the server only egresses a single interface. This is obviously dependent on the server and operating systems vendor and should be investigated in more detail.

Figure 5–14 shows a second method of implementing multi-homing for object servers. In this example, the interfaces are "bonded" together to appear as one single interface that in Linux terms is labeled bond0 by default. The implementations of interface bonding or trunking vary depending on the operating system and even the type of interface card being used, but in the Linux-based example shown in Figure 5–14, the trunking is complimented on the Layer 2 switch with the configuration of a multilink trunk (MLT). When sending and receiving traffic across the trunked link, the Layer 2 switch and the server will typically use a combination of IP address and MAC address information to determine which physical link should be used. It goes without saying that each packet (and typically each user session) will traverse only a single physical link, and the distribution of IP addresses will ensure that overall traffic is shared equally across each physical link on the trunk. Again, the implementations of interface trunking or bonding are shown here only as an example of mechanisms that can be used to increase resilience through multihoming, and require further investigation based on the vendor equipment involved.

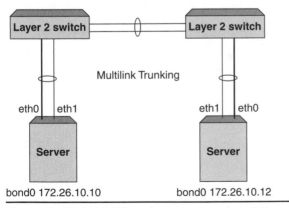

Figure 5–14   Multihoming servers using MLT or bonding.

Layer 4 Load Balancing Metrics

One of the most important concepts in content switching, and server load balancing in particular, is that of the metrics used to distribute load. As we saw earlier, an important role in content switching is to move away from the single server model to one where load can be evenly distributed among a number of different object servers. Understanding the techniques for load distribution and their relative pros and cons is key to successfully deploying server load balancing and other content switching applications.

All distribution metrics will typically be session based. That is to say that they will make a new load balancing decision per TCP session or UDP flow, not on a per-frame basis. While this may seem obvious, it is important to understand that all frames in a TCP session or UDP flow *must* be forwarded to the same real server; otherwise, sessions will be broken. Within most content switching hardware, this is achieved by creating entries in the session table as decisions are made. Consequently, the logic for setting up and maintaining a TCP session would look like:

1. The first packet arrives at the content switch. In a TCP session, this would take the form of a SYN from the client to the VIP.

2. The content switch indexes the session table and searches for the matching entry identified by source and destination IP addresses and source and destination TCP ports. (All TCP sessions in an IP internetwork can be uniquely identified using this combination.)

3. As no session will exist, the load balancing metric is applied and a server selection is made. The content switch will perform the necessary NAT translations and forward the packet, creating a new session table entry for future reference.

4. Return packet from Server to Client arrives at the Content Switch and the reverse translation is performed using the session table information created.

5. A third packet, typically an ACK, arrives from the client to the VIP. The content switch indexes the session table, finds a matching entry, performs the necessary NAT translations, and forwards the packet.

We discuss the individual load balancing metrics next.

Least Connections

Least connections is the simplest distribution metric and is often the default for content switching configurations. It guarantees the best distribution of load among the object servers based on the number of TCP sessions or UDP flows established over time. As the name suggests, when using least connections the content switch will send a new TCP session or UDP flow to the server that has the least number of concurrent sessions at the time.

The primary advantage of least connections as a metric is even load distribution. Over time, the number of sessions handled by each server should be even based on the relevant processing capability of each. Consider an example where two servers are being load balanced, one comprising a faster CPU, more memory, and a gigabit interface card, and the other with slower CPU, less memory, and only a 10Mbps Ethernet card. The faster machine will be able to cope with a higher number of sessions per second, and this would be best reflected using least connections as a load distribution metric.

The disadvantage, as with many other simple Layer 4 metrics, is that least connections provides no persistence between client and server. That is to say that a client retrieving a simple Web page using a HTTP/1.0 browser might have its first GET request serviced by server 1, it's second by server 2, and so on.

Round Robin

Round robin is also a very simple load distribution metric and is very effective for sharing load evenly among object servers. Again as the name suggests, incoming sessions will be load balanced on a round robin basis, with the first session going to server 1, the second to server 2, and so on.

The advantage of round robin as a distribution metric is even numbers of sessions per server. Whereas with least connections, the processing power and performance of each object server plays a part in the distribution, this is not the case with implementations using round robin. Each server will receive the same number of connections over time irrelevant of how fast it is able to process and deal with them. For this reason, round robin is less effective in environments where the relative processing power of the object servers differs, unless used with a per-server weighting as described later in this chapter.

Round robin also suffers the same flaw as least connections in that it does not achieve even a simple level of persistence, and different servers may service subsequent requests from the same client.

IP Address Hashing

IP address hashing is the first metric that is able to provide some form of limited persistence. The term *hashing* is used to refer to a deterministic algorithmic calculation based on the IP address information contained within the TCP session or UDP flow, and it is this uniformity that gives this metric IP address-based persistence.

There are many address and port combinations that the content switch might want to include in this calculation, typically depending on the application being deployed. Let's take a simple example of using the entire 32 bits of the source IP address as shown in Figure 5–15.

While many content switching vendors will employ far more complex hashing algorithms to calculate the result, the concept remains the same. All available real servers are referenced using an index table with, in this instance, eight entries. This index table would usually hold far more entries, typically the same as the total number of real servers supported. Using some form of numeric folding, the IP address will yield an index into this Real Server Index table and from this, the content switch can successfully assign the appropriate real server for the client connection. It follows that all subsequent connections from the same client IP address will yield the same entry point into the index table and thus the same

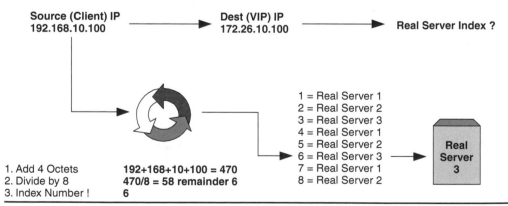

Figure 5–15   Simplistic example of IP address hashing.

real server. We'll see other examples of content switching applications where this consistency of the deterministic algorithms provides an elegant means to solve some implementation issues.

So, why would you use different IP and port information when performing such calculations? Well, for different applications of content switching, different results might be desired. Take an example of simple Layer 4 server load balancing where the repeated connections from the same client should be bound to the same real server. Using source IP address hashing would give us just such a result. If we take this one step further and assume that all connections from multiple client machines are being proxied behind just a single address, our load-balancing model would break, as all connections from these clients will only ever be forwarded to the same real server. In such instances, including the source TCP or UDP port information would again include a randomizing element resulting in connections being distributed among all real servers.

For applications such as Web cache redirection, discussed in Chapter 8, *Application Redirection*, using the destination rather than source IP address will give greater optimization of the caching resources as all connections to the same destination Web site will be serviced by the same cache. Table 5–1 lists some simple examples of hashing combinations and where they would be deployed.

Table 5–1   When and Where to Use Different Hashing Techniques

APPLICATION	IP AND TCP INFORMATION TO HASH
Basic server load balancing	24 or 32 bits of source (client) IP address —Good distribution, basic Layer 3 persistence
Server load balancing with clients proxied behind single IP address	24 or 32 bits of source (client) IP address + source TCP or UDP port number —Good distribution, no persistence
Firewall load balancing	Full 64 bits of source and destination address —Achieves stateful load balancing of firewalls
Web cache redirection	32 bits of destination IP address —Optimization of caches with better hit rate

Response Time and Server Agent

While least connections, round robin, and hashing can, at best, provide only limited visibility of the resource availability of the real servers, the use of either a server-based agent or measurements on the server responses can help to provide a clearer picture of the actual ability of a real server to cope with incoming requests. Response time metrics typically use the health-checking mechanisms to influence the traffic distribution by taking measurements over a period of time of how long the health checks take to complete. This process may range from a simple ICMP ping, the opening and resetting of a TCP connection, or even the running of a fully scripted health check.

One example of where this might provide greater visibility is in the use of an intelligent server-based script that produces a measured result, often requiring the pulling of information from an application server or database. At busier times for each real server, the time taken to complete such a request will increase and thus the weighting on the real server can be gradually decreased to relieve it of processing incoming requests.

Some content switches take this approach further with the inclusion of software-based agents that reside on each real server, feeding back information about the ongoing performance. These agents are typically capable of tracking information on the CPU, disk, and memory performance that the content switch can then use to influence traffic flow and session distribution.

Bandwidth

One other performance-influenced metric is that of *bandwidth monitoring*. In certain instances, typically other than standard server load balancing, it is useful to identify trends in the amounts of LAN bandwidth being used by each real server and use this information to influence server distribution. Monitoring the bandwidth transmitted out toward a particular server MAC address over time and adjusting the weighting of the real server accordingly is one mechanism used to achieve this.

Bandwidth-based load balancing is most useful in environments where data transfer rates are key to the application's success, or in instances where firewalls or routers are being balanced.

Weighting and Maximum Connections

While not a metric in its own right, *server weighting* is a technique that can be used to influence traffic distribution in conjunction with the metrics described previously. Assigning a "weight" to a server will bias traffic flow toward larger or more powerful real servers based on a defined value, usually an integer in a specific range.

Consider an example where two real servers are weighted "2"and "1," respectively. Using a metric such as round robin with these server weightings, the first server would, over time, expect to see twice the number of connections as the second. As one would expect, server weightings are typically only applicable in conjunction with metrics that are performance based (such as round robin, least connections, response time, and bandwidth) and not deterministic metrics such as IP address hashing.

Another further enhancement to standard Layer 4 metrics is the use of a maximum number of connections, definable per real server to indicate the total number of concurrent TCP sessions or UDP flows that the server can handle. This is a useful mechanism to ensure that the resources of a particular server or group of servers are never overloaded, especially when servers of different sizes are used in combination. If the maximum number of connections is reached, new incoming sessions are assigned to alternate servers in the group. It's worth considering that if a persistent distribution mechanism is being used and the maximum connections for a given server is reached, the persistence will likely be broken. The answer to this conundrum is simple—more servers need to be added because while the content switch can make best use of the available resources, it cannot, certainly at the time of writing, produce these resources from nothing. One common approach for dealing with the maximum connections being reached is to define an overflow server or group of servers to deal with requests by displaying a tailored error message indicating that the site is busy. While this approach does not *solve* the problem of insufficient resources, it can help in preventing the user from experiencing a "black holed" connection.

Server Health Checking

We saw in the previous section that the distribution metrics are a very important factor in a content switch deployment; now, let's consider another—that of determining the health status of the associated real servers or network resources.

Clearly, the distribution metric you select to implement will determine how a certain server or resource is selected, but what's equally important is deciding on a set of criteria that show the server to be "*healthy.*" Before we look at some of the commonly available health checking mechanisms, we should first consider what it means for a server to be healthy.

In the context of an HTTP server, for example, we might consider that if we can open a TCP connection to the server, that this is sufficient. This view, however, gives us little indication of the server's ability to actually serve the *content* that the user requires. In considering this, we're introducing the concept of what layer we health check at. Clearly, sending an ICMP request, commonly known as a "ping," to the interface of the device really proves nothing more than the IP stack on that interface is operating and there is a valid IP route between the source and the server. By moving our health check intelligence up the seven-layer model to the Transport and Application layers, we're able to associate the health check with the very thing that the user is interested in: content.

Most modern content switches are able to offer health checking at Layers 2 through 7 and use techniques such as scripting to extend this even further. The type of health check that you choose to deploy will depend largely on the nature of the application and how it is deployed. For many implementations, Layer 4 health checks, such as opening and closing TCP sockets, are sufficient. For more complex deployments where the application is potentially spread across multiple server resources, the use of Layer 7 health checks and beyond might be required. Let's look at some of the most common approaches.

Link-Based Health Checks

The most basic form of health check works effectively at Layer 2 and checks the link status on the port through which the real server can be reached. This type of mechanism offers no insight into the IP layer or above on the real server, but might be useful for devices that operate in stealth mode and do not operate an IP stack on their network interfaces such as IDSs.

ARP Health Checks

Still working at Layer 2, an ARP health will cause the content switch to send an ARP request for the real server's IP address, or that of the next hop route if the server is off subnet. Again, the ARP health check offers little insight into the correct operation of the real server from an application point of view. ARP health checks are useful for devices such as firewalls that will typically block all non-essential forms of IP traffic. Even firewalls with the strictest of enforcement policies will accept ARP requests for their interfaces. Obviously, an ARP health check does not extend further than a local subnet, so if the real servers are located another routed hop away, then the health check will only extend to the router interface leading to the real server.

ICMP Health Checks

Ping is a commonly used network diagnostic and troubleshooting utility. ICMP Echo Request packets are sent from the content switch to the real server and, if the IP stack is operating correctly, the real server will send an Echo Reply to indicate that the path is up. ICMP health checks offer the first real indication that the path between the content switch and the real server is operational from an IP perspective, but still does not prove that a particular application will be available on that server. ICMP health checks are useful for health checking IP devices and paths where there is no concept of an application endpoint to test.

TCP Health Checks

With TCP health checking, we're able to begin to determine the health of not only the path to the real server, but also which applications will be listening there. Typical TCP health checks will initiate a TCP three-way handshake between the content switch and the real server to prove that the application is listening correctly on the assigned port. The content switch will then either perform a graceful TCP FIN and FIN-ACK teardown, or will simply issue a TCP RESET to end the connection.

TCP health checks will presuppose one thing: that the application will close the TCP listening port if it is terminated. It is possible that an application that is not terminated gracefully, or has "crashed," will leave an erroneous TCP listener on its application port. In this instance, a TCP-based health check will be unable to determine that the application itself has failed and will probably continue to send user requests to that server.

Application Health Checks

Many content switches now offer pre-written application health checks for many of the well-used Internet type applications, such as HTTP, SMTP, FTP, POP3, and DNS, although this is by no means an exhaustive list. Application health checks work by allowing the administrator to define a piece of application data that is to be used in order to interact with the application on the server. In HTTP terms, for example, this might be the URL of a test Web page that should be retrieved. In this instance, the content switch will open a TCP connection to the real server on port 80 (or another defined port) as described earlier and send an HTTP GET request for the configured URL. In terms of FTP, this might be a username and password combination to log on to the FTP server and perform a directory listing.

Application health checks are useful for determining things such as inter-server dependencies. Imagine, for example, that a Web server requires the functionality of an associated application or database server in order to accept incoming user requests. By defining the application check URL as a CGI or ASP page, for example, the Web server can be instructed to do further checks that can be called through such a page. This creative use of application health checks gives some indication of their usefulness in understanding the user application on the server and using this to determine the true server health.

Health Check Scripting

If application health checks allow some level of flexibility in how the content switch interacts with the real servers, then scripted health checks take this even further. Many content switches also offer the ability to write custom scripts to interact with the real server in opening and closing TCP ports, sending and receiving application data and a whole host of other options. Scripting languages and capabilities differ between different vendor products, but in general, they offer the flexibility to interact with the real servers and resources in order to get around problems presented by even the most complex applications.

Summary

So, now we've seen the first real application of content switching—server load balancing. From the examples given in this chapter, you'll have been able to build up a picture of the types of issues that server load balancing, even in its most basic guise, can address. Many areas of additional value can be gained from making object servers and the applications which run on them scalable and resilient. Some of the less obvious advantages of server load balancing, such as the elimination of operational issues, can provide great drivers for deploying exactly this type of technology. In Chapter 6 we'll take a look at how we can further extend the advantages of server load balancing with greater application intelligence—looking at Layer 7 information.

Case Study: Layer 4 Server Load Balancing

Foocorp Inc., like most large organizations, has started to Web enable their applications. They also have many traditional applications that use TCP/IP. Their initial requirements are:

- Centralize access to each application.
- Provide resilience in case of a server failure.
- Use private address space for servers—this provides security and minimizes their limited private address pool.
- Ensure that certain applications are sent to the correct servers.

This provides Foocorp the advantage of having a centralized data center or server farm that can share the resources associated with deploying the hardware such as power, cabling, cooling, and so forth.

Deploying Load Balancing

Foocorp has also decided to deploy the content switches in high availability mode for resilience. Here is a checklist of the most important steps:

1. Ensure that you have enough private IP addresses to cover interfaces, VIPs, VRRP addresses, and so forth.

2. If you are going to use different VLANs for the different services, ensure that your upstream firewall has a route to them. Typically, this will be via the VRRP addresses of the content switches.

3. Ensure that you update the DNS with the new VIP addresses that will be used for the service(s).

4. Configure the real servers to be part of a group, and associate the VIP and its necessary service to that group.

5. Ensure that the servers are listening on the correct port for the service(s) they are load balancing. The health checks will show whether this is the case.

6. Make sure that you select the correct load balancing metric. This will be key if you require Layer 3 persistence.

7. Ensure that you set up VRRP for not only the Layer 3 information, but also the Layer 4 if possible.

8. Ensure that you have routes to any internal networks and that they have a route or routes back to the content switches and associated VIPs.

9. Test failure of a switch using VRRP to ensure that you do not have an asymmetric route, as the content switch will need to see the return packet in order to manipulate it back to its original form.

We can see how this has been achieved in Figure 5–16.

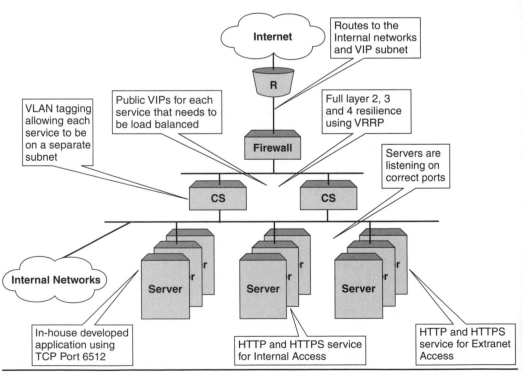

Figure 5–16   Foocorp, Inc. Layer 4 load balancing.

By deploying Layer 4 load balancing, Foocorp has been able to achieve the following:

- Increase user response time.
- Minimize disruption caused by server failure or critical upgrades during the business day.
- Ensure that servers can be added or decommissioned with no change to the user or to DNS.
- Allow statistics of server and application usage to be centrally located and analyzed.
- Secure their servers by using private IP address space and only allowing access to them for the configured service.
- Allow new services and applications to be deployed with no or very little new hardware.

The options and benefits are endless. What this has allowed Foocorp to achieve is the ability to scale and add new and exciting applications with very little disruption to the existing environment.

6

Content-Aware Server Load Balancing

We've seen the benefits of introducing Layer 4 server load balancing into an Internet infrastructure, but there are instances when this alone is not sufficient. For some applications, the use of information contained within the payload—actual *user* data—when making the decision can offer many benefits. In this chapter, we will look at when and where the use of Layer 7 techniques can be useful, why the introduction has an impact on the frame flow in TCP sessions, and a series of examples of using Layer 7 information for server load balancing.

What Is Layer 7 Server Load Balancing?

We saw in Chapter 2, *Understanding Layer 2, 3, and 4 Protocols*, what information is available at each of the layers defined by the OSI Seven Layer Model, from basic Ethernet and IP addressing information used by traditional Layer 2 and 3 switches, to identification of protocols and applications at Layer 4. Layer 7 server load balancing, along with other Layer 7 applications such as Web cache redirection, raises the stakes once more by examining information being generated by the application itself. This could be anything from the URL the user is requesting, the name of the video the user wants to watch, or even the name being requested in a DNS request. Typical applications of Layer 7 server load balancing, which we will look at in more detail later, are:

- **HTTP URL parsing**: Using the location and page being requested via HTTP.
- **HTTP header inspection**: Using other information in the HTTP request, such as language or browser type.
- **HTTP cookies**: Reading, rewriting, and inserting HTTP cookies for persistence and preferential user services.
- **FTP parsing**: Translating information in the FTP Control Channel to ensure correct operation when implementing Server Load Balancing.
- **DNS parsing**: Using the requested domain or host name to decide on the DNS server to send to.
- **RTSP stream parsing**: Identifying the video or audio stream requested by the user and serving the content from the correct resource.

In general, Layer 7 server load balancing enhances the user experience by making best use of the available resources.

Why Use Layer 7 Server Load Balancing?

Basic Layer 4 server load balancing addresses a number of issues regarding the delivery of IP services; namely, performance, reliability, and scalability. When deploying load balanced services, the addition of Layer 7 configuration can further aid in these issues, specifically when looking at some of the nuances of protocols such as HTTP, FTP, and DNS. Let's look at a number of examples specific to HTTP and FTP.

Example 1—All Servers Are Not Built Equally

Imagine the Web site of our friends at Foocorp.com, who might have two basic content types served from their Web site. First, simple static brochureware material such as brochures, manuals, HTML content, and so forth; and second, dynamic content allowing users to buy goods online directly through the Web. Both of these content types impose different requirements on the object servers hosting the site. Serving brochureware material requires larger, faster disk storage and access with less overhead imposed on the CPU and memory resources. Dynamic, transactional content, on the other hand, may require access to network storage and increased CPU and memory resources to handle the transactional nature of the request. In implementing generic Layer 4 load balancing, the site would need to be able to cope with these differing requirements on the same group of object servers.

Example 2—All Content Must Be Available Everywhere

Another potential drawback of implementing load balancing at Layer 4 only is that each object server must be able to server all content for the virtual server. Why is this important? Well, even busy applications have some elements that are more heavily accessed than others, and as a consequence occupy more of the server resources. Take Foocorp.com as an example. Their registration and login services might be particularly compute intensive and would be one area of the site they might want to ensure that users always get a good response from. To keep up with growing demand for these resources on the site, more servers might need to be added, which with Layer 4 server load balancing would mean the need to replicate the entire contents of the site to each of the new servers. There are many other methods to deal with this type of scenario, such as using HTTP redirects to different fully qualified domain names (FQDNs), but implementing Layer 7 intelligence offers by far one of the most elegant solutions.

Example 3—You Get What You Pay For

Looking at our first example again in a little more detail, let's take the concept of implementing different capacity servers one step further. Using Layer 7 server load balancing, we could make best use of the difference in performance by offering subscribing users different levels of response based on service they have paid for. "Gold" subscribers might have access to faster performing resources for which they have paid a premium, whereas "Standard" subscribers are shared among the remaining, lower powered resources.

Example 4—Future Proofing

All examples shown previously might not be required from day one in a simple deployment; however, having the ability to implement Layer 7 server load balancing at a later date often proves useful. Consider being able to tackle application issues that might arise through the use of intelligent traffic handling rather than simply throwing more resources at the problem.

Dealing with Layer 7 Traffic

The process of dealing with Layer 7 traffic inspection, be it for server load balancing, firewall load balancing, Web cache redirection, or any other application, is inherently different from that of Layer 4. We've seen in our coverage of how Layer 4 protocols, such as TCP, and Layer 7 protocols, such as HTTP, operate so that certain information is only available at certain times during the session. Figure 6–1 shows a simplified HTTP session, demonstrating that any useful Layer 7 information which may be needed for a server load balancing decision does not appear until at least the fourth packet of the session.

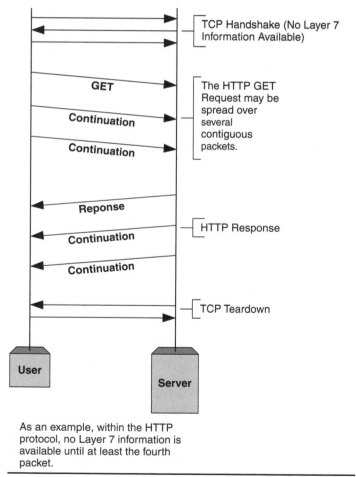

TCP Handshake (No Layer 7 Information Available)

GET

Continuation

Continuation

The HTTP GET Request may be spread over several contiguous packets.

Reponse

Continuation

Continuation

HTTP Response

TCP Teardown

User

Server

As an example, within the HTTP protocol, no Layer 7 information is available until at least the fourth packet.

Figure 6–1   An example of one issue when dealing with Layer 7 inspection in content switching.

The consequence of this behavior has a major impact on the performance of many content switches. In general terms, dealing with Layer 4 processed traffic is computationally easier than Layer 7. If the decision-making information is not available until the fourth packet of a TCP session, the content switch must be able to buffer and store these packets until the relevant information arrives. This process is commonly referred to as *delayed binding*.

Immediate vs. Delayed Binding of Sessions

All of the examples we saw in Chapter 5, *Basic Server Load Balancing*, are what we will refer to as *immediate bindings*. What we mean by this is that the very first packet in the session contains sufficient information to make a load balancing decision. When using a standard IP hashing distribution, for example, the TCP SYN packet from the client that initiates the session will contain the VIP, the destination TCP port, which identifies the service being requested, and the client IP and TCP details to enable a hash calculation to be made. Figure 6–2 shows a simple traffic flow in an immediate binding session.

For Layer 7 services, delayed binding of sessions needs to be implemented. In order for the content switch to parse the required information, it must perform the following tasks:

1. Terminate the TCP from the client by completing the three-way TCP handshake.

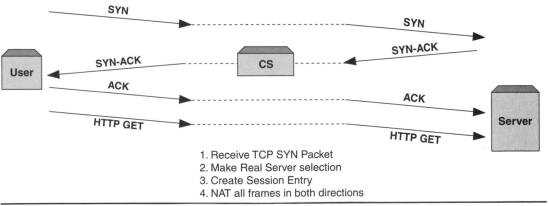

Figure 6–2   Traffic flow example in an immediate binding.

2. Buffer the incoming packets containing the user data. This might not necessarily be as simple as buffering the first frame as, within HTTP for example, the information may not be contained in the first packet.

3. Parse these packets for the required Layer 7 information, such as URL, HTTP headers, FTP control commands, or DNS requests.

4. Make a load balancing decision based on the information found in the user request.

5. Open a new TCP connection from the content switch to the appropriate real server.

6. Forward the buffer request packets on to the real server.

7. For all subsequent packets in the session, the content switch must "splice" these two separate TCP connections together by altering information such as TCP ports and sequence numbers.

Figure 6–3 shows a traffic flow example for a delayed binding session.

It's easy to see from Figure 6–3 that the amount of work required within the content switch to implement Layer 7 server load balancing is considerable when compared to simple Layer 4 processing.

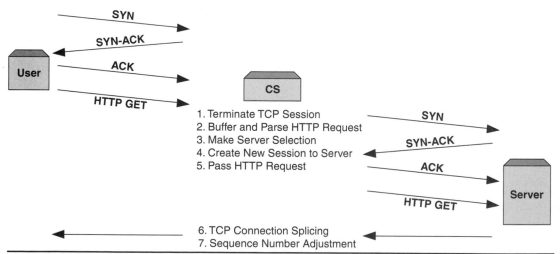

Figure 6–3   Traffic flow example in a delayed binding.

Using Delayed Binding as a Security Mechanism

Delayed binding has a secondary use when implemented in content switches—as a security mechanism to help prevent denial-of-service (DoS) attacks and in particular, SYN flooding attacks. SYN flooding is an easily instigated attack that aims to fill the backlog buffer of an operating system.

The SYN Flood Attack

All operating systems maintain what is known as a *backlog buffer*. This is an area of memory reserved to handle new TCP sessions that are not yet currently fully established. When a client sends a TCP SYN to an object server, the server operating system will create an entry in the backlog buffer as a record, which is used to show that the connection is under establishment. Once this buffer entry has been created, the server will send back a SYN-ACK to the client that, typically, would be responded to with a final ACK and thus complete the session establishment.

During a SYN flooding attack, however, the attacking client or clients will send the SYN packet but never the final ACK of the handshake, thus leaving the backlog buffer with an entry that will never be completed. Such an entry would have to be allowed to time out based on criteria specific to the operating system. If the attacking client can send enough SYN only packets, convincing the operating system that each is part of a valid new session, the backlog buffer can be filled easily, thus preventing other, valid client connections to be established. For a valid client during this period, the server would appear to be unavailable because none of the client-side SYN packets would ever be acknowledged.

The process of generating a SYN flooding attack is trivial, and many tools exist to perpetrate such attacks with minimal resources. Most content switches are capable of providing a layer of protection against SYN flooding attacks given that they are typically one of the first devices in the topology that are session aware. Inherently, the content switch must be capable of protecting both itself (as it too has a session table that may be susceptible to such attacks) and the object servers it is load balancing.

Solution 1—SYN Cookies

The first solution is for the content switch to implement a mechanism known as *SYN cookies*. The concept of SYN cookies uses two ideas: first, not creating a session entry in the content switch until the third packet (the ACK) has been received; and second, using information contained in the initial client-side SYN to generate the sequence number for the resulting SYN-ACK. By taking information from the client-side SYN packet, hashing information from the IP and TCP layers, and using this together with some form of time-dependent information to form the initial server-side TCP sequence number, the content switch can delay making a session entry until a valid third packet in the handshake arrives.

This approach means that only sessions originating from valid Internet clients will complete the TCP three-way handshake and consequently occupy session table space on the content switch.

Solution 2—Session Table Management

The second approach for dealing with this DoS threat is in how the content switch manages entries in its session table. A content switch will typically have a session table much larger than the backlog buffer on an object server, which will offer some resistance in the first instance. Many content switches will also implement an aging process for dealing with sessions that are either idle or have terminated ungracefully, and this process can be extended to deal with "half-open" TCP sessions where the handshake has not completed correctly; for example, during a SYN flood attack. Most implementations of this type of mechanism will offer configurable timers for aging out the half-open sessions.

No content switch manufacturer would position their platforms as a single security point against unauthorized entry or attack prevention. However, when used as part of a many layered security approach, techniques such as those described previously can be very effective in providing extra network security.

Layer 7 Parsing and the `Connection:Keep-Alive` Header

From our description in Chapter 2, *Understanding Layer 2, 3, and 4 Protocols*, you'll remember that the client-to-server connection does not necessarily follow the model of one TCP request per object being retrieved. Indeed, it is most common in modern browsers for the underlying TCP connection to remain alive across the retrieval of numerous HTTP objects, and this has a knock-on effect in Layer 7 traffic handling from the content switch's point of view. Imagine that the content switch has gone through the process described previously and offered the client a delayed binding in order to parse the Layer 7 information that may have arrived several frames later. Once the server-side connection for the session has been made, there is nothing to stop the browser sending a request for a different content type, not suited to the selected server, across the existing TCP session.

What the content switch must be able to do in this situation is maintain and manage the tear-up and tear-down of multiple backend, server-side connections, while parsing the client-side connection for incoming HTTP requests. Take the example show in Figure 6–4—on the client side, a single HTTP/1.1 connection will present two GET requests for two different content types. On the server side, the content switch must bring up a connection to the first object server to service the request for "index.html," and then tear down the connection and establish a new connection to the second server group for the request of "other.asp."

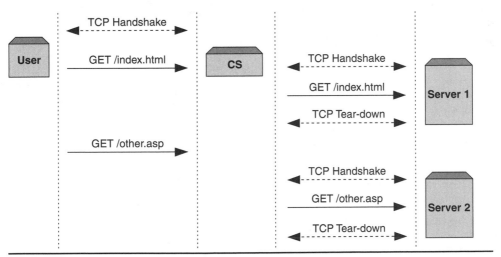

Figure 6–4   If the client uses HTTP/1.1 or the `Connection: Keep-Alive` HTTP header, the content switch must manage the tear-up and tear-down of TCP connections to different servers in the back end.

HTTP URL Parsing and Load Balancing

As our first application of Layer 7 server load balancing, let's look at one of the most widely implemented applications—URL parsing. In basic terms, as we saw in Chapter 2, the URL is "the thing you type in the Web browser," although the precise definition of what distinguishes a URL is a little more subtle. Definitions and examples of each, including a URN, are as follows:

- **Uniform Resource Name (URN)**: Used to identify a page, object, or resource without the use of a scheme by which it is to be retrieved; for example, *www.foocorp.com/brochures/aboutus.html*.

- **Uniform Resource Locator (URL)**: Used to show both the resource and the scheme used for retrieval; for example, *http://www.foocorp.com/ brochures /aboutus.html*.

- **Uniform Resource Indicator (URI)**: Used to show the resource, scheme, and any markers within a page; for example, *http://www.foocorp.com/ brochures /aboutus.html#whereweare*.

In general, and for the purposes of this chapter, the term *URL* is used generically to cover all three instances of document descriptions. If you consider the following HTTP GET request from a client, the elements that would be considered during a URL parsing decision are those after the GET header.

```
Hypertext Transfer Protocol

GET /brochures/aboutus.html#whereweare HTTP/1.0\r\n
Accept: image/gif, image/x-xbitmap, image/jpeg, image/pjpeg\r\n
Accept-Language: en-gb\r\n
User-Agent: Mozilla/4.0 (compatible; MSIE 5.01; Windows NT 5.0)\r\n
Host: www.foocorp.com\r\n
Connection: Keep-Alive\r\n
\r\n
```

It's worth noting that in terms of dealing with the request, the full path, document, and markers are separated from the *www.foocorp.com* host information, which has been moved to its own unique header. We'll look at how to use these other HTTP headers later in this chapter. Depending on the vendor of the content switch, the decision may optionally include the HTTP version, which is included at the end of the GET request line, giving the ability to make a load balancing decision based on the version of HTTP being supported by the client browser.

Examples of URL Parsing

Now that we've got an understanding of the components which make up what is commonly known as the URL, let's look at some examples of how and when URL parsing can be used.

1. Separating Static and Dynamic Content Types

As an example implementation of URL parsing, let's assume that Foocorp.com needs to separate out the static and dynamic content for their Web site. By *static content* we mean the images and HTML that make up the static content of the pages—these can be identified by parsing the URL for file extensions such as *.gif, *.html, *.bmp, and so forth. Other, *dynamic content* such as executable scripts and ASP pages can be identified by file extensions such as *.asp and *.cgi, and strings such as /cgi-bin/. This approach allows a site designer to maintain two different profiles of server hardware to handle the difference in the nature of the requests. Serving static content requires access only to the static content store, and its delivery is typified by lower requirements on memory and CPU. Dynamic content, on the other hand, requires access to application servers or backend databases, and its delivery incurs greater demands on the memory and CPU resources of the server. Figure 6–5 shows an example of separating static and dynamic content types.

2. Introducing New Site Elements

A further example of the use of URL parsing is adding new sections to an existing site. Consider Foocorp needing to add another promotional section to the existing Web site, which might run for a limited time and the content for which may be managed by a separate administrator. By adding another URL string match of "/promotion/," for example, a new group of object servers can be used to segregate this subsection of the site. Figure 6–6 shows our previous example expanded to include the introduction of a new sub-site.

HTTP Header Load Balancing

Once it's clear that we can have access to the HTTP GET method and the data that follows it for load balancing decisions, it's easy to see that further inspection of other HTTP headers is also applicable and useful to solve a number of issues

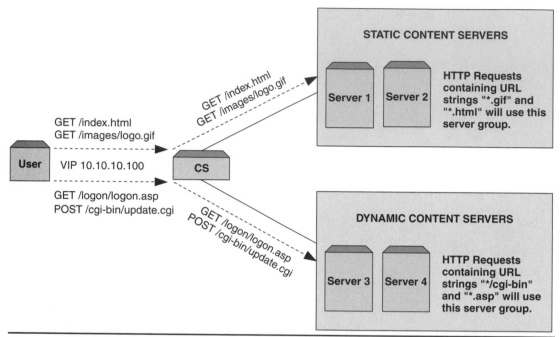

Figure 6–5   Using URL parsing to separate static and dynamic content types.

in scaling HTTP services. The HTTP RFCs 1945 and 2068 (for HTTP/1.0 and HTTP/1.1, respectively) define a large series of HTTP headers as standard, although it is possible for either the client- or server-side application to insert custom headers if required. Some of the more useful and commonly implemented of these standard headers are listed in Chapter 2, and the following example shows some of these from a HTTP packet capture:

```
Hypertext Transfer Protocol

GET /brochures/aboutus.html#whereweare HTTP/1.0\r\n
Accept: image/gif, image/x-xbitmap, image/jpeg, image/pjpeg\r\n
Accept-Language: en-gb\r\n
User-Agent: Mozilla/4.0 (compatible; MSIE 5.01; Windows NT 5.0)\r\n
Host: www.foocorp.com\r\n
Connection: Keep-Alive\r\n
\r\n
```

In configurative terms, most content switches will require the definition of the header name (e.g., "User-Agent") and the values per real server to match against.

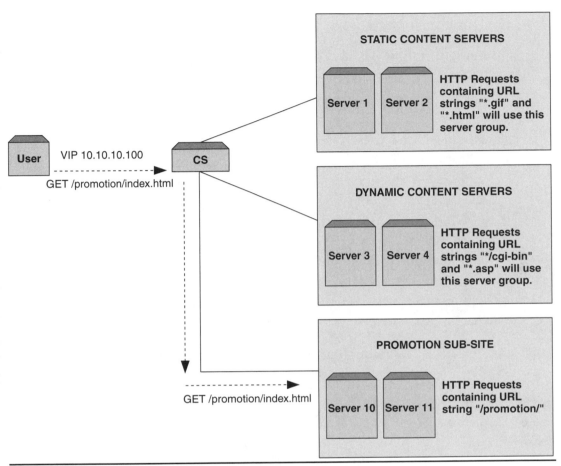

Figure 6–6   Introduction of a new subsite using URL parsing.

Applications of HTTP Header Load Balancing

1. Virtual Hosting with the Host: Header

One of the most common implementations of HTTP header load balancing is through the use of the Host: header. When a user enters a URL into the client browser, the host portion—the *www.foocorp.com* element—is stripped out and included in the HTTP request as the Host: header. As the Host: header was only formally introduced into the HTTP/1.1 specifications, it is likely that some older browsers will not support the passing of this header. Many modern browsers will implement this and other newer header options even when forced to perform object and page retrievals using HTTP/1.0 after the method.

In considering why Host: header load balancing is useful, let's consider an example involving a shared hosting environment that houses a number of different Web sites. This implementation methodology has become increasingly popular during recent years, owing to the fact that it allows Web hosting businesses to offer increased value for money while keeping costs low by sharing hardware resources among larger numbers of customers. Prior to the ability to inspect the HTTP Host: header, each customer would have assigned an IP address per unique host or had to house content for all host-based Web sites on every object server. Figure 6–7 shows an example of this type of implementation. Here we see that each of the individual Web sites is separated by a unique IP address (10.10.10.100 and 10.10.10.101, respectively), which, given that registered Internet addresses are relatively expensive, does not provide cost-effective scalability.

A far more effective and scalable implementation model for these types of shared resource scenarios is to use the HTTP Host: header. This allows the provisioning of a system commonly referred to as *virtual hosting*, something that can also be implemented on Web servers directly. Virtual hosting basically

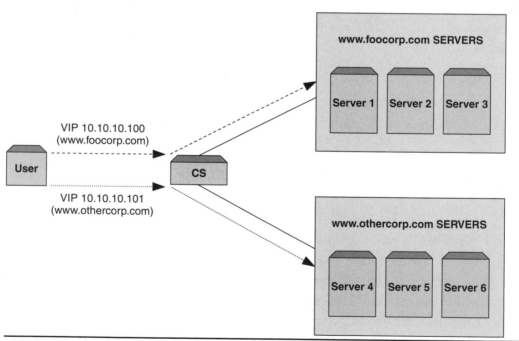

Figure 6–7   Implementing a shared resource model using unique IP addresses per Web site.

means to use a single IP address to represent multiple hosts or Web sites. From a content switch perspective, this implies that we can use a single VIP to represent a series of sites, the host names of which are distinguished using the `Host:` header. Enabling `Host:` header load balancing on the content switch in our previous example gives us the scenario shown in Figure 6–8.

2. Optimizing Content for Browser Types

For any experienced user of the Internet, one thing is clear: not all browsers are created equal. Ask any site designer to name his or her top five technical issues when implementing new pages and styles, and the incompatibility between Web browsers will feature highly. This can be anything from the simple and subtle differences between Microsoft Internet Explorer and the Mozilla-based browsers such as Netscape, through to the challenges of not knowing whether the content viewer is using a WAP phone or PDA to view the site. Clearly, delivering the site content back to users in a form most suitable to their browser choice is a challenge that needs to be met.

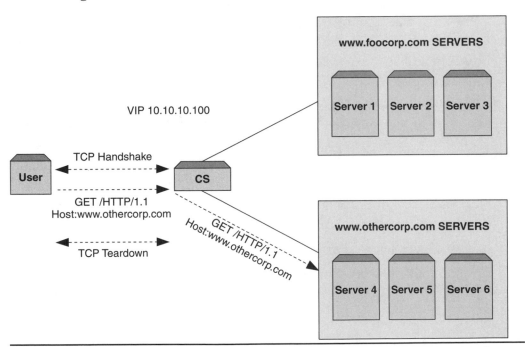

Figure 6–8   The shared resource model implemented using HTTP `Host:` headers for virtual hosting.

Within the HTTP specifications, there is a standard header definition for User-Agent, which, as the name suggests, provides information about the browser type issuing the requests, along with supplementary information about the compatibility and operating system being used.

```
Hypertext Transfer Protocol

GET /brochures/aboutus.html#whereweare HTTP/1.0\r\n
Accept: image/gif, image/x-xbitmap, image/jpeg, image/pjpeg\r\n
Accept-Language: en-gb\r\n
User-Agent: Mozilla/4.0 (compatible; MSIE 5.01; Windows NT 5.0)\r\n
Host: www.foocorp.com\r\n
Connection: Keep-Alive\r\n
```

In general terms the User-Agent header contains the base browser type first (as the most significant piece of information), followed by other comments that identify the browser and any subproducts that form a significant part of the user agent. The preceding example shows a User-Agent that is Mozilla 4.0 compatible and is in fact a Microsoft Internet Explorer product running on top of the Windows 2000 operating system (identified by the Windows NT 5.0 comment). (Mozilla is an open-source browser based on the Gecko browser engine. Using this as the User-Agent shows the Web server that the browser claims to be compatible with this layout engine. For more information, see *www.mozilla.org*.)

As we can see from Figure 6–9, the ability to read this header information allows us to implement a hosted solution where the same content is optimized for different browsers and recipient devices.

So, what does this offer in terms of a usable solution? Well, for many Web sites, knowing the makeup of the clients before they view the content can be a real benefit. Many sites might implement a different URL for each different content optimization, such as:

- www.foocorp.com—standard Web browsers
- mobile.foocorp.com—mobile phones, WAP clients, and PDAs
- text.foocorp.com—a text-only version of the site for light clients

or might have links from the main homepage to content optimized for these different browsers. Using the User-Agent string for sites that have large amounts of content for different subscribers can greatly enhance the overall user experience.

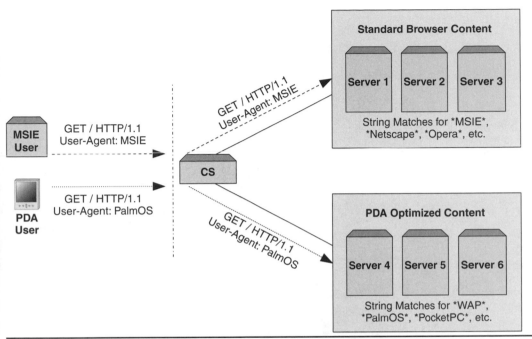

Figure 6–9   Using the `User-Agent` HTTP header means that content can be optimized for delivery to different user types.

3. Delivering Content in the Correct Language

The final HTTP header type we'll look at is `Accept-Language`. This header identifies to the object server the language encodings that are supported and understood by the browser. Within the configuration of most modern browsers, the languages that are to be offered by this header can be configured, as shown for the Netscape browser in Figure 6–10.

The settings shown in the Netscape Navigator dialog boxes in Figure 6–10 would result in the following `Accept-Language` header being inserted into the HTTP request:

```
Hypertext Transfer Protocol

GET /brochures/aboutus.html#whereweare HTTP/1.0\r\n
Accept: image/gif, image/x-xbitmap, image/jpeg, image/pjpeg\r\n
Accept-Language: en-us, en;q=0.66, af;q=0.33\r\n
User-Agent: Mozilla/4.0 (compatible; MSIE 5.01; Windows NT 5.0)\r\n
Host: www.foocorp.com\r\n
Connection: Keep-Alive\r\n
```

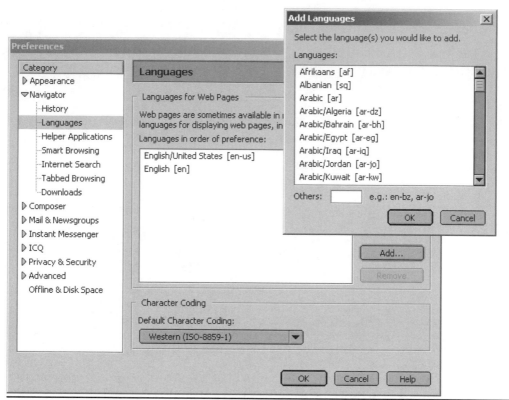

Figure 6–10   Most modern browsers, such as Netscape Navigator, allow the user to select the languages to offer in the `Accept-Language` HTTP header.

In the GET request we can see the `Accept-Language` header with the three language types: en-us, for U.S. English; en, for UK English; and af, for Afrikaans. Each of these parameters is described also using the "q" option, which indicates the preference specified by the browser. In this case, en-us is the preferred language with a q=1 (not shown as it is the default), followed by en with a quality of 0.66, and, finally, af with a quality of 0.33.

The inclusion of the `Accept-Language` header into content switching implementations has a very similar effect to that of the `User-Agent` header. Its use can improve the user experience of a Web site by eliminating the need to deliver only standard English language content or offering the user a manual choice.

In all, given the wide range of standard Request and Response HTTP headers included in the original specifications, the implementation of header-based load balancing offers the chance to solve numerous problems associated with

Web site deployment. Some content switches will offer the ability to load balance based on commonly used headers such as those discussed previously, some will allow you to define *any* HTTP header to load balance on, and others will combine a mixture of both.

HTTP Cookie Load Balancing

In Chapter 2, we saw that HTTP has its own client-side state mechanism commonly known as cookies. A cookie is simply a small piece of information implanted into the HTTP content by the server and used to identify the client on all future visits to the site. Cookies can be permanent, in which case they are stored on the hard disk of the client machine; or temporary, when they are stored temporarily in memory while the browser session is open. Later in Chapter 7, *Persistence, Security, and the Internet*, we'll see how cookies can be used to tackle issues of persistence on the Internet, but for now let's consider their use in cookie-based load balancing. When used for persistence, the cookie value is used to determine which object server the client's TCP connections should be spliced to in order to preserve a persistent user experience. When filling an online shopping cart, for example, many retail Web applications will require that all TCP connections for a given user transaction reside on the same physical server.

Cookie load balancing is similar in concept to using cookies for persistence, but offers the ability to provide a tailored user experience based on their cookie value. First, let's see how a user's browser comes to have an implanted cookie in the first place. Figure 6–11 shows a user visiting a Web site and receiving a temporary cookie.

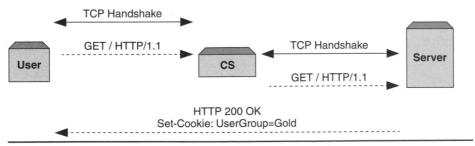

Figure 6–11   A server-implanted cookie reaches the client browser and will be included in every HTTP GET to that domain.

When the client first visits the Web site, or in subsequent HTTP GET requests and responses, the site has the ability to insert the cookie into the user's browser to act as a reference point later during the transaction. In the case of a memory resident or temporary cookie, the information may only be interesting during the lifecycle of that particular user session. For example, a user purchasing items from a shopping site potentially need only be identified during each purchasing cycle. For cookies resident on the hard disk of a user, otherwise known as *persistent* cookies, the information may be used to identify the client on *every* subsequent visit to the site. In either scenario, the cookie value also contains information on the domain that implanted it and is presented by the user in every HTTP GET to the Web site. We'll see the persistence mechanisms that can be implemented with cookies later, but now let's see how they can be used for preferential services and other applications.

Applications of Cookie Load Balancing

Cookies can be used very effectively to improve the operation of many HTTP based applications. Now we've seen the types of cookies and how they operate, let's take a look at some examples of how cookies can be used in content switching applications.

1. Effecting Client Logon

The first scenario we'll look at is using cookie load balancing to enforce a strict login and authentication model for a Web site. Let's imagine that Foocorp.com wants to implement a partner-only Web site to provide certain premium, chargeable services for their partners. One of the main drivers of Internet commerce, or *e-commerce*, is the value of the content and services being offered. In being able to distinguish between different customer groups and enable a different charging model based on the quality of content to which the user groups will have access, the costs of implementing the types of infrastructures we've considered can be paid back far quicker. The first stage of this model is being able to identify users accessing the content. The first stage of the identification for access to the site will be a user logon through the browser. After a user has successfully identified and authenticated himself, the object server doing the logon can implant a temporary or permanent cookie so that the client can be identified on all subsequent visits and directed toward the content type he has paid for. There are other scenarios, even with the use of permanent or hard disk resident cookies, where the user might have to log on again in future visits. First, the client may be using a machine he has never used previously to access the site and, as cookies are local to each physical machine, the cookie will not be on the client's current machine. Second, most modern browsers offer users the ability to clear all cached files and cookies from their machines. In this instance also, the users would not have a previously implanted cookie to identify them.

Figure 6–12 shows this scenario in more detail. Implemented here are two groups of servers. Group 1 contains servers that are dedicated solely to performing logon and authentication for the site. Group 2, and subsequent other groups as we'll see, contain the actual content.

Once the user's TCP connection has been completed by the content switch, the incoming HTTP GET request can be parsed and searched for cookies. If the correct cookie name with an associated value cannot be found, the content switch will splice the connection into the server group designated to handle "No Cookies." In some content switch configurations, this group may have the

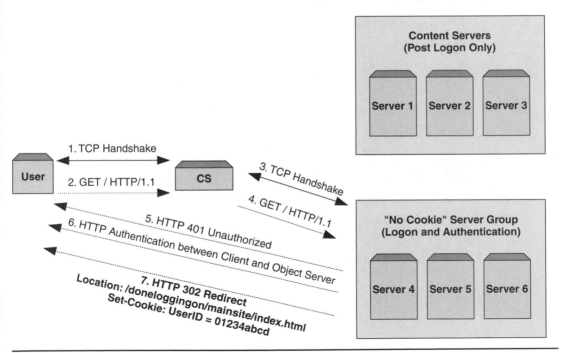

Figure 6–12   Using cookie load balancing, a user who does not have a cookie can be directed to a captive server group to authenticate.

option of being explicitly defined as containing real servers to handle requests with no cookies. In other configurations, these servers might simply be defined to handle a cookie value of "any" and will receive the request based on the fact that this will be the least accurate match for any valid request. In either case, the client request will be directed toward the captive servers for logon. The complete session between the client and the site looks like:

1. The client establishes TCP session to content switch via delayed binding.

2. The client sends an HTTP GET request with no cookie value currently set.

3. The content switch parses the HTTP GET request and, seeing there is not a cookie set, establishes a new TCP connection to the "No Cookie" server group.

4. The recipient server receives the HTTP GET request and issues the client an HTTP 401 Authentication Required message to show the browser that a username and password are required.

5. The client provides the username and password in a subsequent HTTP response and the credentials are validated by the logon server.

6. Provided that the username and password combination are valid, the server will issue an HTTP 302 or 301 redirect to the correct URL for the main part of the site. This HTTP redirect will also contain a `Set-Cookie` header, which will implant the cookie into the client browser.

Once this process has completed, all subsequent GET requests from the client (which will contain the cookie) will be directed to the main content servers for the site. In our basic example, what we've achieved by the use of cookie load balancing is the capture of unauthorized user sessions and their consequent logon and authorization, thus ensuring that clients who have not identified themselves are never allowed IP access to the servers containing the real site content.

2. Preferential Services

As a second example, let's look at using the cookie value implanted in example 1 to determine the quality of service or content to which is a user is entitled. As the cookie value can effectively be any string value, many different service levels could be implemented using such a model; however, let's take a simplistic example using "Gold," "Silver," and "Standard" service levels. Based on our previous example, let's assume that the logon server has implanted a second cookie called UserGroup, which has these three possible settings. Once the user has successfully logged on and authenticated, this cookie will allow the content switch to direct the user requests to the appropriate user group based on the services the user has paid for. This premium charging model might be used for additional processing and availability of resource, such as larger numbers of servers or more processing power, or simply premium rate content such as enhanced information or better quality images, movies, or music files.

Figure 6–13 shows two users who have logged on being directed to the resource to which they are entitled based on the cookies' values inserted during the logon and authentication process described in example 1.

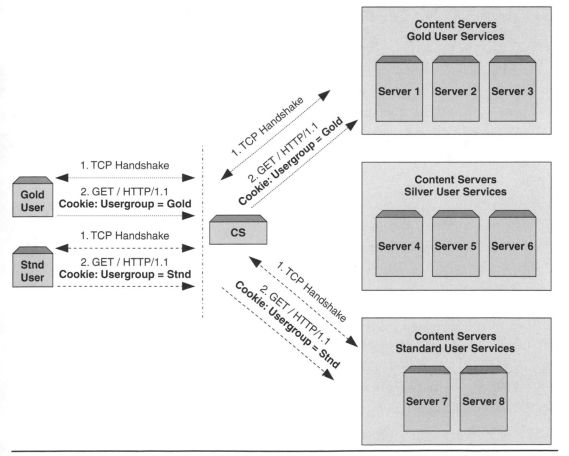

Figure 6–13   Users can be differentiated by services using cookie-based load balancing.

Load Balancing FTP

Our next application of Layer 7 server load balancing is somewhat subtler than those we saw previously. Some protocols are more complex than a single TCP connection from the client to the server and require multiple interoperating, bidirectional TCP connections to operate correctly. One good example of such an Application layer protocol is FTP. In Chapter 3, *Understanding Application Layer Protocols*, we saw the fundamentals of how FTP operates in its two modes—Active mode and Passive mode—so now let's apply what we already know and see how the protocol scales in a content-switched environment.

The issues of implementing FTP into content-switched architectures can be loosely summed up by two main points. First, as there are two separate TCP connections operating in conjunction, the details and control of these separate sessions must be combined within the content switch to ensure that mechanisms such as address translation and server selection are common between the two. Second, FTP is an example of an Application layer protocol that embeds IP address details within the Layer 7 application data payload between client and server. For any Layer 7 aware device performing NAT between the two end points in an FTP conversation, the challenges are common, so the issues that we'll see in the next few pages for content switching also hold true for other NAT devices such as stateful inspection firewalls. Let's look at both modes of FTP operation in turn—Active mode and Passive mode.

Load Balancing FTP in Active Mode

In Active FTP, the client opens an FTP Control connection to the server to carry control commands, and the server opens an FTP Data connection to the client to carry the actual data being transferred, which might be anything from a directory listing to a large file. To initiate this return connection from the server, the client issues a PORT command across the established FTP Control connection showing the server the IP address and TCP to which it should connect for the FTP Data connection. Once this command has been issued, the server will establish the FTP Data connection using the details provided by the client and begin the data transfer.

In Active mode operation, the responsibilities of the content switch are as follows:

- Perform delayed binding between itself and the client to establish the initial part of the FTP Control connection.

- Select a real server, open a TCP connection between itself and the real server, and splice the two together.

- Receive the client PORT command and forward to the real server.

- Allow the server to establish the FTP Data connection through the content switch to the client, ensuring that the source IP address for the TCP session is translated to the same VIP to which the client has established its FTP Control connection.

It's really this last point that is important in making the solution work. Imagine a scenario where the content switch is front-ending multiple VIPs for many different FTP services. The content switch must be able to parse the PORT commands from various clients attaching to all of these services and correctly translate the source IP addresses of the FTP Data connection to ensure that the clients see this coming from the same source they are attached to for FTP Control. Failure to do this would result in an application failure for most FTP clients. Figure 6–14 shows the process in more detail.

Let's look at the four stages of the example in more detail:

1. The client opens the FTP application and enters the site URL or IP address. This causes the application to open an FTP Control connection to the VIP on the content switch, which will in turn be load balanced to one of the real servers. Once the client-to-server connection has been established, the client will be challenged for a username and password to authenticate. At this point, the client has a full FTP Control connection to the real server.

2. The client will issue a command within the FTP application that will require the use of an FTP Data session. Within FTP, all data transfer between client and server is carried over the FTP Data connection. whether it is a file download or simply a directory listing. In many GUI FTP applications, the directory listing for the home directory will be requested, automatically triggering this process. The result is that the client will issue a PORT command instructing the server which IP address and TCP port the FTP Data connection should be opened to.

3. The server now initiates the FTP Data connection back to the client. When the clients FTP PORT command was issued and parsed through the content switch, session information was recorded that can now be

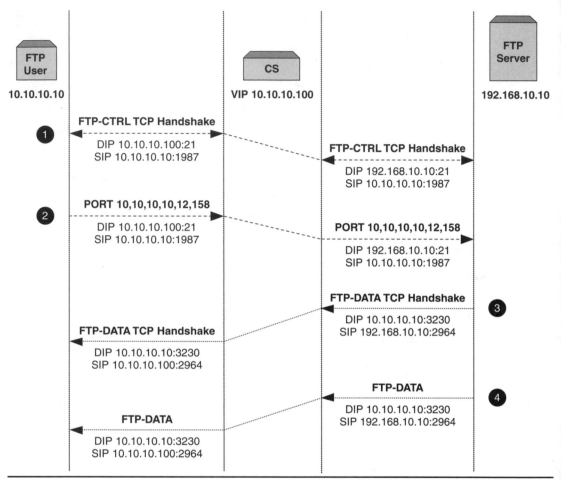

Figure 6–14   The traffic flow, parsing and address translation for an Active FTP session through a content switch.

used to correctly map the source IP address of the real server FTP Data connection to the VIP the client is talking to. This ensured that if the client opened its FTP Control connection to 10.10.10.100, the resulting FTP Data connection will also appear to originate from this address. As the FTP Data session is initiated, the content switch will perform the required source NAT on this connection.

4. All subsequent frames in the FTP Data session will be translated (destination IP address from client to server and source IP address from server to client).

Load Balancing FTP in Passive Mode

Passive mode FTP works differently from Active mode. In Passive mode, the FTP Data connection is established from the client to the server, meaning that both channels in the FTP session are established in the same direction. The reason that Passive mode FTP is popular within secure environments is because of the way the PORT command in Active mode opens a number of attacks commonly known as "FTP Bounce attacks." These Bounce attacks have several variations and can be used to perform subsequent intrusions such as portscans and even the bypassing of filtering or stateful firewalls. These attacks are based around the fact that an FTP client operating in Active mode can send a PORT command with a different IP address (and TCP ports) to that that initiated the FTP Control connection. Imagine if the client issued a PORT command with an IP address of a machine that is on the same subnet as the FTP server, and consequently on the *inside* of a firewall. This would give the attacker the ability to open a TCP connection to any IP address and TCP port by simply placing that information inside the PORT command. Other, more elaborate attacks can be formulated based on these principles, which are outside the scope of this book.

It is for this reason that Passive mode FTP is popular in Internet facing environments where security requirements are typically higher than in simple internal networks. For Passive mode FTP within a content switched environment, the content switch must perform the following functions:

- Complete a delayed binding with the client on the FTP Control connection.
- Select a real server, open a TCP connection between itself and the real server, and slice the two together.
- Parse the FTP Control connection for the PASV command, which the client uses to indicate to the server that it wishes to initiate a Passive FTP mode connection for data transfer.
- When the server issues its command 227 "Entering Passive Mode" argument, showing the client which IP address and TCP port to connect to, the content switch must change the Layer 7 information in the command and replace the IP address (and optionally the TCP port) to the VIP.
- For Passive FTP parsing, the last point is very important. If the real server is located on an internal subnet with a nonroutable IP address,

this will be passed in the PASV response. If the content switch does not successfully translate the PASV response from the server, the client will try to open an FTP Data connection to this incorrect address. Figure 6–15 shows the packet flow and translations for a Passive mode FTP session through a content switch.

Let's look at the five stages of this Passive FTP example in more detail:

1. As with Active FTP, the client FTP application will open an FTP Control connection to the VIP on the content switch. The content switch will perform a delayed binding on the connection and select a real server based on the Layer 4 distribution metric or other criteria. Once the real server has been selected, the content switch will open a TCP connection to the server and splice the two connections together.

2. The client will issue a PASV command to indicate to the real server that a Passive mode FTP session is required or preferred.

3. The real server will respond to the client's PASV command with a response code of 227—Entering Passive Mode (192,168,10,10,11,150)—indicating that the client should open an FTP Data connection to the IP address 192.168.10.10 on TCP port 3543. As the packet containing this FTP response passes through the content switch, the response code and argument will be translated to 222—Entering Passive Mode (10,10,10,100,11,150)—replacing the server's IP address in the Layer 7 payload with the VIP on the content switch. The content switch will also create some form of session reference to allow the expected client-initiated FTP Data connection on TCP 3543.

4. The client will then open an FTP Data connection to the VIP on TCP port 3543, which will be directed to the correct FTP server dealing with this client session.

5. All subsequent packets in the FTP Data connection will be translated based on this session information, transparently to the client and the server.

In summary, FTP load balancing is a good example of an Application layer protocol that typically does not need explicit configuration in the sense of URLs and so forth like many HTTP configurations, but requires some subtle Layer 7

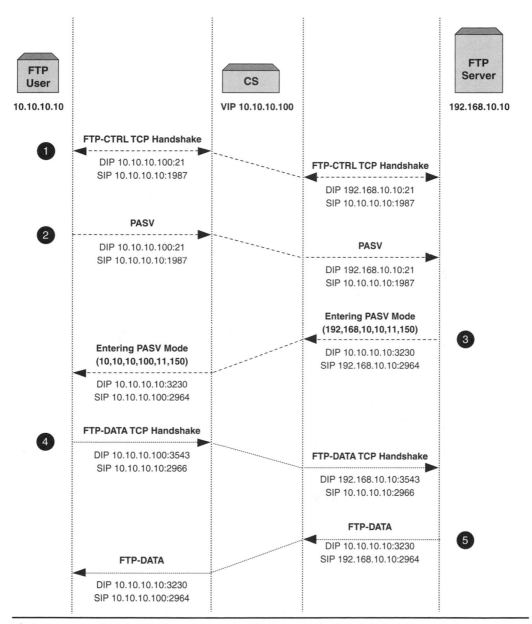

Figure 6–15   The traffic flow, parsing and address translation for an Active FTP session through a content switch.

information manipulation within the content switch to address the problems of a multiconnection application. We'll see another example of a multiconnection protocol that requires similar manipulation later in this chapter.

Load Balancing DNS at Layer 7

The final Layer 7 load-balancing example we'll consider is DNS. In Chapter 2, we saw that DNS can be either TCP or UDP based, although for the purposes of this discussion we will look at the UDP-based model more typically used for the request-response mechanism of resolving domain names within the Internet. While the primary reason for implementing a load balancing solution for DNS is the resilience of having more than one server, for some instances, such as ISP infrastructures and the root name servers for the Internet, sheer volume of traffic can also represent a problem. The UK-based root name server, "K" (*http://k.root-servers.org*) handles somewhere in the region of 4000 DNS requests every second at peak periods. At the time of writing, this is handled by three physical servers operating as a single cluster. Adding the intelligence to be able to deal with DNS requests based on the host or domain information means increased flexibility for large-scale DNS infrastructures.

The other advantage of using Layer 7 based DNS load balancing is that it offers the ability to deal with a problem known as "Split DNS."

Before we look at some deployment examples for DNS load balancing at Layer 7, let's look again at the nature of a DNS request. The following code shows a standard DNS request, in this case for www.foocorp.com, sent by a client machine. When we refer to DNS load balancing at Layer 7 it is specifically the parsing of the Name field in the Query section of the request. Using this information, the content switch can match the variables in this field against the regular expressions and text strings assigned to each real server and forward the UDP-based request to the correct server.

```
Domain Name System (query)
    Transaction ID: 0x0b84
    Flags: 0x0100 (Standard query)
        0... .... .... .... = Response: Message is a query
        .000 0... .... .... = Opcode: Standard query (0)
        .... ..0. .... .... = Truncated: Message is not truncated
        .... ...1 .... .... = Recursion desired: Do query recursively
        .... .... ...0 .... = Non-authenticated data OK:
    Questions: 1
    Answer RRs: 0
    Authority RRs: 0
    Additional RRs: 0
    Queries
```

```
www.foocorp.com: type A, class inet
    Name: www.foocorp.com
    Type: Host address
    Class: inet
```

The main difference from the other Layer 7 examples we've seen so far for things like HTTP and FTP is that DNS request/response traffic for resolving Internet names is typically UDP rather than TCP based. This effectively reduces some of the overhead on the content switch, as it removes the need to perform a delayed binding between the client and the server in order to parse for the Layer 7 information. In a UDP-based DNS query, the Layer 7 information is available in the first frame.

Applications of Layer 7 DNS Load Balancing

As a UDP-based service, layer 7 DNS load balancing has some less obvious applications in the network. Let's take a look at how intelligent DNS load balancing can provide some advantages.

1. Providing Large Scale DNS Infrastructure

The first example of implementing Layer 7 DNS load balancing is very simple—provide more intelligent distribution of UDP-based DNS requests into a DNS server farm. By using the ability to parse the Name field of the DNS query, client requests can be distributed based on the domain name being requested. This might take the form of using the first letter of the domain name, such as www.**f**oocorp.com, defined by regular expressions, or by using the top-level domain as a mechanism, such as www.foocorp.**com** or www.ietf.**org**. Figure 6–16 shows this type of implementation in more detail.

2. Implementing a Split DNS Infrastructure

For many enterprises, there exists a challenge when implementing DNS services for client machines or other DNS servers that is commonly referred to as *Split* DNS. With many network devices to configure, it is advantageous to implement a single IP address for DNS services within the network. However, many enterprises have different requirements for internal and external DNS naming. For example, imagine two groups of resources that are used by internal clients—one group containing internal only resources, such as *intranet.internal.foocorp.com*,

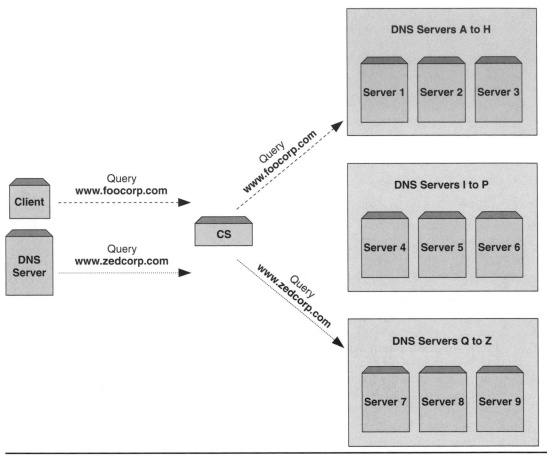

Figure 6–16   By parsing the Name field in the DNS query, DNS requests can be load balanced effectively using string matches against the host, subdomain, or top-level domain.

expenses.admin.foocorp.com, and so forth, and the second containing publicly accessible resources such as *www.foocorp.com* and all other Internet Web sites. The enterprise will require that internal only resources are resolved using internal, privately administered DNS servers, while external resources and all other Internet domain names are resolved using DNS servers provided and managed by their ISP. Implementing these DNS resources as defined real servers on a content switch and using string definitions to direct the DNS requests to the correct internal and exter-nal DNS resources based on Layer 7 inspection allows the enterprise to deliver dif-ferent, or split, DNS servers represented via a common IP address—the VIP on the content switch. Figure 6–17 shows an overview of a Split DNS infrastructure.

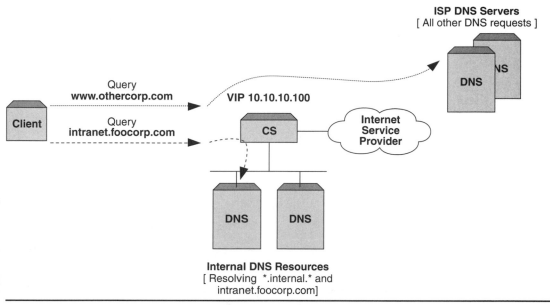

Figure 6–17   Implementing a Split DNS infrastructure with content switching.

Here we see a client with a DNS server configured as the VIP 10.10.10.100. The content switch is configured with two server groups:

- **Internal DNS servers**: These servers handle internal names such as intranet.foocorp.com or any host in the subdomain *.internal.foocorp.com.

- **External (ISP) DNS servers**: These servers handle any publicly accessible *.foocorp.com resources, such as www.foocorp.com, and all other Internet domains.

When the client's request arrives at the content switch, the Name field in the request is parsed and forwarded to the correct DNS server group based on host requested.

Load Balancing RTSP Streaming Media

The delivery of either real-time or delayed feed streaming media can be very compute intensive on the resources of object servers. As we saw in Chapter 3, the delivery of streaming audio and video data requires not only the use of a combination of TCP- and UDP-based delivery channels, but also potentially the interpretation and encoding of a live video or audio feed. The attraction of load balancing standard HTTP traffic is increased many fold when you consider the horsepower required to deliver high quality media streaming. However, as we've seen with other multithreaded protocols such as FTP, the load balancing of RTSP has issues all its own.

Load Balancing RTSP at Layer 4 Only

Before we look at the subtleties of RTSP load balancing at Layer 7, let's look at the basic frame flow when we use Layer 4 only. Figure 6–18 shows the basic traffic flow for Layer 4 load balancing of RTSP and RTP traffic. If we consider the steps in turn, we'll see where the problem lies.

1. The client initiates a TCP-based RTSP connection to the VIP on the content switch. In the instance where only Layer 4 load balancing is used, the VIP will only be configured with a service port of 554 for RTSP. Typically, no form of delayed binding is used and the connection is load balanced to a selected server.

2. The client and server exchange OPTIONS, SETUP, and DESCRIBE header messages to agree on the RTP and RTCP delivery mechanisms and other variables.

3. The client issues a PLAY command to instruct the server to commence delivery of the UDP-based RTP and RTCP frames containing the data and control, respectively.

4. Here is where we see the potential problem. As the server initiates the UDP (or potentially TCP) based RTP delivery, the content switch has no understanding of this flow, nor any way to associate it with the RTSP connection established in step 1. As a result, the source IP addresses on the RTP and RTCP UDP streams from the server to the client are not translated to the VIP on the content switch.

The net result of this type of configuration can be summarized as *IP address bleeding*, whereby the real source IP addresses of the object servers are revealed to the client on the UDP streams carrying the video and audio data. In many instances, this might not create a problem, as the RTSP and RTP specifications do not require that the source address of the RTP delivery be the same as the destination IP address for the RTSP connection. Where this might cause issues is in the following scenarios:

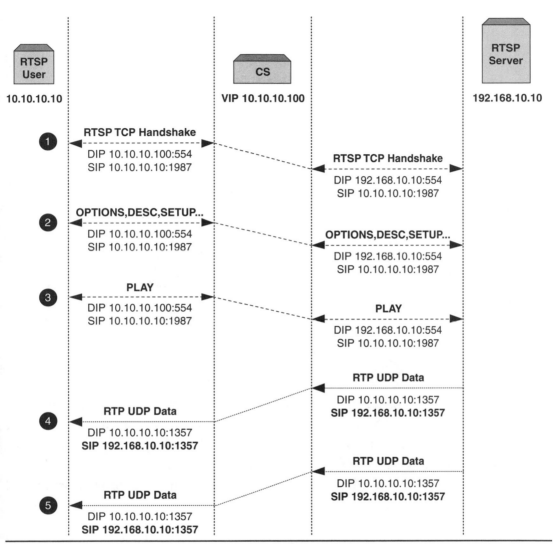

Figure 6–18   One of the main issues with load balancing RTSP at Layer 4 only is that the real IP addresses of the object servers are "bled" back to the client, as the corresponding RTSP and RTP streams are not associated in the content switch.

- If the service is hosted by an ISP or hosting service implementing anti-spoofing policies on perimeter routers of firewalls, the real servers will need to be located in public, routable address space. In many implementations, the ISP or hosting service will filter out source IP addresses that do not belong to the assigned address block. One solution for this scenario is to locate the servers in routable address space, although this will incur greater cost as many ISPs will charge for larger numbers of addresses.

- Some stateful firewalls implemented in the transitory networks between the client and the server may parse the RTSP connections to determine the expected RTP connections and open corresponding UDP source and destination ports. If the source IP address bleeding occurs, the firewall may reject the UDP-based RTP stream and force the server and client to negotiate down to the less efficient interleaved mechanism.

Therefore, our golden rule for implementing the Layer 4 only server load balancing for RTSP as described is to locate the servers in public routable address space such that once the source IP address bleeding occurs, fewer problems will be experienced.

Applications of Layer 7 RTSP Load Balancing

Adding Layer 7 intelligence to the load balancing of video and audio streaming services with RTSP has a number of applications. Some are less obvious and simply improve the overall operation while others can have tangible benefits in improving how different video and audio content types are delivered.

Tying RTSP, RTP and RTCP Channels Together

The first application we'll consider is a solution to the issue described in the preceding section. The correct source IP address translation will provide the client application with the illusion that both the RTSP connection and the consequent RTP and RTCP streams all originate to and from the VIP on the content switch. Without describing in detail the individual workings of specific vendor implementations, the basic traffic flow can be seen in Figure 6–19.

The basic stages of the traffic flow as shown in Figure 6–19 are as follows:

1. The client initiates a TCP handshake to the VIP on the content switch, which in turn facilitates a delayed binding to the client. If no parsing of the URL is required to decide on the object server (see Application 2), then the content switch will initiate a TCP connection to the object server.

2. The content switch will parse the RTSP data for the passing of the SETUP command from the client and the consequent RTSP 200 OK message from the server, extracting the client_port and server_port arguments as shown here:

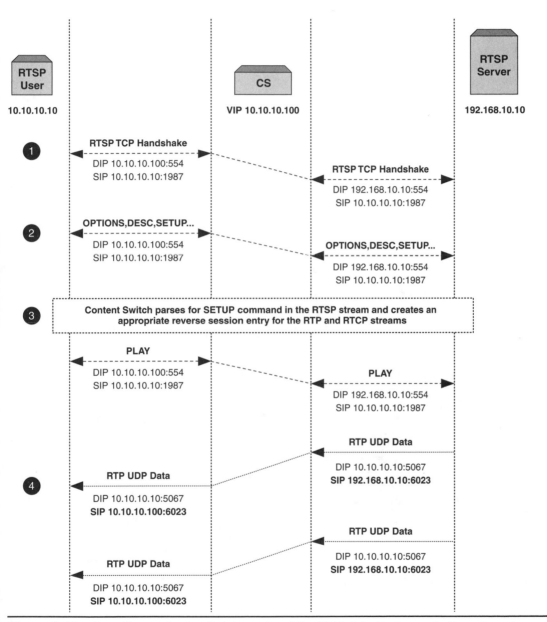

Figure 6–19   Once the content switch has parsed the RTSP data, it can create the relevant session entries to ensure the reverse NAT takes place for the RTP streams.

```
C->S    SETUP rtsp://video.foocorp.com:554/streams/example.rm RTSP/1.0
        Cseq: 3
        Transport: rtp/udp;unicast;client_port=5067-5068
```

```
S->C      RTSP/1.0 200 OK
          Cseq: 3
          Session: 12345678
          Transport: rtp/udp;client_port=5067-5068;server_port=6023-6024
```

3. Once the content switch has extracted the correct source and destination UDP port numbers, it can create a session entry for the UDP data flows from the server to the client ensuring that the correct source IP address (and optionally source UDP port) translations occur.

4. For the RTP data flow, all packets are properly translated, leading the client to believe that the source of the UDP-based RTP streams is the same VIP to which it has established the RTSP connection.

While each vendor's implementation of Layer 7 RTSP parsing for this type of issue may differ slightly, the fundamental outcome remains the same—the object servers from which the RTP content will be delivered can now reside in RFC 1918 non-routable address space, and the content switch will ensure that none of these addresses appear to the outside world.

Parsing the URL of the RTSP Stream

As we saw earlier in the chapter for HTTP content, there are often many good reasons to separate different content types across backend object servers. In the case of RTSP-based video and audio streams, this reasoning is often accentuated, as different stream types will require different resource types. Live video streaming, for example, requires large amounts of processing power in terms of CPU and memory to allow the object server resources to convert the live video and audio in the correct compression and format for delivery to the client, as well as access to the live feed itself via directly attached cameras, satellite feeds, or TV type input. Static, or prerecorded, might typically require less power CPU and memory resources, as the compression and encoding will already have taken place during the recording and positioning of the content. This type of service might more typically require NFS or SAN access to large data stores containing the prerecorded movies, programs, and clips. Other requirements may be to separate out free versus pay-on-demand content, authenticated versus nonauthenticated content, or even using the URL to distinguish between paying customers in a shared hosting environment. Whatever the requirement, the ability to parse the URL being passed within the

RTSP stream can be a very powerful addition to a media streaming implementation. Figure 6–20 shows an example of separating live and prerecorded streams on the object servers using a content switch.

In the same way that FTP requires intelligent parsing and translation of IP addresses and TCP ports, and HTTP offers the ability to segregate content types, Layer 7 RTSP load-balancing combines both of these requirements and capabilities. With RTSP being an open, RFC defined protocol, many content switch vendors now offer support for the mechanisms described previously.

Summary

In the course of this chapter we saw some of the many ways in which Application layer data can be used to switch traffic. We saw four of the most commonly implemented Layer 7 protocols for load balancing—HTTP, FTP, DNS and RTSP—and some of the issues that can be solved with content intelligent switching. One thing is for sure—as the processing power of content switches

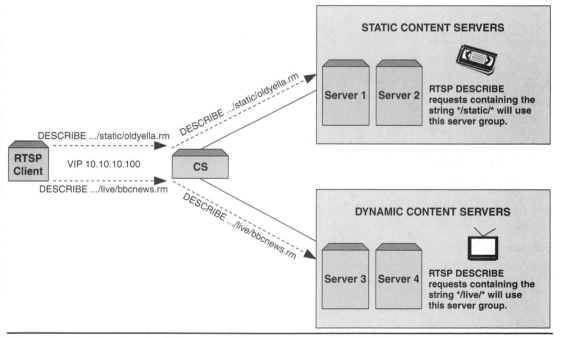

Figure 6–20   A content switch parsing the DESCRIBE commands of an RTSP stream offers the ability to separate different content types such as live and prerecorded streams.

increases, the deeper into application data network designers will be able to look, opening a whole new set of applications for this type of technology.

Case Study: Content-Aware Server Load Balancing

Having deployed Layer 4 load balancing and ensured that the design and servers are capable of handling the necessary traffic, the IT staff at Foocorp, Inc. would like to create a more personalized and easy to manage environment by having certain servers distribute specific high value content.

Using these powerful content switches will allow Foocorp to activate the Layer 7 load balancing functionality with very little infrastructure changes, merely configuration changes. What Foocorp is hoping to achieve:

- Provide application persistence based on user rather than IP address
- Increase the server capacity to handle specific applications and objects for image based files
- Use the same IP address for some of their online e-commerce businesses
- Still maintain the Layer 4 functionality previously deployed

When Enabling Layer 7 functionality, the basic requirements and features provided by Layer 4 are still available, such as private address space for security, VRRP for high availability, and so forth.

Deploying Content-Aware Server Load Balancing

If deploying Layer 7 content switching from day one, you should review the checklist from Chapter 5. However if adding it at a later date, remember to cover these important steps:

1. If using cookie persistence, decide on the best method for your requirements. If you are using Passive or Active Cookie mode, make sure that you discuss with the server administrator what values to associate with the server-generated cookies.

2. Understand that Layer 7 processing, while fast in some content switches, will be slowly than Layer 4 processing. Determine the throughput required and ensure that the calculation will be acceptable.

3. If using URL load balancing, make sure that the policies or rules for this configuration will send data to a server if a Layer 7 load balancing string is not matched. There should always be a back-end server that will accept the incoming session.

4. If using `Host:` header load balancing, remember to configure the correct header for the associated VIP.

5. Remember to update DNS with the new site names, even though they are using the same IP address.

6. Test failure of a switch using VRRP to ensure that you do not have an asymmetric route, as the content switch will need to see the return packet in order to manipulate it back to its original form. Ensure that this works for Layer 7 traffic as well.

We can see how this has been achieved by Foocorp in Figure 6–21.

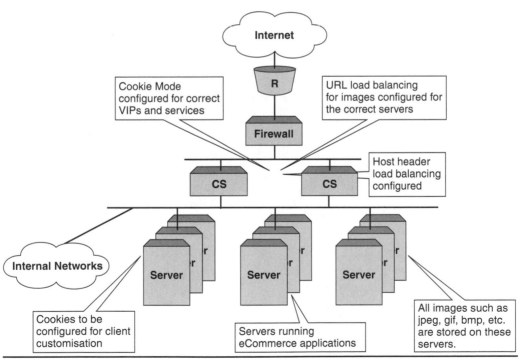

Figure 6–21   Foocorp, Inc. Layer 7 load balancing.

By deploying Layer 7 load balancing, Foocorp has been able to achieve the following:

- Personalize user access offering a better customized service
- Ensure that specific servers respond to specific content types
- Allow multiple online e-commerce business to use the same precious public IP address
- Allow new services and applications to be deployed with no or very little new hardware

Content networking at Layer 7 allows for very tight control of the networks. We discussed a brief and simple area of this exciting technology in this case study. We recommend engaging the content switch manufacturers who will provide quality resources who will be able to work with you to identify the best methodology for your Layer 7 infrastructure.

7

Persistence, Security, and the Internet

Persistence, or "stickiness" as it is sometimes referred to, is the mechanism used to ensure that the same user is connected to the same load balanced service for the duration of the session. With the advent of content switches and their load balancing ability to direct users to different backend servers, the need to maintain persistence has increased. Different load balancing metrics can be used to distribute the load and can often send the user from one server to another for different sessions as part of a single conversation. For a lot of content, this is satisfactory, as it increases site performance and enhances the user experience. However, the users' experience will be severely diminished if they are in the process of performing a transaction and are suddenly sent to another server that has no idea about the information just submitted. Persistence can be implemented in many ways, which we will look at later in this chapter.

The application will dictate whether persistence is required. E-commerce applications, or those that are connecting to a backend database, are the most common, as they have information that is specific to the user and require this when a user is filling out forms or adding items to his or her shopping basket for check out and payment. This transaction needs to be handled by a single server to ensure that all online information entered is tracked and associated to that user. Figure 7–1 shows what happens when a session that requires persistence is broken. In addition, the use of persistence ensures that there is no duplication of data, the database records are opened by one process, no data is lost or corrupt, and the record is cleanly closed and updated on completion. Sharing this among

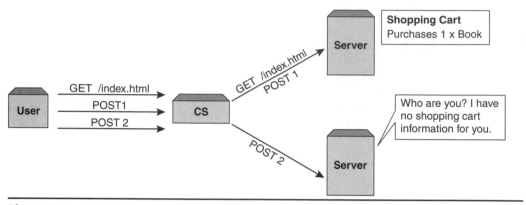

Figure 7–1   Why persistence is required in e-commerce transactions. Without persistence, we can see that a session from a user breaks.

multiple front-end servers is not a recommended mechanism. Each server will need to communicate with one another in order to have visibility of the entered data. If encryption is being used, each server will need to perform the processor-intensive key exchange, and to make matters worse, if a load balancing metric such as round robin is used, this process will have to be repeated as each session is closed and reopened. This is not a viable option and would place far too big an overhead on the transaction servers. These servers should be concentrating on processing data as quickly as possible before sending it back to the origin in order to increase performance and site availability.

Therefore, with persistence, we need to understand that there are certain issues when trying to implement it into your networks. This is further exacerbated when connecting to the Internet or other infrastructures not under our control.

Internet Service Providers—Proxying and Traffic Volumes

Anybody connecting to the Internet today, be it for individual use or for a business requirement, will typically use an Internet Service Provider (ISP). ISPs offer a centralized point for users to connect to the Internet. This eradicates the need for each individual user or business to provide their own infrastructure and participate in routing updates, DNS configuration, and so forth. All of this is handled by the ISP, who in addition will have a resilient network and have peering agreements with other service providers to connect into their infrastructures. This provides a transparent view to the end users; they merely have to sign up with an ISP and connect to a predetermined end point within the ISP, and all onward communication is carried out seamlessly. This makes connection to the Internet a relatively painless operation, but brings with it design issues for network architects. These can vary depending on the ISP used, but mainly revolve around proxy issues and Network Address Translation (NAT).

Proxies

In the days before content switching, the only way to provide access and some form of control was to point all the users at a single device. Traditionally, a single proxy always handled access out to the Internet. This device was configured to perform NAT, provide a minimum level of caching, and allow access to external devices. As the Internet has evolved and more users are online, large ISPs are now under pressure to provide a comprehensive and cost-effective service. As ISPs may have hundreds of thousands of subscribers, managing IP address allocation to all these remote devices is a major concern. Moreover, with the IP address shortage being experienced it makes no sense to allocate hundreds of thousands of individual addresses when only thousands of people are online simultaneously. ISPs have an obligation to preserve address space as effectively as possible. The way the ISPs get around this is to allocate everybody a private IP address as described in RFC 1918. This allows every subscriber to connect to the ISP concentration point, or proxy, using his or her allocated private IP address. Then, using NAT, each private IP address is translated to a single public IP address using Port Address Translation. Port Address Translation uses the source TCP port to differentiate the different users. It allows many thousands of addresses to be translated to a single public address, as illustrated in Figure 7–2. This is often called a *mega proxy*.

As each user is now connecting through a proxy with access to the Internet, it makes sense that these proxies also perform other functions. With the drive to increase revenues, other applications and services are provided at a small increase to subscription costs. These services typically include:

- Personal firewalls
- Virtual private networks (VPNs)
- Personal content portals
- Antivirus checking

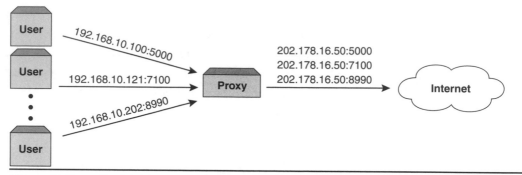

Figure 7–2   Port Address Translation. This maximizes the use of IP addresses and ensures that thousands of devices can access the Internet using a single IP address. This is often referred to as a mega proxy.

However, one of the biggest advantages of a proxy is its caching ability. Caching allows the content being requested by one user to be stored locally at each ISP POP and therefore will be available to other users who require the same data at a later date. This increases performance while minimizing bandwidth usage, since subsequent requests do not have to be sent out across the Internet, as the data is already local. Caching breaking news stories or major sporting events are typical examples of how we can increase the user experience and reduce bandwidth usage. Web cache redirection is discussed in detail in Chapter 8, *Application Redirection*.

Therefore, it is a compelling argument for ISPs to deploy a proxy to handle these functions. These are known as mega proxies. However, due to the sheer volume of users and content being served, a single proxy, while it can handle thousands of users simultaneously, is not a viable option when effective throughput is required. To overcome this, multiple proxies are deployed and are often load balanced to provide better performance and resilience. This brings with it a whole host of other issues that can play havoc on persistence.

Proxy servers from different vendors also throw their own unique issues and quirks into the mix. Proxy servers can communicate with one another and distribute the load between them for the same user session. The thinking behind this is that the requesting device is oblivious to any optimization of its request. All the requesting device requires is that is gets a response back from the device to which it sent the request. If all the acknowledgment and sequence numbers are valid, the cyclic redundancy checksum calculates, then the packet is processed. Therefore, proxy servers can manipulate and distribute load without the user knowing. This in itself can be a major pitfall in environments requiring persistence.

Once a user connects to a mega proxy, all onward connections into a site appear as if they have come from that proxy. As these proxies are handling sessions for many thousands of users, all of these connections appear to have come from that same device. While this is great because it conserves the rapidly diminishing IP address space and allows routing tables and updates to be reduced, it causes serious issues when persistence is required. As these proxies are load balanced, sessions for a single page of HTML objects can be seen as coming from different devices. In an HTTP environment where every HTTP GET or POST is seen as a single session, this doesn't affect the user. However, in environments that require the same server to handle the session, this obviously is not a feasible solution. Based on this we will see that IP address hashing, while an excellent method for persistence, is not a scaleable and preferred solution when large mega proxies are involved. Figure 7–3 illustrates the potential hazards of using proxy servers when persistence is required.

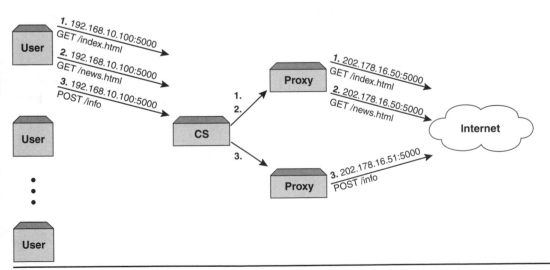

Figure 7–3   Issues with load balanced proxies and persistence. By load balancing requests across multiple proxies, persistence is not maintained, as the request appears to have come from multiple sources instead of a single source as is required.

IP Address Hashing

The most common persistence mechanism is to use the IP address of the requesting device and bind all subsequent requests from that device to the selected server. For a TCP session to operate, a source IP address (SIP) and a destination IP address (DIP) are required. Normally, these values are unique for each flow from different devices and provide an excellent pointer to which the session can be associated. As discussed in earlier chapters, load balancing can be done using multiple variables. The most common method is to use the IP address. The SIP, DIP, or a combination of both can be used. How this approach is implemented is a large area of discussion, but to simplify matters we have summarized the process here:

1. When a packet ingresses the content switch, an algorithm runs against the incoming SIP, DIP, or SIP/DIP combination, and a value is calculated.

2. The algorithm differs from vendor to vendor, but all solutions will yield a value that will be used to select the appropriate destination server.

3. All further communications from that source to that service will be sent to the selected server, thus providing persistence.

This is also true for DIP hashing. Depending on the algorithm, it is generally accepted that this method is excellent for load distribution.

However, the problem here is that when using SIP hashing, this only provides Layer 3 persistence, and when used with a mega proxy, or even a medium-sized proxy, all sessions will be sent to the same server. While this might not be a major issue, it can have detrimental effects when we see how mega proxies are used and how prevalent they are in today's networks.

Mega proxies are very common in large ISPs and because of this can negate the use of SIP persistence. Again, this will occur if the SIP and DIP are used in conjunction. Obviously, while DIP hashing provides persistence, it will select the same server for every session on that service (HTTP, DNS, etc.), as all users, regardless from where they are coming, will be destined for the same address, which therefore defeats the object of load balancing. DIP hashing is, however, used in Web cache redirection and other such applications discussed later.

To get a better spread of traffic even when mega proxies are used, the TCP or UDP source ports in conjunction with the SIP and/or DIP could be used to provide a more granular method of persistence. This would allow for an even flow of load balanced traffic, but could still break the persistence model if different proxies are used that change the SIP during the transaction or when switching between HTTP and HTTPS.

Hashing is one of the best methods to use if you are designing a site and are not sure of what applications are going to be deployed. A point to note here is that many sites do use IP address hashing and have created successful and exciting applications with it. Remember that just because mega proxies are being used does not mean that you cannot use hashing as a method for persistence. It all depends on the site requirement, applications being used, and the site's public availability—as our former boss would say, "when in doubt, hash." Chapter 5, *Basic Server Load Balancing*, has more detailed information on hashing.

Cookie-Based Persistence

Another more accurate mechanism to use is something that is unique to the user and is always used during communications between the client and server. Cookies are the mechanism used to achieve this. To understand this concept, let's first find out what cookies are and how browsers make use of them.

Cookies

A cookie is just another HTTP header. Every browser has the ability to use this information. It is stored in memory while the browser is operational and then can be copied to the hard drive of the user's device for later use. Cookies are text strings that consist of specific information set by the device issuing the cookie. They will have a name or ID and each will have a value. It is this value that is unique to each TCP session and can be used to differentiate between users. In addition, cookies will also have a date, time, and an expiration date. Cookies can also be embedded within the URI string and can be inspected by content-aware switches. The following is an example of a cookie stored on the hard drive of a PC:

```
PREFID=0b8a58957b6eb7d0:TB=1:TM=1012536298:LM=1012536298:S=7tVGQN2iyDM
Foocorp.com/15362618878336321116343222235948829469397*
```

To further demonstrate the cookie location and value, Figure 7–4 is a trace of the HTTP header using the preceding cookie. The name (PREF ID) is typically

```
Hypertext Transfer Protocol

GET /search?client=navclient-auto&ch=51554150042&freshness_check=3Mpsk9VuX
HTTP/1.1\r\n
Accept: */*\r\n
Accept-Encoding: gzip, deflate\r\n
User-Agent: Mozilla/4.0 (compatible; MSIE 6.0; Windows NT 5.0)\r\n
Host: www.foocorp.com\r\n
Connection: Keep-Alive\r\n
Cookie:
PREF=ID=656210d555a653:TB=1:TM=2029086665:LM=2029086665:S=qIL-CZYmB_o\r\n
\r\n
```

Figure 7–4   Packet trace showing HTTP header with cookie information.

used by the content switch to search on, and it is the associated value to the name that is used to create persistence.

There are typically two types of cookies—permanent, and temporary. A permanent cookie has an expiration date and is used each time that particular site is visited. This cookie is stored on the local machine. A temporary cookie is used only for the duration of the session; in other words, only while the browser is open. Once shut down, that cookie is no longer valid and is deleted. Temporary cookies do not have an expiration date in order to differentiate themselves from permanent cookies.

Using cookies for persistence is an extremely compelling argument, as each session can be seen as unique regardless of the source IP address. We are now making decisions based on content and not just Layer 3 and/or Layer 4 information. However, one of the requirements when using cookies is to ensure that the server issues cookies back to the user or requests a cookie from a user on initial connection. This process will require liaison with the application development team and will normally require changes to the server setup. In some instances, this is not possible or practical. To overcome this, content switches are able to insert and strip out cookies on sessions to and from the user without the server being aware of this. This allows the network administrator to control the environment and not rely on server software changes to aid in the quest for cookie persistence. One key element here is that the browser needs to be set to accept cookies. This can be turned off on browsers and is an individual choice, dependent on your security required. If a browser does not accept cookies, the best mechanism for persistence is to use IP address hashing.

Before we go any further, let's look at the steps involved for cookie persistence when a client connects to the VIP. This is a typical setup and would be used even if a content switch were not installed to provide load balancing.

1. The user and server set up a TCP three-way handshake via the content switch VIP.

2. The user sends an HTTP GET to the VIP.

3. The content switch examines the request, confirms that there is no session information pertaining to this session, and selects a server based on the load balancing metric set for that group.

4. The server responds to the request and inserts the cookie in the return packet.

5. The content switch examines the cookie and inserts the session into the session table, including the server that responded. If cookies are to be inserted or rewritten by this switch, this would occur at this point as well.

6. All subsequent sessions with that cookie value will be sent to the same server, thus maintaining persistence.

A point to remember is that delayed binding, also known as TCP splicing, will be enabled when a content switch is used, because the switch needs to determine what content is being requested before sending a user to the selected server. Delayed binding is discussed in more detail in Chapter 6, *Content-Aware Server Load Balancing*.

Cookie Types

In most content switches, there are three types of cookies used for persistence:

- Temporary mode
- Permanent mode
- Insert mode

Let's first look at Temporary mode, where a temporary cookie is used only for the duration of the session and expires on shutdown of the browser. These cookies are not stored locally on the user machine and are issued each time a user attaches to a server. Therefore, each cookie value could be different on each visit to the site. This requires that the server be set up to issue cookies on request. Once the cookie has been issued, the content switch checks for the cookie ID and ensures that subsequent cookies are sent to the selected server.

Permanent mode allows cookies to be stored on the user machine. The duration for which they are stored is dependent on the cookie expiration date. Expiration dates are set by the server administrator for the servers that issue cookies. The date can be any length from a few hours to many years. This is beneficial when using applications or services in which the users will need to take one of the following actions:

- Renegotiate their connectivity
- Resubmit certain information
- Provide further payment to continue enjoying access

Insert mode is unique to content switches and can be implemented by the network administrator without input from the server administrators. The reason for this is that the cookie is inserted when the session leaves the switch back to the user and is stripped out on the subsequent return. The server never sees this cookie and as far as it is concerned, the cookie never existed. Obviously, Insert mode places additional overhead on content switches, as they need to inspect every packet and manipulate it on ingress and egress. Insert mode supports both temporary and permanent cookies.

Cookies in Action

Using cookies is an extremely powerful approach that allows for a more granular view of content switching. Cookies can be used to single-handedly allow the administrator to determine different levels of access, performance, and status based on user cookie values. This gives the administrator the ability to create different services and revenue streams using cookies. Figure 7–5 demonstrates the ability to assign different class or service levels to each user. The level of service purchased (or granted) can be associated to cookie values; in this case, bronze, silver, and gold cookies are used, with bronze being the basic service and gold the premium. Dependent on the value of the cookie issued during login, the user is granted access rights and privileges commensurate with the level of service purchased.

However, when using cookies as a persistence mechanism we need to be able to detect the cookie within the HTTP header or within the URL. This is done

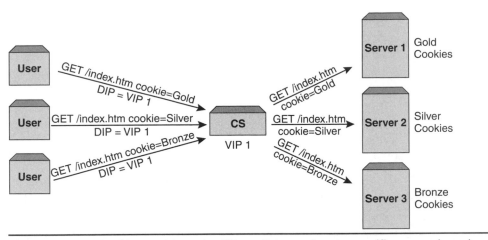

Figure 7–5   Cookies enable us to differentiate services to specific servers based on the uniqueness of the cookie. It is the cookie that is unique to each user.

by parsing the packet and looking, from the HTTP header onward, for the cookie value. Parsing is explained in more detail in Chapter 6. This works great for HTTP applications, but we break the model when using HTTPS. The reason for this is that with HTTPS, the data portion is encrypted and the cookie ID that we use to associate the value is no longer visible. Figure 7–6 shows why this occurs.

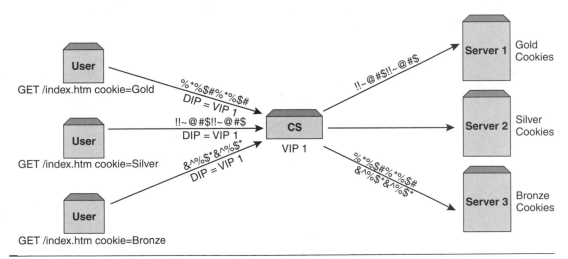

Figure 7–6   Using cookies with SSL brings its own challenges, as SSL has encrypted the very thing we want to inspect.

Obviously, persistence is no longer possible so we are left with two options: IP address hashing or SSL Session ID. We have seen the drawback of using hashing with mega proxies, so SSL Session ID is an alternative.

SSL

SSL is a protocol developed by Netscape in the early 1990s that allows certain applications running over TCP/IP to be encrypted, as well as providing authentication mechanisms. It is typically used across public and private networks. SSL has evolved into Transport Layer Security (TLS) with the guidance of the Internet Engineering Task Force (IETF). We will refer to this protocol as SSL throughout the book, as this is the accepted terminology. SSL sessions encrypt the data portion of the session providing no clear content other than the IP, TCP, and SSL headers that can be used for persistence. For example cookies, URLs, and so forth will be encrypted, as they reside in the data portion of the packet.

SSL is a fairly complex protocol and in order to provide insight into this important protocol we covered the basics in Chapter 3, *Understanding Application Layer Protocols*, which will be extremely helpful when we discuss SSL Offload in this chapter. However, should more detailed information be required, many good articles and books are available on this subject exploring it in far more detail than we have here.

SSL Session ID Persistence

As we have seen, the use of IP address persistence can have many issues if mega proxies are being used, but would work when using SSL because any other information you might want to use is encrypted. Using hashing in this scenario would depend on network design. If used in a network where all users have unique addresses, hashing is a simple and effective method to maintain persistence. Unfortunately, in most cases, this is not always possible, and other more intelligent mechanisms are required. Now that we have seen how SSL works and the importance of the SSL Session ID, we can understand why it makes session persistence really simple when other unique identifiers are encrypted.

The SSL Session ID is part of the unencrypted SSL header, and each time a client connects to the server and sets up a SSL session, a unique SSL Session

ID is used. This is a simple and easy to implement method against which to ensure distributed persistence when all clients are using the same SIP. Unfortunately, using SSL Session ID persistence is flawed, not because of the content switch's ability but rather the functionality of the Microsoft Internet Explorer (IE) browser. In order to enhance security, the MS IE browser renegotiates the SSL Session ID every two minutes. This provides erratic and unstable behavior for sessions requiring persistence that are longer than 120 seconds. Windows 2000 browsers have been changed to allow the SSL Session ID to wait 60 minutes before renegotiating the ID with the server. All Netscape Communications browsers do not exhibit this behavior. This again does not resolve this issue permanently, and as Microsoft's IE browser is one of the predominant browsers used, the use of SSL Session ID for persistence is basically obsolete unless you can ensure that all users connecting to your Web site are using Netscape browsers.

We are now basically faced with the issue that we cannot guarantee persistence in an encrypted session unless we use hashing. This hinders the ability to provide an effective service. However, this can be fixed. It does require additional hardware and design, but allows for intelligent persistence in encrypted sessions.

Fixing the Model with SSL Offload

Moving the point of SSL processing from a server to a dedicated device has many benefits. Let's look at these benefits before we explore the workings of SSL offload and the different models and deployment scenarios.

One of the primary benefits is a massive increase in performance. As we all know, a slow responding site can be extremely frustrating and in some cases can be the difference between doing business or moving on to a site that provides rapid and efficient service. Many studies have been carried out to try to determine the cost of a slow site when performing online transactions, and while the results indicate that many millions of dollars are lost, the only true gauge is how you feel and what you would do if faced with a painfully slow connection. Human nature dictates that we would react differently depending on the day or mood. What we all know is that the faster a site responds to our needs, the better we feel. Therefore, our goal should always be to enhance the user's experience.

Unfortunately, SSL is typically a slow performer. SSL transactions, due to their nature, need to be encrypted and decrypted. As discussed earlier, the larger the encryption algorithm and key, the more processor intensive they are. Processors have a finite amount of capacity, and as we increase SSL sessions into a site, the more processing a server has to do. Remember, it is not only the initial transaction that needs to be decrypted, but all subsequent ones as well. Sure, the setup process is by far the most compute intensive, and it is this reason why servers tend to buckle under heavy SSL loads. The setup session rate can very quickly bring a server to its knees.

Servers all have the ability to listen on TCP port 443 for SSL connections. On completion of the three-way handshake, it is up to the server to perform the key exchange and decryption. Most servers are also processing HTTP traffic, responding to health checks from a content switch, answering management requests regarding availability, and generally keeping their house in order with all the other processes required by the operating system. All of this requires CPU cycles. With heavy SSL session setups, the CPU can quickly become swamped, and the server not only degrades the service for SSL but as all other processes are competing for a slice of the CPU, they in turn will begin to decline. This has a knock-on effect and ultimately affects the user who is trying to access your site—the one person you want to keep happy. Therefore, SSL can impact an entire server and all its processes in busy sites. The secret is to offload this function.

SSL Offload Types

How do we perform SSL offload without degrading server performance? A popular method has been to install an SSL encryption card within the server itself. This is a hardware-based solution and has its own CPU for carrying out all SSL encryption and decryption. This relieves the CPU of the server from having to perform this, and allows it to concentrate on serving files and maintaining an adequate level of speed. In small organizations with a single server, this solution is seen as cost effective and provides an increase in performance that cannot be beaten. However, using SSL cards in larger sites comes with a few issues that are not insurmountable, but definitely require a fair amount of thought before committing to that solution.

SSL cards do not provide the same performance increase as dedicated SSL offload appliances because they are using the processing capabilities of the host server. In addition to this limitation, and probably one of the most crucial issues in large sites, is the management of certificates. Some leading-edge dedicated SSL offload appliances can provide central management of these. While it may only be a single certificate to begin with, as the site grows and more services are required (remember that certificates are tied to domain names), more certificates are required. Another point to remember is that the cards are third-party products; operating system upgrades could affect the drivers and the workings of the card. Therefore, care must be taken when performing an upgrade. This may require that additional software be loaded to allow the card to function.

Dedicated SSL offload appliances allow for a huge increase in performance as they perform the task themselves, which allows a server to perform its function (i.e., respond to requests) without impacting performance. There are many appliances dedicated to this on the market today, but due to the deployment models supported, not all are created equal.

A SSL offload appliance's sole purpose in life is to listen for SSL traffic, typically on TCP port 443, and encrypt and decrypt this traffic. How this is done differs from vendor to vendor but ultimately the end result is the same.

1. Traffic ingresses the device, is decrypted, and is sent to the server.
2. The return traffic enters the device, is encrypted, and is sent back to the client.

This occurs until the session is complete. The issue all designers have to address is how to get the SSL traffic into the appliance. Simple, place the appliance in the data path. However, this creates performance and resilience issues. What if the device fails, then all SSL and other non-SSL traffic to and from the site ceases. In addition, all non-SSL traffic has to pass through the appliance, thus degrading performance, and we are almost back to where we started. It is much better to let the SSL appliance concentrate on what it is designed for. In this case, however, it is the SSL processes that are compromising non-SSL data. To overcome this, it is easy to place a pair of these SSL appliances in parallel as can be seen in Figure 7–7. This provides a resilient route in to and out of the site. Again, the scalability of this approach has to be questioned. Not

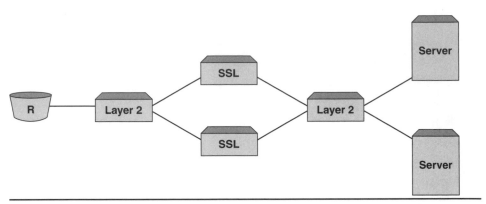

Figure 7–7   SSL offload appliances in parallel offer some resilience, but any failure of an appliance will impact half of the network traffic.

only is the above still true, but also a single failure of an SSL appliance will degrade access to and from the site by 50 percent.

Adding additional devices in parallel merely adds complexity without providing the benefits of a device that sits out of the data path. However, many vendors have manufactured these devices, and deploying them in parallel, while not optimal, is still seen as a step up in performance from SSL cards in the server. The best method is to place the device out of the data path and rely on another device to intercept and forward only SSL traffic to the appliance. This method is by far the most efficient and allows for performance, scalability, and resilience unmatched by the other methods.

To make this work, a content switch is required. A content switch has the ability to understand Layer 4 information. Most switches are able to perform this function by redirecting TCP port 443 traffic into a SSL offload appliance without impacting other protocols. By sitting out of the data path, the SSL offload appliance does not have to forward other traffic. Most importantly, if it fails then there is no degradation to the site for all other protocol types. This allows designers to deploy this method, understanding that they only need to provide enough capacity to cater for SSL throughput only.

Let's now look at how this is done. We'll also examine some of the design pitfalls and benefits that can be achieved by implementing this.

To begin, you need a content switch and it has to sit in the data path—this is true for all content switches as discussed in previous chapters. There are a few approaches that can be used to send required traffic to the SSL offload appliance:

- Redirect all traffic with a specific IP address
- Redirect all traffic on TCP port 443
- Sending all traffic using a combination of both

Using the IP address only method is typically not used, as most sites use the same domain for both HTTP and SSL (HTTPS) traffic (e.g., *http://www.foocorp.com* and *https://www.foocorp.com*), which would break this specific deployment model. Once the content switch has determined the criteria, it forwards the traffic on by maintaining the source and destination IP addresses. The only thing that should change is the destination MAC address. Some SSL appliances can act as a proxy and therefore are seen as the end device to the client and the source device to the server. Using proxies has its advantages and disadvantages. However, most sites are not fond of using the SSL appliances as a proxy, as all requests are seen as coming from the SSL offload appliance and not from the actual user. This makes tracking and logging difficult. We will discuss ways to overcome this later in the chapter. For now, let's see what happens to the traffic from here on.

1. Packets are forwarded to the SSL offload appliance with the DIP being that of the domain that the user requested.

2. The SSL offload appliance performs the three-way handshake back to the client and then begins the intensive task of exchanging keys and agreeing on a cipher spec as discussed earlier in the chapter. All this time, the backend servers are unaware of this session.

3. On completion of the SSL handshake, the device then creates a new TCP session with the backend servers on another unencrypted port. This can be configured on any port.

4. The server receives the request in clear text, carries out the requested function, and sends the response back to the client. Because the server has no knowledge of the SSL offload appliance, it will send this back to the client on the "new" unencrypted TCP port.

5. The content switch intercepts this and based on its session table forwards this back to the SSL off load device that originated the initial session.

6. The SSL off load device, using its session table, encrypts the data and sends it back to the user over SSL with all the right TCP acknowledgement and sequence numbers.

7. This continues until the session is complete.

While it appears that there is an increase in processing, the ability to split the load and have different devices providing this service can increase the SSL performance from 20 to 50 transactions per second on a traditional server with no SSL offload ability up to the 750,000 mark—dependent on offload appliance and deployment model. This far outweighs any perceived overhead and latency that might be introduced by the content switch and SSL offload appliance. Figure 7–8 shows a resilient SSL offload design.

One issue that is often raised is that of using a clear TCP connection for the decrypted traffic from the SSL offload appliance into the backend servers. This is seen as a potential security breach, as data that should be secure is now flowing over your network in an unsecured fashion. Sure, this is true, but is often allowed since it takes place within a secure data center. The perception is that if people can trace this, they have to have access to the data center. If they do, then they typically have access to the backend servers where the "crown jewels" are stored, and performing a packet capture is irrelevant as access to the servers and their databases becomes the major concern. Saying that, however, there are organizations that require true end-to-end encryption, and in some cases,

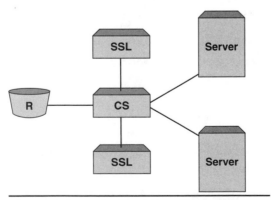

Figure 7–8　　Resilient SSL offload design offers true redundancy, as the appliances are not in the data path and will not impact network traffic.

particularly financial companies, this can be a regulatory requirement. Using an SSL offload appliance at first glance appears to have no benefit, as the server still has to decrypt the data and therefore has to perform those compute intensive transactions that we have been desperately trying to minimize over the last few pages. While this is certainly true, we mustn't forget that the SSL offload appliance still plays an extremely important part in this process. For starters, the SSL offload device is the only thing that can actually decrypt the traffic, and while it is still inside the device (therefore secure), it can scan for cookies or any other Layer 7 parameter defined. Once it has found a match, it can maintain persistence using the associated values as seen in the section about cookie persistence earlier in this chapter. It will then encrypt the data and send it to the correct server, thus maintaining persistence on information that is normally considered encrypted in an SSL transaction. It should be pointed out that not all vendors are able to implement this solution today and some provide a clumsy approach to this, as it sends clear text out over the infrastructure albeit for a small amount of time. The goal of end-to-end encryption is to ensure that no clear text from a secure session ever traverses the network.

While this solves the persistence problem in an end-to-end encryption session, it does not appear to decrease the backend servers' load. Let's look at the ways around minimizing the load on the servers for SSL traffic.

Backend Encryption

To achieve this, there are multiple methods that can be used. One of the easiest to implement is to use a very low encryption strength for the backend servers so they do not have to perform such a compute intensive function for every connection. This adheres to the requirement for end-to-end encryption, but still forces the server to create and tear down an SSL session for each user request. This can negate the effects of carrying out end-to-end encryption, as busy sites may receive so many new user requests that the CPU may still become the bottleneck.

Another approach makes use of "old" connections. When a new session has been created and then another new session is started, the server and user will always try to reuse their existing keys to minimize SSL session setup. With the SSL offload appliance actively participating in all SSL sessions, it has an understanding of sessions that have expired and has the ability to put these aside for later use. This is known as *connection pooling* or *connection splicing*. This method requires that the SSL offload appliance must act as a proxy. Again, for logging purposes, this is not always acceptable, but we will discuss later how to overcome this in a secure encrypted environment.

When a new session is created between the SSL offload appliance and the user, the offload appliance looks in its pool of unused, but still potentially active sessions to the backend servers. It selects one and performs the session setup reusing the key from the original session. As discussed earlier, this makes a huge difference to performance, as it is the new key exchange that requires the most computing power and this process is no longer needed. The server can receive encrypted sessions without worrying about the huge CPU overhead required for new session setup. This is an ingenious method and one that provides true back-end encryption without compromising the performance associated with servers and SSL termination.

Let's now address the final point in this—how we provide the ability to perform logging, when using the SSL offload appliance as a proxy.

Every session that is created has a unique Session ID that can be forwarded within the HTTPS header to the backend server. The source IP address can also be forwarded to the server using the *X-Forwarded-For* header. This provides the ability to determine how many unique connections were used and allows network and server administrators to provide accurate reports on user connectivity in a secure, encrypted environment.

Summary

We discussed the need for persistence throughout this chapter and the issues associated with this, particularly in a security environment. The simplest approach is to use the source IP address (or destination) for persistence. The only issue here is what happens when we have many hundreds, if not thousands, of users connecting from behind a proxy. Fixing this problem is what makes working with persistence challenging. We need to move up the protocol stack to achieve this and start to use content. Encrypted sessions again cause persistence problems, and they need a unique approach that can involve additional hardware.

All persistence issues can be resolved; it merely depends on your requirements and how granular you want to be.

Case Study: Persistence

Now that we have completed our discussion of persistence in the Internet, let's take a look at how our favorite company, Foocorp, Inc., would deploy these techniques.

When designing a network to support IP-based applications, it is important to understand the criteria of the application; in other words, is user persistence required?

Foocorp, Inc. developed an application that requires a user to log in, specify the information they require and then search through the database based on the required criteria. The problem is that they offer a business-to-business service as well as a consumer service. Typically, the business-to-business users are hidden behind a proxy and require different levels of service to that of the consumer. Moreover, the business users may work from home so there is no way of knowing who is who in this scenario.

In addition to this, the existing information and service levels cannot be jeopardized by the deployment of SSL for security and authentication. The IT folks at Foocorp, Inc. have decided to use an SSL offload device, as they realize that this provides an increase in performance as well as scalability should this service become popular. They have also selected one that can be deployed outside the data path.

Deploying Persistence

Let's look at the steps needed for a successful implementation.

1. Install the SSL offload appliance(s). These should typically be 100Mbps or gigabit connected. Dependent on available port density, this can be connected to a Layer 2 device. They must, however, only have one path, and that is through the content switch.

2. Create a CSR and send the CSR off to a CA for signing.

3. On receipt of the certificate, copy it into the device and associate it with the required domain name and IP address.

4. If backend encryption is required, ensure that the servers are listening on the correct TCP port and that that service is active.

5. Configure redirection policies or filters on the content switch to redirect the SSL connections to the SSL offload appliance.

6. If the content switch is not acting as a proxy, redirection policies or filters will need to be created on the content switch to redirect responses back to the SSL offload appliance. If this mechanism were not in place, traffic would be routed directly back to the user either on the wrong TCP source port or with the wrong SIP, which would cause the user to be reset.

7. If health checks are being performed from the content switch, ensure that responses reach the switch by inserting an allow policy or filter before the redirection policy or filter used for the return packets. This policy or filter must be specific to the IP address of the Web switch; otherwise, all packets will be allowed and will not hit the redirection policy or filter, thus causing the site to fail.

8. Configure the cookie persistence mode required; Temporary, Permanent, or Insert mode on the content switch, remembering to ensure that the cookie name and the size of the cookie are determined.

9. If server changes are required to implement cookie persistence, remember to involve the server administrator in order to get the necessary information from them.

10. Once these steps are completed, the site should be operational.

We can see how this has been achieved by Foocorp in Figure 7–9.

By deploying SSL offload and persistence, Foocorp has been able to achieve the following:

- Increase site response time for online transactions
- Delay the capital outlay for server upgrades to cope with SSL transactions
- Provide true end-to-end application security from any geographical location
- Ensure that users remain connected to the server for the duration of the transaction
- Control client access to and from the site
- Provide end-to-end encryption for key services
- Use Layer 7 information on encrypted sessions

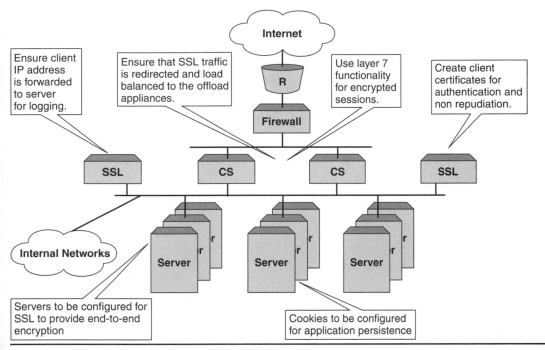

Figure 7–9   SSL off load and persistence.

By deploying a dedicated appliance to perform process intensive tasks such as SSL, Foocorp has managed to easily and effectively manage their site for future growth.

8

Application Redirection

If you take a long hard look at application redirection, it is enough to give the security administrator within your network sleepless nights. Application redirection gives you the ability to intercept a flow of traffic based on the application it is using and redirect it to a different location totally transparent to the user. That location could be anywhere, local or remote. However, before you start to worry, let's understand why this feature is an extremely powerful utility that can increase the performance of your network and minimize operational costs. Therefore, while you might have a nervous security administrator, you should at least have a relatively happy chief financial officer.

A content switch is an intrusive device by its very nature. For it to provide its services, it needs to be able to see what information is being sent. This can be equated to that of a letter. Traditional routers are the postal workers. They see an address and send it to you regardless of the content. They are only interested in getting the letter to the addressee; sending it to the destination IP address in Layer 3 terms. What if this letter was urgent and you needed it at work but it was addressed to your home? How would you get it there? What if this letter was junk mail and you decided you had no need for it? Where would you send it? What if this letter needed to be sent to your accountant instead? How would you do this? The postal worker could never remember everything about you and your requirements without impacting everybody else's needs. Therefore, to make matters simple, he delivers it all to the address on the outside and it is up to you to sort it out when you get home.

While this works and has for many years, we are building more intelligent networks that require us to increase the level of service we offer, and to do this we need to see more than just the front of the envelope. Application redirection gives us this ability. We must stress that being able to transparently send a session to a remote location or to be able to scan the contents of an HTTP header are not security threats, but rather a mechanism by which we can accelerate the network and offer a rich set of services to enhance the user experience.

Application redirection allows us to indiscriminately intercept a data flow based on its destination, application, URL, or even its cookie value and steer it to another location entirely. This is done transparently to the user. So, what would we use this for?

The Requirement for Application Redirection

To cope with the ever-increasing spread of information, we have begun to build faster, bigger, better, and more intelligent networks to allow the world to communicate. These forms of communication are already evolving, and voice data and video have converged onto our PC. With televisions, mobile phones, and PDAs becoming extremely popular methods to provide constant access to this media, the amount of data in any form that we send and receive will undoubtedly increase. Network manufacturers and providers will continually push the boundaries in order to provide more than is required by the ravenous consumer. Being able to intelligently manage the network is a fundamental requirement that is already being addressed. Content switching, while seen as a new technology, will become as widespread as hubs and switches are today. Application redirection is one of the mechanisms available that gives us the ability to offload tasks to devices without impacting performance. These devices, or appliances, are typically designed to cater for that particular application. They are configured and tuned purely to provide a specific function.

However, as application access and popularity increases, so does the load on the server or devices running it. Load balancing is the answer, but in many cases, as we will see in the next section, server load balancing and application redirection, while both having their roots in content switching, are two different animals indeed.

Application redirection requires that the device receiving the data is transparent. In other words, it is a proxy type of application and knows what to do with the request. Typical devices that can benefit from application redirection functionality in a load-balancing environment are:

- Caches
- Firewalls
- SSL offload appliances
- Content routing
- Proxies
- Bandwidth managers

As can be seen, application redirection gives us the ability to control certain types of traffic and send it to specifically suited devices. This allows us to implement devices within the infrastructure to improve performance by handing the load to multiple devices, and to do this transparently. This means that there is no configuration or intervention required at the user desktop. This can save an organization vast sums of money, as deployment can be carried out relatively quickly. Visits to each and every user are not required in order for them to make use of the service. When you have thousands of remote users, coordination of a network upgrade or application enhancement is extremely difficult and time consuming.

VIP-Based SLB vs. Application Redirection

We saw in Chapters 5 and 6 how to perform server load balancing. The most common model is to create a VIP and let that be the target or destination to which the user connects. Based on the ability of the content switch, the manipulation of the addresses and inspection of the data is the function of the load balancing process. This process, which replaces the DIP with that of the real server, is by far the most common. It is extremely simple to implement, as all the intelligence is inherent within the switch. Why, then, would you want to use anything else to perform load balancing?

Applications that require the source and destination IP address to be maintained are a prime example of why you would use application redirection.

Application redirection does not do any manipulation of the IP addresses; it merely substitutes the destination MAC address with that of the destination device selected by the load balancing metric and maintains the original source and destination IP address. The difference between this and a traditional router is that a load balancing decision has been made at this stage. This obviously makes our traditional load-balancing model a little harder to implement, as we do not have a VIP we can use as the pivotal point (or destination) of the session. In the normal load-balancing model, you would not use application redirection. However, if you require a session, based on its service (TCP port) used, to be sent to a set of servers or even to a VIP, application redirection is the most efficient mechanism to achieve this. Figure 8–1 shows how we can intercept certain applications and steer them to different devices.

Web Cache Redirection (WCR)

We covered SSL redirection in the previous chapter and will be discussing firewall load balancing in the next, so this chapter will focus on one of the most common uses for application redirection—WCR.

WCR is one of the most deployed services in the Internet today. As the Internet has grown and content has become available, ISPs have seen the bandwidth and usage of their infrastructure increase. Imagine an ISP with 300,000 subscribers, and 10,000 are online simultaneously. What if 10 percent of those on line all wanted to look at the same Web page? Without the content being local, every user would have to be routed to the content source. This is a huge duplication of data, a massive drain on resources, and excessive use and waste of bandwidth. So, why not

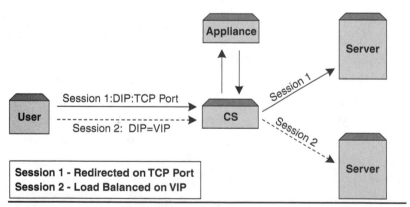

Figure 8–1   Application redirection shows how the content switch inspects the data and redirects sessions, based on service used, to the appliance. Other sessions are passed through normally.

provide a device that stores or caches this content locally? Caching is not a new concept and has been used in PC network devices for many years. It was only in the late 1990s with the growth of the Internet that caching appliances came to the forefront. Sure, we have early software-based caches that were used, but as access speeds increased, the need for dedicated caching appliances has become an important part of internetworking design. Every major ISP in business today will have some form of caching in place to minimize bandwidth usage and increase user performance as can be seen in Figure 8–2.

Before we rush off and discuss WCR, let's take a step back and spend some time understanding how caching works and the different methods involved in providing this service.

How Caching Works

In short, caching is the function of retrieving data, storing it locally, and then having it readily available for use when next requested. Ensuring that content is current or fresh is a key element that caching manufacturers take very seriously. Today, caching vendors have designed appliances to store and access data extremely quickly. The mechanisms used to do this are typically proprietary and each has its advantages and disadvantages. It is safe to say that caching of data for specific applications is what can differentiate vendors from one another. Some typical examples are:

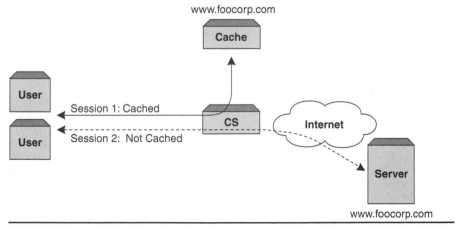

Figure 8–2   Cached content can be served quickly, while uncached content needs to traverse the network back to the origin server.

- HTTP data
- FTP data
- Streaming media such as video on demand

With the advent of streaming media and faster access speeds, users are demanding faster and better services from their ISP. In addition, as compression techniques improve and companies are looking to use media as another aspect to their business, streaming media services have become extremely popular. However, maintaining a steady, jitter-free stream of data from the origin server to the user becomes a challenge in today's overcrowded and oversubscribed backbones. It is here that caching comes to the fore and provides a solution that allows for data to be retrieved and viewed without the impact to the origin server or the backbone. This is true for all forms of data.

Cache Hits

Cache hits are used to describe how successful a cache is. Caches can use both memory and hard disk space to store data. Vendors design algorithms to ensure that the most frequently accessed objects are stored in memory, and some also allow the network administrator to force (pin) objects into memory. The reason for this is that a cache's function in life is to be hit as often as possible and serve that data back to the requesting device. Monitoring cache hits indicates how successful a cache is. A cache hit is when the object requested has been found in the cache store, either in memory or on the hard disk. Hit successes over 50 percent are seen as adequate, and obviously the more cache hits your cache performs, the less your bandwidth or servers are being hit. We will see later that maximizing cache hits is a key design criteria, and simple things such as load balancing metrics can affect the cache hits.

Caching Fundamentals

There have been many studies carried out about how many objects make up a typical Web page, and results vary between 30 and 80 different objects. As Web design becomes more intricate and innovative, a typical Web page will only increase in size. If each object is seen as a single HTTP GET, then between 30 and 80 TCP sessions will have to be created in order to download a typical Web page. We should point out here that the use of HTTP/1.0 causes this to happen. HTTP/1.1 was developed to overcome this limitation, as it allows a TCP session to remain open and multiple HTTP GETs to be sent down this single connection. This has the benefit of reducing TCP session setup and tear-downs and increases performance. Figure 8–3 illustrates the difference when using HTTP/1.0 and HTTP/1.1.

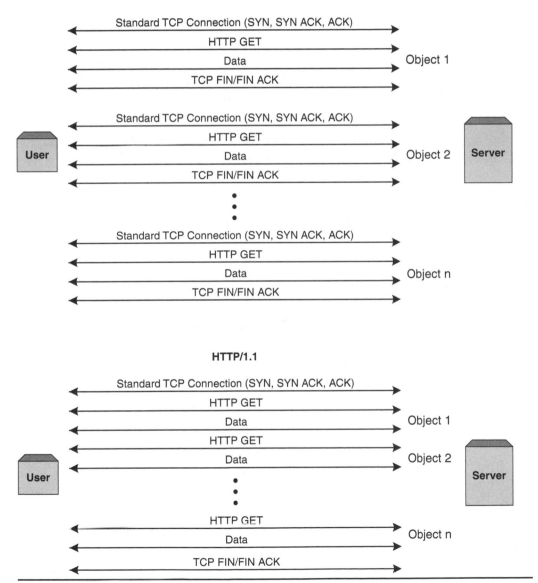

Figure 8–3   HTTP/1.0 vs. HTTP/1.1 shows how session setup is reduced when using HTTP/1.1.

Of the objects that make up a Web page, some of these are dynamic and some are static. By *dynamic*, we mean that they change often (every second to every few minutes or even hours). A typical example of dynamic content would be news services, stock price tickers, sports scores, and so forth. Static content, on the other hand, can be around for hours before it changes. Classic examples of this would be the date on a Web page, which would obviously change every 24 hours. Site names, banners, borders, company logos, and so forth would very rarely change. Therefore, if this site has been accessed before, why should another user coming from the same place have to consume bandwidth in order to download static content that could very easily be stored locally? It is here that caches make use of the HTTP/1.0 and HTTP/1.1 protocol header information that determines which objects need to be refreshed and which are still current. While developers also often try to force content to be refreshed (or not) by embedding messages within the HTML, this alone cannot guarantee content freshness. We need to make use of the HTTP headers. HTTP headers are discussed in detail in Chapter 2, *Understanding Layer 2, 3, and 4 Protocols*, but we will run through the most important headers that we use when performing caching.

HTTP/1.x

Lets look at what happens when a device accesses a Web page and understand the different HTTP headers used. There are many different types of HTTP headers, but the one at which we will look a little more closely is the General header. This header contains the Cache Control header, and it is this that determines what the cache must do with this request. The cache cannot disobey this and must honor the request specified in the Cache Control header. The following are the three most common Cache Control header directives used in HTTP/1.1:

- Probably the most common is the no-cache command. This indicates to the cache that it must retrieve the data from the source. It cannot send any content to the requester without first ensuring its validity from the source. This obviously impacts caching performance and is not ideal for content that can be cached.
- The max-age command indicates to the cache how long before the cache must update the object
- The last-modified and if-modified-since commands allow the caches to determine the age of the content and whether it should be updated.

Let's now look at the process that takes place when retrieving a Web page.

1. A user initiates a TCP session with the origin server.

2. The user performs the three-way handshake and then sends an HTTP GET.

3. The cache inspects the request to determine the directive set in the HTTP Cache Control header (or Pragma: No Cache header used in HTTP/1.0).

4. If the header directs for "no cache," then the cache requests the data directly from the origin server, even if the content is stored on the cache.

5. If the "no cache" header is not set, then the cache will determine if it has the content, and again, if not, will retrieve it from the origin server.

6. Assuming the cache does have the content, then it will first confirm the freshness of the content. This is based on the manufacturer's algorithm but will basically see if the content needs to be updated. If not, the cache will serve it directly back to the user.

7. If it does need to confirm the content's validity, it will send an HTTP header with an "If Modified Since" directive asking the origin server to confirm if the requested content has changed.

8. If the origin server has not changed the content, it will serve it directly back to the user. If the content has changed, the cache will then request the modified object from the origin server.

9. On receipt from the origin server, the cache will update its freshness table with the new content and expiration timer based on the HTTP Cache Control headers and serve the data back to the user.

This may seem like a long-winded and time-consuming function, but it must be remembered that only very small requests are sent across the Internet, therefore imposing minimal delay. The more a cache is used, the more effective it becomes, and the quicker the response will be.

Understanding how caching operates is an important function when discussing WCR. Unfortunately, we will not go into a great deal of caching principals, as this is a subject in its own right and there are many books and articles that cover only this topic. We have tried to give a brief overview to assist in understanding the fundamentals while reading this chapter.

HTTP Status Codes

Part of the HTTP protocol specification is to provide a mechanism for feedback to the application (and user) on the success or failure of a request. We will also see that content switches, as well, make use of this feature when performing advanced features such as firewall load balancing and global server load balancing. There are generally five different areas of status codes:

- **1xx**: These cover information aspects on initial connection and indicate that the connection process is proceeding.
- **2xx**: These are used to determine the success of the connection; the 200 OK being the most famous.
- **3xx**: These indicate if redirection needs to take place. This is often seen in the caching environment where a 302 Moved Temporarily or Redirect is used.
- **4xx**: Indicates a client error; the dreaded 404 Not Found being the most popular (or unpopular).
- **5xx**: Indicates a server error; the most typical is 503 Service Unavailable.

It is important to be aware of HTTP status codes when troubleshooting a network, as these can indicate what is happening upstream or downstream from your location. In addition, it can also point clearly to the fact that the server is not issuing content and it is not the fault of the content switch.

Cache Types

There are many different modes in which to deploy a cache, with each having certain benefits over the other. The most common deployment modes are:

- Forward proxy
- Transparent proxy
- Reverse proxy

We will look at each in a bit more detail and understand their capabilities as they are intended to function in stand-alone mode. Caching vendors design their products to be able to operate without the intervention of a content switch. While this is possible, protocols such as WCCP and ICP (discussed later in the chapter) have been developed to overcome the lack of a content switch. These protocols provide some level of scalability and resilience, but fall short of the mark when competing against the functionality of a content switch. It would, however, be safe to say that using a content switch to provide the redirection, intelligence, and resilience greatly enhances the caching appliance's performance. Speed and intelligence are what differentiates caches from each other, so it makes sense not to overload it with other tasks not directly associated with serving content quickly.

Forward Proxy

This is an extremely popular method of deployment, as the cache is seen as the device to which all data is sent. Users and servers configure themselves to point to the cache. When the packet arrives at the cache it terminates that session, determines what content is required, and then requests the content from the origin server on its behalf. The client IP address is not passed to the origin server, and all requests appear to have come from the forward proxy. There are many benefits to using a forward proxy.

- The most important is performance increase. Caches are designed to serve data very quickly, and by being the first point of contact, data, even if it is not the whole page, can be served locally.
- Caching of data can save bandwidth usage, minimize operational expenditure, and defer link upgrades.
- Filtering for inappropriate content that can be detrimental to a company's reputation can be controlled and logged.
- Software updates can be carried out by proxy caches. Browser software can be downloaded on execution of a script providing a simple, user-controlled update saving administrators valuable time.
- Access via a single device to external networks allows security administrators to allow only that device external access, thus protecting the internal network.
- Authentication via a directory service or radius type implementation can ensure that only those authorized can use this proxy service, as well as maintaining logging and in some cases billing records.

When using a forward proxy, the destination TCP port is usually set to 8080 or something similar. This allows the proxy server to listen on that specific port for all incoming traffic knowing that this is the traffic it must proxy out onto the Internet for. On receipt, the forward proxy opens a new session with the original destination address. The source IP is that of the forward proxy, and the destination TCP port is changed to 80.

While forward proxies are an excellent method for accelerating network access and providing a certain level of control they also have certain disadvantages:

- The proxy is the single point of failure. As users are pointed to a single device, should this device fail, then external access is not possible.
- The forward proxy caches need to maintain all the cached pages so any distribution of content is very difficult and will rely on the caches communicating with one another.
- The scalability of this service diminishes rapidly as you add more users to the network. Sure, adding another cache is a fix, but this requires additional desktop visits to change browsers to point to the second cache. In addition, determining who uses which cache requires user intervention, thus minimizing any administrative and manageability benefits.
- Logging is probably the single biggest factor when using forward proxies, as the source IP address will always be that of the cache. While this does not impact the provider of the caching service, it certainly makes life difficult for upstream sites and their logging ability.

Figure 8–4 illustrates a forward proxy cache.

It must be noted that there will always be pros and cons to any deployment, and it is up to the network architect to determine the best solution in order to complement and maximize the design. Forward proxy caching can accelerate

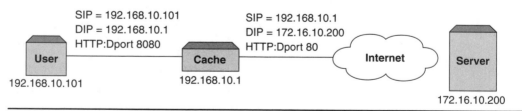

Figure 8–4   A forward proxy cache handles all traffic destined for the external network using itself as the intermediary.

your network and increase availability while providing a simple, manageable access point. Understanding the benefits and weighing them against the disadvantages will ensure a successful implementation of a caching service.

Transparent Proxy Caching

In contrast to a forward proxy cache, a transparent cache is exactly that—transparent. Typically, it sits in the data path and interrogates every packet to determine what is Web-based traffic and what is not. On receipt of a packet for which it is proxying, albeit transparently, the cache either retrieves the data from its local cache or retrieves it from the origin server. Most transparent caches can also preserve the source IP when requesting data. This allows the origin server to see exactly who accessed the data. This is a fundamental difference between the forward proxy and the transparent proxy; however, a transparent proxy is not obliged to perform IP spoofing. It can function in exactly the same way as a forward proxy and request the data on its behalf.

The key difference between the forward and transparent proxy is that the transparent proxy sits in the data path. Therefore, in effect it could be set up as the default gateway and will receive all traffic destined for other networks. Transparent caching is a popular method of deployment, but is usually deployed in conjunction with an external device. Deployed on its own, it has the following disadvantages:

- All traffic, cacheable and noncacheable, is sent through this device, providing a potential bottleneck in the network.

- Trying to provide a resilient, scalable solution creates a problem when more caches are needed. Some caches provide their own form of load balancing between themselves, which can overcome this resilience issue but requires expertise on these protocols.

- If acting as a proxy, then mega proxy (discussed in Chapter 7) and logging on upstream sites again rears its ugly head.

Saying all that, transparent proxy caching is still an extremely compelling solution when caching is involved. Deploying this allows zero desktop administration, as the requests are intercepted en route to the destination. This means that no browser changes are required. The advantages of using a transparent cache are almost the same as that of a forward proxy:

- First and foremost, it will increase the performance. Caches are designed to serve data very quickly, and by being the first point of contact, data, even if it is not the whole page, can be served locally.
- Caching of data can save bandwidth usage, minimize operational expenditure, and defer link upgrades.
- Filtering for inappropriate content that can be detrimental to a company's reputation can be controlled and logged.
- Access via single device to external networks allow security administrators to allow only that device external access, thus protecting the internal network assuming IP spoofing is not configured.
- Authentication via a directory service or radius type implementation. This can ensure that only those authorized can use this proxy service, as well as maintaining logging and in some cases billing records

Figure 8–5 illustrates a transparent proxy cache.

Reverse Proxy Cache

Reverse proxy, server acceleration, Web server acceleration, and server-side caching are all names that are used to describe this method of caching. Whichever one you use, the bottom line is that this method increases site performance. While all the caching fundamentals are the same, this method is typically deployed by the content owner. They want to increase site performance in order to better serve the customer. The advantages of this are as follows:

- Large portions of the site content can be prepopulated onto the cache, providing much quicker access to the site. Caches typically are much faster at retrieving and serving data than a normal file server.
- Access into the site can be from a single source IP address if this is a requirement and no logging is needed. This enables a much tighter security policy for public facing sites.

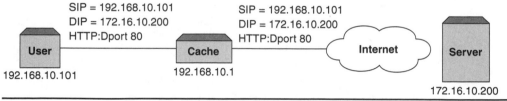

Figure 8–5   Transparent proxy cache.

- Performance can be further increased if the cache is deployed in front of the firewall. This solution is not always recommended due to the security implication, but it can be very beneficial in intranets and extranets where, typically, access is from a trusted network.

- As we progress into serving rich content across the Internet, streaming media applications can and will consume massive server resource. Using a dedicated appliance to provide a "front-end" cache allows for better throughput and performance.

- Cost of server upgrades can be deferred or minimized, as reverse caches can service the majority of requests.

Like all deployment models, there will always be some disadvantages. However, reverse proxy caching has very few disadvantages as it benefits both the user and content owner. The content owner who installed this benefits from increased site performance and user retainment. These advantages are typically what the user requires anyway, so in most cases a reverse proxy cache is a "win-win" situation for both user and content owner.

Figure 8–6 illustrates a reverse proxy cache.

While server and network administrators look to enhance their networks, caching provides an excellent mechanism to do this and without doubt is an important part of any site that wants to accelerate and maximize its existing infrastructure. However, deploying caching on its own, without using a load-balancing device, brings with it many challenges. Ensuring scalability and resilience are foremost in any network administrator's mind. There are protocols available to provide some form of communication between caches. The two most common today are:

- Internet Cache Protocol (ICP)

- Web Cache Communication Protocol (WCCP)

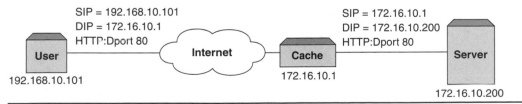

Figure 8–6   Reverse proxy cache.

While there are a few others, these two have evolved and emerged as probably the most widely deployed. We will look at each in a little more detail to understand its advantages and disadvantages.

ICP

ICP is a mechanism that allows caches to be configured in a hierarchical fashion. Caches understand who is the parent and who are their peers in this configuration. ICP allows a cache to communicate with its peer or parent if it does not have the content requested. This allows caches to make use of local or hierarchical content from other caches, rather than sending this information across the Internet. This maximizes a caching farms' hit rate and allows for sharing of content. A cache will not send out an ICP request to its neighbors if the content is local. If the content is not found, the cache will send an ICP request to its peers requesting a reply from them. If the content is still not found, the request is sent up the hierarchy until it is found or retrieved from the origin server. It is then sent to the original cache that serves it back to the user. It must be pointed out here that ICP adds an overhead to any request, as the caches first have to communicate using ICP, and then, if required, initiate an HTTP connection in order to retrieve the data. This might be acceptable in a small cache deployment, but can complicate matters in large, dispersed cache deployments.

WCCP

WCCP was developed by Cisco Systems and is used within routers and caches. A WCCP-enabled cache will signal a WCCP-enabled router, informing it of its IP address. When the router receives HTTP requests, it will automatically select a cache based on a hashing algorithm and forward the packet. This process is transparent to the user. On receipt of the packet, the cache will either serve the content or request it from the origin server. Using WCCP allows network administrators to deploy WCR seamlessly into the network. While this is an open protocol and has had many enhancements, there are a few aspects that often deter the network designers at high-performance Web sites.

- Placing additional overhead on software-based routers can heavily impact basic router functions such as updates, forwarding, and convergence times. In addition, routers might not be managed by the business and be in the control of an outsourcing provider.

- Encapsulation of all packets between the router and the cache adds over-head to both devices.
- Layer 7-based Web cache redirection is not possible.

While both these protocols offer a form of scalability and cache meshing or clustering, nothing beats using a content switch to provide load balancing of large cache farms without impacting performance of the cache or other key net-working devices.

WCR

WCR, simply put, is making use of the intelligence of a content switch and steering or redirecting the traffic to the cache farm. This method requires no caching protocols such as ICP or WCCP. By using the content switch, caches can retrieve and serve content extremely quickly. There are no processing over-heads required in order to understand which device has what data. In addition, routers can perform the function for which they are designed, and that is to route. Overloading them with other tasks can impact other business critical traf-fic, delay routing updates, and degrade convergence times. There are typically two methods for WCR:

- Layer 4 WCR
- Layer 7 WCR

Using Layer 4 WCR is often seen as the traditional method, as it typically redirects TCP port 80 to the cache farm. Some tuning of load balancing metrics can maximize cache hits, but other than that, no more intelligence is achieved. Layer 7 WCR, on the other hand, offers much more granularity and allows for caching on:

- URL/URI information
- HTTP Host header
- URL hashing
- Browser based
- Layer 7 streaming protocols

This functionality allows a much richer and intelligent spread of traffic, as caches can be configured to handle specific types of content and management of this is more easily achieved. Before we progress, let's quickly cover a topic that can determine and influence how WCR on a content switch is implemented.

IP Spoofing

Just mentioning this can get security administrators in a spin. IP spoofing disregards traditional network rules and allows a transparent proxy device to perform the request on its behalf, but, and it is this that causes security concerns, uses the IP address of the source device. In other words, the proxy device will receive the request and forward it on maintaining both the SIP and DIP addresses but expect the response to come back to the proxy device. This function is seen as a security breach, and some firewalls and routers will alert the security administrator that there is a possible intruder or hacker within the network. Care must be taken when deploying a cache (or any appliance) that performs IP spoofing. It is the content switch that ensures that the spoofed packet returns to the "correct" device, which in this case would be the cache (or appliance). IP spoofing is an important function when upstream sites want to understand who is accessing them. ISPs also like to use IP spoofing to ensure that they are not seen as masquerading as a mega proxy.

Layer 4 Web Cache Redirection

Regardless of which cache method is used (forward, transparent, or reverse), Layer 4 WCR can be deployed. By its very nature, the cache will receive a packet either destined for it or for the origin server. By inspecting the HTTP header and understanding the location of the content, the request is then forwarded on.

In Figure 8–7, we can see that using a content switch and its redirection filters or processes ensures that packets get sent to the cache. This is relatively simple to set up, as all we are redirecting on is port 80. On redirection, the destination port could be changed by the content switch if required (e.g., from 80 to 8080) in order to adhere to the cache's listening port. Understanding how we ensure that the packets get to the cache is easy. The cache then requests the data and the request is routed to the origin server. If the cache is not performing a proxy function but rather maintaining the users source IP address, also known as IP spoofing, how will we ensure that the packet returns

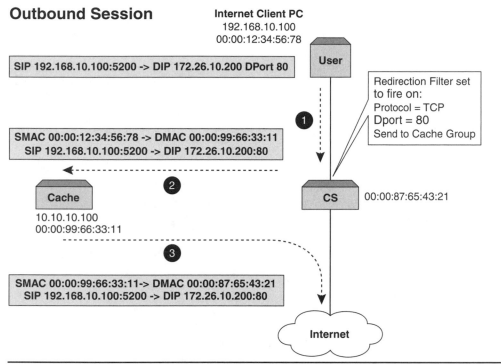

Figure 8–7.a   Layer 4 WCR showing traffic flow and address substitution.

to the cache? The problem here is that the response packet will have a destination IP address equal to that of the user, and the content switch should route it directly to the user in order to adhere to the Layer 3 rules. It is imperative that the cache gets this request back in order to store it for later use. If it did not allow this, then the function of caching would be severely jeopardized. In addition, as the cache is out of the data path, there is no way of it seeing this traffic. So, what do we do with the return packet? Well, it is the content switch that needs to be configured to ensure that the return packets are sent back into the cache. This can be easily achieved, as all that is required is that the inverse of the redirection filter set up for outbound traffic needs to be configured for inbound traffic as illustrated in Table 8–1.

This ensures that all HTTP traffic is returned back to the cache that requested it. There is, however, another problem here: How do we ensure that traffic is returned to the correct cache if more than one cache is deployed? The next section describes how to solve this problem.

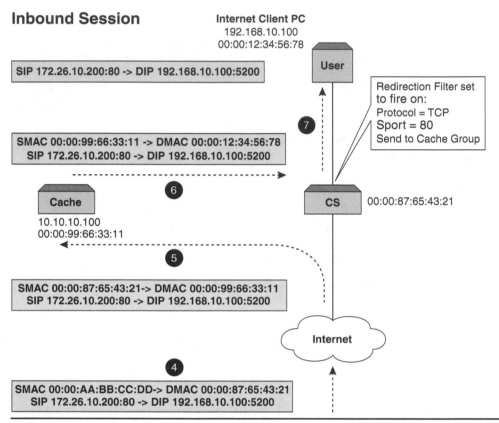

Figure 8–7.b   Layer 4 WCR showing traffic flow and address substitution.

Table 8–1   Redirection Filters

	OUTBOUND FILTER	INBOUND FILTER
Source IP	Any	Any
Destination IP	Any	Any
Source Port	Any	80
Destination Port	80	Any
Redirection Port	None	None

WCR and Load Balancing Metrics

Without doubt, understanding the traffic flows and what will happen when configuring WCR on the content switch is critical to ensuring a successful installation.

In Chapters 5 and 6, we discussed load balancing and the different metrics used to provide persistence versus load. With caching, persistence is not a definite requirement but one that makes a lot of sense. If we had a request leaving our device and it was redirected to a cache farm, surely we would want the response to return via the initiating cache and not another cache within the farm. The reasons for this are:

- Better use of caching hardware, as all content for that request will be accessible via a single cache.
- Minimizing duplicated requests for the same data from different caches.
- Enhances logging functionality. Information for access to that entire site will be stored on a single cache, thereby ensuring collation, and generation of reports is simplified.

It is important to understand that caches are treated exactly the same as real servers within a load balancing configuration. They are health checked just like any other device, they can have a load balancing weight associated to them, have maximum connections configured, or any other valid real server parameter that may be required. They are added to a group and are seen as a group of devices with equal resources that can be selected by the content switch when performing redirection. Because redirection is to a group of servers, and a group must have a load balancing metric associated with it, it is imperative that we understand what happens with the different types of metrics.

For starters, the classic round robin and least connections are nonstarters because this would severely minimize your cache hits. As we have discussed throughout this book, IP address hashing is an excellent method for ensuring persistence. Addresses are typically unique, and it is this that we exploit when using Layer 4 WCR.

Using DIP hashing is an extremely popular method for WCR as it allows for maximum cache hits and ensures that all data for that DIP (or site) is serviced by that particular cache. Using SIP hashing can also yield persistent results, but will not maximize cache hits. As can be guessed, the SIP will be unique for all users; therefore, caches would need to store all content, as a request to the same

Web site from two different source addresses could get serviced by two different caches. This is not making optimal use of the caching infrastructure.

However, depending on vendor, SIP or DIP hashing is not always the answer when performing IP spoofing to the caching farm. Let's look at what would happen if redirection was carried out and the content switch maintained no session information relating to the request.

We can see in Figure 8–8, what happens when we enable hashing on the DIP. The initial packet gets redirected or steered to the cache farm and then is sent on to the origin server. On return, without some rule set up on the return path it would get sent directly back to the user bypassing the cache. This is not acceptable, as the content would not be returned to the cache and would not be stored for later retrieval. This totally negates the deployment of the cache, as it breaks what we are trying to achieve. A rule needs to be configured to ensure that the requests are sent back to the cache. Now with no session information, the content switch would just run the same redirection filter as seen in Table 8–2. If the

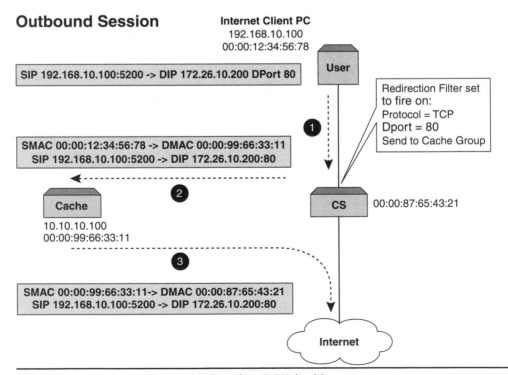

Figure 8–8.a   IP spoofing and WCR using IP DIP hashing.

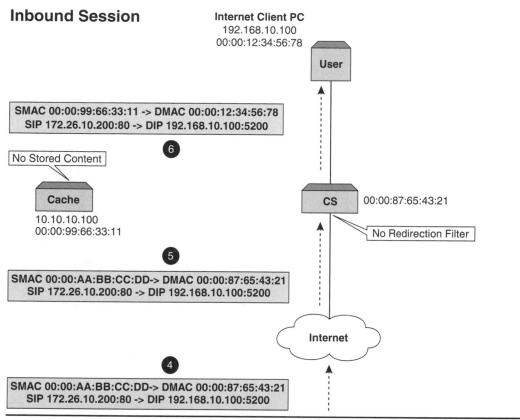

Figure 8–8.b   IP spoofing and WCR using IP DIP hashing.

Table 8–2   Redirection Filters

	OUTBOUND FILTER	INBOUND FILTER
Source IP	Any	Any
Destination IP	Any	Any
Source port	Any	80
Destination port	80	Any
Redirection port	None	None

DIP was used, the request could get sent to the wrong cache because the DIP will not be the same on the return path, so the switch's algorithm would potentially calculate a different cache to answer the request. The same would apply if the SIP was used. It must be pointed out that this is a vendor-specific issue and would need to be investigated when deploying WCR and IP spoofing.

If the cache is acting as a proxy and using its address as the source for all requests, then obviously this issue is nonexistent because the DIP on returning packets will be that of the requesting cache. Dependent on requirements and content switches, it will always be possible to set up a solution that works. By using Layer 7 WCR we can ensure that the correct cache is resolved regardless of SIP or DIP address.

Layer 7 WCR

Inspecting further into the packet to determine what content is being requested is an extremely attractive method of WCR. A number of different attributes can be inspected to provide more granular traffic management:

- URL/URI information
- HTTP Host header
- URL hashing
- Browser based
- Layer 7 streaming protocols

Before we look at each, let's quickly point out the advantages of Layer 7 WCR:

- Separation of data types; different files can be accessed via different caches.
- Allow the cache to bypass noncacheable content.
- Ensure that all requests for a specific URL are serviced by a specific cache.
- Allow different browser types to be serviced by different caches.
- Allow for high bandwidth usage applications such as streaming media to be handled by specific caches.

URL/URI Information

As a refresher, let's look at the difference between a URL and a URI.

http://www.foocorp.com—the host portion or URL and typically refers to the protocol type and network location.

The URI, on the other hand, typically includes the entire argument and as well as the actual file, object application, and so forth, that is requested.

http://www.foocorp.com/products/content_switches/technical_specifications/data.pdf

Both of these make up a URI that is used to determine Web objects and their location. Using URL/URI information to perform WCR on is a very powerful mechanism that allows the network administrator to set up different content rules to intelligently steer traffic to different caches, and in some instances, to totally bypass the cache farm when noncacheable content is being requested. In addition, the content switch can now also look at the HTTP header information, and in some cases can ignore the header directive (discussed earlier in this chapter) and send it on to the cache farm.

By using the intelligence within the content switch, the caches can be optimized to cache on a per-page basis rather than a per-site basis. This also allows for certain types of content to be stored on certain types of caches. For example, a low-end cache could be used for small text type objects, while a large high-end cache could be used for caching large files and in some cases streaming media. This is shown in Figure 8–9.

Host Header

Caching on Host header allows a similar functionality to caching on DIP. Typically, the Host header is associated to a single DIP. However, in the case of virtual hosting, multiple Web sites (or domain names) are associated with the same IP address.

As can be seen in Figure 8–10, the use of Host headers can distribute the content to multiple caches that would otherwise have all been serviced by a single cache if DIP hashing was used. This particular mechanism is popular with service providers who often provide smaller organizations with this function. By using reverse proxy caching on the Host header, the cache farms would be optimized for cache hits even though all requests were destined for the same DIP.

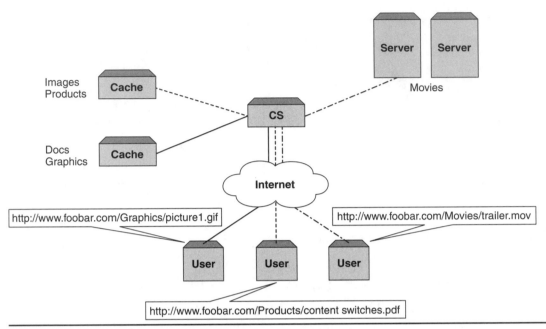

Figure 8–9   Layer 7 URL WCR.

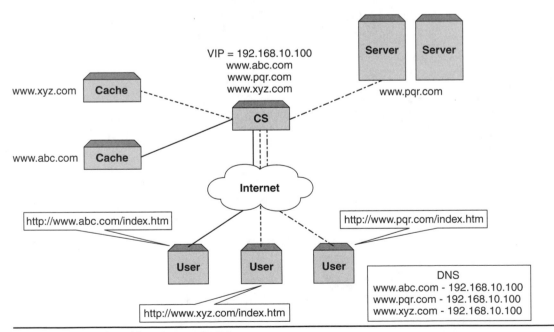

Figure 8–10   Virtual hosting and WCR.

URL Parsing

This approach is very similar to IP hashing except instead of using an IP address the content switch takes the URL and parses it (parsing is discussed in Chapter 6). Based on the value, it then sends all requests for that URL to the selected cache. This means that all requests for a specific object such as .gif are sent to a specific cache regardless of host header. Due to the granularity of this the spread and retrieving of data is much more efficient than SIP or DIP hashing.

Browser Based

Using the User-Agent (or browser type) HTTP header to determine which cache, or group of caches, to select provides network administrators with the opportunity to allow multiple different topologies to use the same infrastructure. The thought process behind this approach is that it allows for different formatting for different access devices. In a wireless world where a PDA or mobile phone is accessing Web content, formatting this to fit the device output format is important. Mobile phones and PDAs do not have the computing power to operate in 16-bit color or have large 15" or 17" screens, so ensuring that content requested is specific to them is key. In a world where we will always have access to content, service providers and content owners will not know what end device a user is using based on IP address. However using the User-Agent allows content for those specific devices to be cached and returned, thus optimizing both the user experience and the infrastructure.

Layer 7 Streaming Media

With streaming media being seen as a high bandwidth application, caching of this makes a lot of sense to enterprises wanting to minimize operational and bandwidth costs. However WCR is typically configured to use TCP port 80, and caches are also configured for this port. Streaming clients, while TCP port 80 is configurable, prefer to use their native TCP and UDP ports and protocols that in most cases are unique to each application. Having the ability to determine that the content is a streaming application and redirect it to a Web cache offers network administrators a compelling reason for bandwidth savings and user performance. Let's take a quick look at what makes up a streaming session.

Streaming Media Protocols   While most streaming media applications allow the content to be sent over HTTP and played at the end device, this method of delivery does not allow for controlling the stream like a video (fast forward, pause, etc.) as it does when using the native protocols. Streaming media expects the client to set up bidirectional signaling and control channels in order to receive data. These channels typically run over TCP and UDP and use the standards-based protocols RTSP and RTP .

To understand the complexities of using streaming media, we will look at just a single delivery method—RTP over UDP. It should be pointed out that there are different methods in which to carry out these communications, but for simplicity's sake, we will look at only one.

When a session is set up, the RTSP client will set up a bidirectional TCP channel between the RTSP server and itself for control and negotiation of the stream. In addition, a unidirectional RTP UDP channel is set up from the RTSP server to the client and this is what the data will flow down, while any synchronization or packet loss information is provided over an additional bidirectional UDP channel. Figure 8–11 demonstrates this.

As Real Networks and Apple QuickTime both use RTSP as their protocol of choice, the content switch needs to be able to redirect this into the cache in exactly the same fashion as its HTTP cousin. Obviously, this is a little more complex than HTTP, as there are two other TCP/UDP sessions associated with this single user stream. It is imperative that the content switch can correlate these streams and understand that they belong to the same user. This functionality is a key requirement when performing Layer 7 streaming protocol redirection. As the cache is handling these streams on behalf of the origin server, it is important that the associated user streams (control, signaling, and data) are sent to the same cache. In a single cache environment this would be simple as there is only one destination, but as cache farms increase, then the

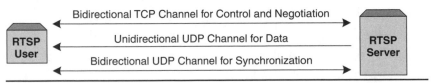

Figure 8–11   Signaling and control channels set up when using RTP over UDP for delivery of streaming media.

need to use Layer 7 properties is key to ensure that all sessions associated to one stream are delivered to a single device in order to function correctly.

Redirection of Microsoft's MMS protocol is also possible and would benefit the user and provider in exactly the same way.

Noncacheable Content

Some content cannot be cached due to its dynamic nature, and there is some that maybe the content owner or network administrator does not want to cache. As an example, financial stock pricing and online games may not be able to be cached and are usually configured to bypass any caches in the request response path. In addition, some sites require IP address authentication, and using a proxy cache will disallow this to happen. Therefore, caching vendors allow for dynamic bypass and if not supported, content switches can be configured to allow these types of request through without being sent to the cache. Whatever the reason, there is no sense in sending it to the cache and incurring processing overhead on files that cannot be cached. Most content switch manufacturers also include a list of known noncacheable content and these typically include the following:

- ASP files
- CGI scripts
- HTML extensions
- Executable files
- Scripted HTML files

These are not fixed in stone, and any decent content switch will allow you to delete or add to the list when deploying WCR.

Vendor Issues

While it is not our intention to determine what each caching and content vendor can and cannot do when interoperating, we feel that we should point out a few areas where issues have existed and could potentially do so in the future. By being aware of these and understanding the symptoms, troubleshooting can become much simpler.

MAC Address Substitution

An area where content switches and cache vendors can bump heads is on the use of MAC addresses in redirection. In some content switches, when redirection takes place only the destination MAC address is changed. This is acceptable and allows the device to see the SIP and DIP as well as the source MAC address, which hasn't been changed. Now, if this redirection was to another subnet, and the source MAC address was not changed to that of the content switch, there are some caches (and firewalls) that will make a note of the source MAC address. On response instead of routing it via the correct gateway, it merely substitutes this MAC address in the destination MAC address field and forwards the packet. No device will receive the packet, as the MAC address is not on that particular network. Therefore, the response will be dropped and the user will finally time out.

To overcome this "feature," some content vendors allow for the source MAC address to be substituted with that of the content switch. This ensures that all return packets are sent to it where the session table can then be scanned and the correct process is run against the returning packet.

Firewalls and SYN Attacks

One of the main functions of a cache is to retrieve data quickly and efficiently. This is what manufacturers strive to achieve and one goal we all feel is beneficial. Caches also try to "anticipate" your next request by downloading links from within the requested page to ensure that should you require the content, it is already available. When accessing content quickly and intelligently, caches will set up many TCP sessions simultaneously. This is of particular relevance when HTTP/1.0 is used. By being proactive, caches can often cause a firewall to deny it access, as it appears that a SYN attack is being processed. This typically will only happen in a proxy mode, as the SIP will be that of the cache and in some instances thousands of sessions can be set up in a single second causing the firewall threshold to be breached. It is important to understand this potential pitfall and ensure that the security and network administrators are aware of this in order to create the necessary rules and polices to allow this to occur.

Without doubt, using WCR for Layer 7 functionality allows the ability to perform total control over your site. It must be noted, however, that using Layer 7 functionality does incur higher latency than blindly sending all port 80 (or

554) traffic to a cache farm. This is obvious, as the content switch will need to first perform delayed binding or TCP splicing as discussed in Chapter 6. This allows the cache to then scan the HTTP portion and determine what content is being requested. In addition to this, WCR relies on caching vendors to provide an appliance that is up to the task that the content switch is performing. While some content switch manufacturers also provide caching solutions, by its very nature a content switch is cache agnostic. Any caching product, be it software or appliance based, will work with any content switch today.

Security Redirection

With security in the forefront of most network administrators' minds, anything that can facilitate or assist in providing security becomes an attractive proposition. By making use of the powerful redirection features, packets can be scanned for malicious virus strings or certain inappropriate content, matched against a set of rules and redirected to a logging server or to a server that displays a warning. This form of security can be used to detect anything from known virus strings to a telnet session on TCP port 23. How and what is done when the match is made, is up to the network administrator. The most common use of this type of redirection is for virus protection. Due to its popularity, some content switch manufacturers have designed specific rules that allow for a TCP RST to be sent to the offending user.

Router/Link Load Balancing

With the drive for resilient networks, a major requirement (and, in some cases, a regulatory one) is to provide dual feeds in to or out of a network. Taking this one step further, using two different service providers to supply these feeds adds extra protection in the event of a provider network failure and increases performance if one of the networks suffers routing delays or update issues. Having a multihomed feed leads organizations to reason that if two links are being paid for, then why not use them both? From a financial aspect, this makes perfect sense, but from a network and traffic pattern aspect, it is a little more difficult to achieve.

The goal of using this form of redirection is to allow organizations to maximize their infrastructure and increase performance—the goal of any network

administrator. Another aspect that appeals to companies is to be able to intercept and steer traffic to different "next hop" routers that are best suited for that
particular type of traffic, or one that is closest to the actual data but might not
participate in routing updates. Typically, most companies, who have dual feeds
(or even a single feed) from a service provider are not interested in participating
in routing updates and maintaining routing protocols with them. In addition,
service providers are not keen on having customers run routing updates between
themselves and other providers. This can create loops and uncontrolled access
between their networks. Being part of a BGP or OSPF area is not attractive,
and most organizations will opt for a default route for outbound connections,
leaving all the routing complexity to the service provider. However, with dual
feeds, how can an organization ensure that traffic traverses the required links?

Certain content switch manufacturers have created specific devices to cater to
this type of application, and they typically learn routes by understanding the
routing algorithms and can perform some intelligent decision making regarding
which link to use. Most manufacturers, however, use built-in intelligence within
the switches to provide link load balancing. There are a basically two different
types of link load balancing.

Router or Default Gateway Load Balancing

This method of configuration on the content switch allows companies to use
both links from different suppliers regardless of the ingress path. Deploying this
form of redirection is relatively simple and relies on the fact that the return path
does not have to be stateful. Figure 8–12 demonstrates how router load balancing works.

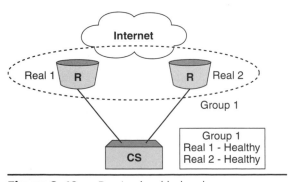

Figure 8–12   Router load balancing.

The upstream routers are set up as two real servers and placed in a group. They are health checked just like any other real server, but due to the probability that they would be unlikely to run a service, ICMP health checking is typically used. However, in today's routers, HTTP can also be used, as most modern routers are configured with an HTTP daemon to allow browser-based management. The group has a load-balancing metric associated with it. This metric is typically "round robin" and ensures that every alternate packet is sent across a single provider's network. This provides great load balancing of traffic and effective use of the infrastructure. One of the problems here is that depending on latencies within the different networks the packets are traversing, they might arrive out of sequence at the destination. This is not good for application performance and network optimization. User retries and negative acknowledgments would incur additional latencies. In addition, certain service providers might run source route filtering and not allow spoofing of IP addresses. Therefore, understanding your network, its limitations, and the applications you are using will be important to determine whether this type of load balancing can be deployed. In most cases, there is little or no problem in configuring this.

Another approach is to configure the primary router interface as a real server, and this real server is backed up by a secondary real server, which is the second router interface. This will ensure that all packets traverse through the primary router and only use the secondary router in the event of a failure. Whichever method is used, the key here is that in the event of a failure, the content switch automatically detects this and routes all traffic through the active router, providing dynamic resilience.

To further aid in this method, some content manufacturers allow for multiple default gateways to be configured on the switch and load balanced. This automates this process, but has the added advantage that only one gateway can be operational if desired with the others in standby. To determine the state of the primary gateway, health checks and ARP health checking is often used, as this allows for firewalls to be configured as a default gateway but still respond to health checks without security alert being raised.

ISP, WAN, or Link Load Balancing

With this form of load balancing, it is important to understand what the end goal is. With dual feeds and a single default route, it is difficult to force traffic back through the router on which it entered the network. Using dynamic routing protocols assists with this, but with equal cost routes being a probability, a mechanism to ensure route stickiness or persistence is required. There are basically two ways to achieve this: at the MAC layer or at the Network layer.

By writing the source MAC address into the session table on the content switch, all returning packets that match that session can be redirected to the forwarding router. All that happens is that the destination MAC address on the response packet is substituted with the source MAC of the original packet. The source MAC address will be that of the upstream router and will therefore be forwarded back to the same device that sent it. Figure 8–13 demonstrates this.

It is imperative that the forwarding devices are the devices that are connected to the different networks. If not, there is no guarantee which path the packets may take. In addition, it should be pointed out that MAC layer information is not an option for sessions initiated on the internal network and using the routers for outbound sessions. It is for inbound sessions only.

For outbound sessions, Network layer information is used. The content switch acts as a proxy appliance, and on a new outbound session will write that entry into the session table and perform NAT by substituting the source IP address of the outbound session with an address associated with that of the service provider's network. This ensures that all returning packets will be forwarded via that network

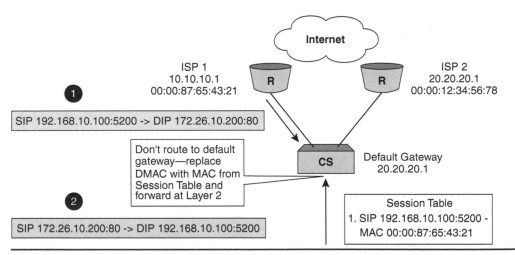

Figure 8–13   MAC layer ISP, WAN, or link load balancing using MAC address substitution to achieve persistence.

due to the IP address used that falls within their range. When the return packet arrives back at the content switch, the necessary address substitution can take place. This ensures that packets are sent back through the routers from which they came. Figure 8–14 illustrates how this works.

To further maximize the dual feeds, companies may not always want to use persistence but may opt for the link with the least delay. This can happen by using advanced load balancing metrics that can test for bandwidth usage or response times. To get the maximum benefit from this form of load balancing, it makes sense to ensure that the real server, which is being health checked against for link status and response time, is a router at the other end of the network. This gives true end-to-end measurement of the infrastructure.

Summary

Application redirection is a very powerful tool and can provide network administrators with many different scenarios for optimizing the network. Understanding the limitations and the traffic flow is key, and will ensure easier troubleshooting . Redirection allows huge flexibility when designing networks and allows for a high level of manipulation of the session entering or leaving your network.

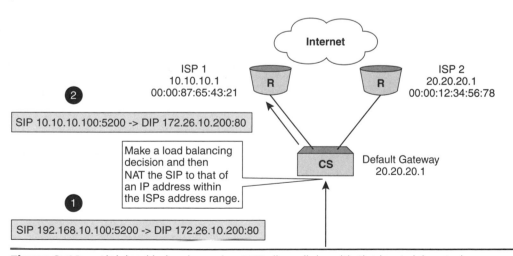

Figure 8–14   Link load balancing using NAT allows links with the least delays to be used per session.

Case Study: Application Redirection

To increase network performance, Foocorp, Inc. has decided to deploy caches to accelerate their Web site for external users and to minimize bandwidth costs for outgoing connectivity. They also want to deploy streaming media caching so remote branches can participate in product updates via Webcasts.

The benefits of using content switches for this function allow the caches to sit out of the data path and allows for truly scalable Layer 7 cache redirection. In addition, they have also increased network resilience by connecting to a second ISP, but now would like to maximize the connectivity by load balancing outbound connections. What Foocorp is hoping to achieve by doing this is:

- Increase network and site performance
- Reduce the capital expenditure by using fewer servers to provide network availability
- Defer bandwidth upgrades by using caches
- Provide streaming media functionality for remote branches to receive training, product updates, and company addresses
- Maximize network bandwidth by load balancing both in and outbound connections

Deploying Application Redirection

WCR is very straightforward to deploy and will be added to the existing configuration deployed in the previous chapter. When using WCR, it is important that these following steps are covered:

1. Confirm which mode of caching you want to use—reverse, transparent or proxy—and determine if your cache can perform simultaneous modes.

2. If streaming media is required make sure you use the correct server and install any licenses required.

3. Set up WCR for URL parsing based on the criteria you need; for example, URL, Host header, and so forth.

4. Ensure that you configure the content switch to not send any noncacheable content to the caches. You can add additional content types to the defaults already configured.

5. If using Layer 4 WCR, ensure that you use a persistent type of load balancing metric, as a round robin type will duplicate content across caches, will not maximize the caches, and most importantly, could increase bandwidth usage.

6. When using Layer 7, ensure that you have a cache that will handle any requests that do not fall into the configured strings.

7. With WAN link load balancing, make sure you have two public IP addresses (one from each ISP) that you can NAT the source IP to for outbound connections.

8. Set up the correct DNS entries for inbound WAN link load balancing.

We can see how this has been achieved by Foocorp in Figure 8–15.

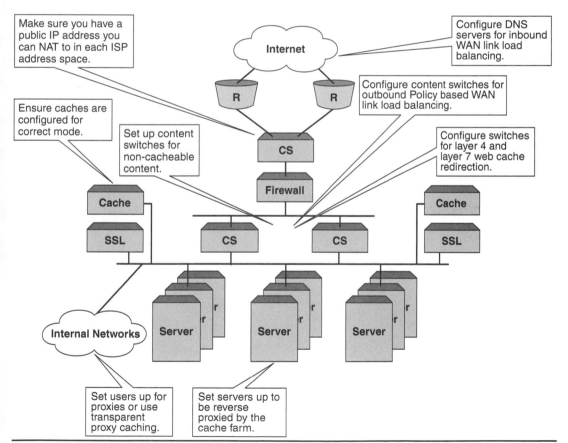

Figure 8–15   Foocorp Inc. using WCR.

By deploying Layer 4 and Layer 7 WCR, Foocorp has been able to achieve the following:

- Increased network and site performance.
- Decreased server hits, allowing them to process more of the important online and business transactions.
- Streaming media allows for e-learning, e-conferencing, and so forth for remote branches.
- Minimizes and defers bandwidth costs.

With WAN link load balancing, outbound connections can be sent over different or selected links based on polices such as protocol type, network address, and so forth.

Foocorp has now deployed a comprehensive network that allows for a very scalable, flexible, and resilient network.

9

Firewall and VPN Load Balancing

Without a doubt, the need to protect digital information from unauthorized access has become a necessary and integral part of any organization in business today. Threats from external, as well as internal attacks are an ever-present reminder of just how vulnerable we are. Not withstanding this, the reliance on the digital medium continues to increase, and therefore our requirement for protection rises in parallel. There are virtually no key elements within society today that are not computerized. The more we computerize our mission-critical processes and services, the more vulnerable we become. While it is not all doom and gloom, it is important to understand that security is typically a number-one agenda item on a CIO's technology list.

Many different products on the market today can (and in some cases cannot) effectively provide network security. The overlying factor, however, is that the more secure you want your network to be, the more latency you will incur. In addition, access in to and out of your network by traveling and remote or tele-working employees is becoming an absolute requirement. Using the Internet, which has global reach and is extremely affordable, to connect to your network makes a lot of sense. The major issue here is that corporate or private information is being transported over a public network. The solution is to create a VPN between the user and the internal network. To further increase the security, encryption is used to protect sensitive data.

Therefore, by protecting your site from external threats while simultaneously allowing users to access your network over a public network, a comprehensive security installation is key. However, as the company grows and access speeds increase, the pressure on those security devices is increased, as users demand more speed and less latency. To overcome this load balancing of these devices to provide security acceleration is an extremely cost effective and scalable solution.

Why Load Balance Firewalls and VPN Switches?

Firewalls are the devices that we use to protect data. By configuring them to only allow certain devices or applications access to our network, we can control who, when, and how accessed is achieved.

By their very nature, firewalls are termed as *stateful* devices; that is, they need to be able to see the entire conversation between user and server to ensure that no rules are broken during the session flow. Therefore, traditional firewalls typically need to inspect each packet to ensure that it adheres to the policy that has been configured (or not), and then perform the necessary action associated to that particular rule. That action can be to allow, deny, or even NAT the packet. By using these features, the vulnerability of a network diminishes, but typically so does performance in to and out of that network. Firewalls, while they offer the best protection available, do impact performance. This is something that organizations and individuals have come to expect and accept, as performance is not a goal if security cannot be assured. Many firewall vendors have tried to increase performance by engineering the software, and in some cases the hardware, to better handle the statefulness of traffic and increase the throughput. Third-party manufacturers provide software that allows firewalls to be clustered and therefore share the load of a busy site. All of this is designed to try to increase performance and minimize the bottleneck that firewalls introduce. Second to this, and sometimes an equal requirement dependent on the organization, is to provide resilience and redundancy to minimize network downtime. Using any software-based solution brings with it the overheads associated with running an additional service on a device that is designed to provide network protection. To overcome this, content switch manufacturers have seen an opportunity to allow their switches to load balance these important devices. With content switches being session aware—in other words, stateful—they can begin to participate in the flow of traffic ensuring that sessions return via the same path that they entered the network. From a firewall standpoint, this is perfect, as they require a stateful session.

In addition to this, the content switch can also handle and direct a lot more traffic through multiple firewalls and ensure that only active firewalls are used. Likewise with a VPN device, the need to provide not only resilience but also throughput becomes paramount. We will discuss later in this chapter the intricacies involved when load-balancing sessions that often have their required data encrypted. Suffice to say at this stage that it is the intelligence of the content switch that enables VPN and firewall load balancing to be powerful and widely deployed content networking applications.

Firewall Overview

Before we progress into the murky depths of firewall load balancing it is important to understand that there are many different methods used by firewall manufacturers to provide security. Today, the majority of firewalls are stateful.

Stateful Firewall

This means that the firewall needs to see the entire session between source and destination and will hold a virtual session open allowing the flow of traffic. This allows network administrators control over all protocol types and ensures that only bonafide initiated sessions are given access.

While a stateful firewall is without a doubt the best method to protect a site, it is easy to see the overhead that can be placed on these devices. A typical TCP session setup would progress through the following steps:

1. TCP SYN arrives at firewall

2. Once the packet has been read in to the software, it will check against its policies to see if it is from a valid network and for a valid service.

3. In addition, the SIP, DIP, Sport, Dport, sequence, and acknowledgment numbers are recorded before the packet is forwarded through the firewall.

4. On receipt of the TCP SYN ACK, the firewall needs to ensure that it is from a valid network and that it is a response to the TCP SYN already recorded in its state table.

5. On determination that this is a valid session, the forwarding of the data portion of this session is passed into a fast path or express forwarding engine. This is done to relieve the overhead associated with inspecting every single packet.

6. On receipt of the TCP FIN and subsequent FIN ACKs, the firewall will delete the session from its state table.

The reason for showing the typical steps associated in session validation is to demonstrate the intelligence and effectiveness of a firewall while illustrating the processor-intensive functions required. Remember that the firewall will need to carry out this type of inspection for every TCP session, and this, in large or busy sites, can be in the thousands, if not tens of thousands, per second.

It would be fair to say that this is a very broad overview, and each firewall manufacturer will have their own algorithm and method by which they first validate the connection and then forward that session as quickly as possible. It is not our intention to discuss each method in detail, but suffice it to say that a stateful firewall is a very complex and intelligent device. Other applications such as NAT also need to be performed somewhere within this process. Again, each manufacturer has their own way and order in which this is implemented. But again, these types of requirements place large overheads on firewall processors and this ultimately impacts network performance.

Firewall Synchronization

To provide resilience, often two firewalls are deployed. These can be in active standby mode or in active active mode. Because stateful firewalls hold those virtual sessions, it is easy to have this session table copied between firewalls, ensuring that they all have the same view of the network. By doing this, firewalls allow for a failure to occur on any firewall and the recovery is transparent to the user. This method is great for resilience, but still needs to rely on some software or hardware to load balance the incoming and outgoing packets. In addition, the total sessions supported are equal to that of a single firewall, as each firewall needs to have an exact replica of the other's session table. This is great for resilience, but does ensure that designs take into account the total sessions possible and deploy the correct firewall to cater for the requirement.

Layer 2 Firewalls

Most firewalls today are routed firewalls. In other words, they have an IP address on the dirty side and an IP address on the clean side and they route the packet from one interface to the other if the policy allows access. Traditionally, this has been the only method and one that is accepted as being satisfactory. However, with the emergence of time-sensitive applications and considerable external threats, some manufacturers offer the ability to provide a Layer 2 firewall.

As can be expected, this relies on Layer 2 addressing for forwarding but still ensures that the packet, with all its Layer 3 and 4 information, is validated for access. It basically sits in the data path like a Layer 2 switch does today and inspects each packet passing through the device. By not actively participating in the Layer 3 routing process, it is able to "invisibly" inspect the data, and it is this that makes it appealing to some customers. This type of firewall has many advantages:

- Organizations that have a large investment in routed networks and legacy application need not make any changes to network topology.
- Deployment is very easy, as no address change to any devices is required.
- Backout or uninstallation is simple, as no address changes are needed.
- As the device has no public facing IP address, it is very difficult to hack or connect to.
- It is invisible to users and can be deployed in environments where there is a tendency to test the extremes and capabilities of any new security device.
- It minimizes network latency, as no Layer 3 routing is required once a session has been established.

Layer 2 firewalls offer no additional protection in terms of the actual software they run, but rather provide transparency and easy-to-install and de-install procedures.

When configuring firewall load balancing, understanding how the firewall will behave is critical, as the different types will require a different configuration and in some cases cannot be effectively load balanced. Further to this, the "dark art" of firewall load balancing can often create uncertainty when dealing with firewall administrators, as the deployment method often breaks traditional Layer 3 rules. Understanding how the firewall operates will certainly assist you not only in troubleshooting the network but also with ensuring that the firewalls are properly configured to allow for firewall load balancing.

Deploying Firewall Load Balancing

Firewall load balancing comes in many guises, and dependent on your requirements, the basic method may suit you. It is important to note that content switches are not always used for firewall load balancing, and we will briefly discuss the other methods available to give you a better insight into the benefits of using content switches.

Using VRRP

By using a mechanism such as VRRP (or in some cases, their own proprietary implementation of this standard), firewall manufacturers allow for firewalls to be deployed and still provide the resilience that organizations demand. While this allows for resilience, it does very little for performance. VRRP is a standards-based method by which multiple devices share a virtual address. This address is typically a Layer 2 MAC and Layer 3 IP address and can either be a different address or one associated with one of the devices.

When deployed on a firewall cluster, all packets are sent to the VRRP address and, based on who is the master, that device will answer the ARP request and ensure that all traffic is sent via its interface. In the case of a failure of the master device, the other devices participating in the VRRP process will negotiate with one another on who will take over as master. This process typically takes about three seconds. In most scenarios, there are only two devices running VRRP, so on the failure of the master the secondary device will detect no response and after three seconds will take over as master. If other devices are involved, this may increase the fail-over time by one second.

It is important to understand that the state table on the firewalls will need to be synchronized, otherwise the fail-over will result in dropped packets. Synchronization of this is typically configured within the firewall software or can be achieved using a third-party software package. This is an effective solution for low usage sites requiring resilience but not greatly concerned with increasing throughput.

Using Software-Based Solutions

Many different third-party manufacturers provide software to allow for load balancing and load sharing of firewalls. These have their merits, but also rely heavily on VRRP or some form of multicast or proprietary method by which to communicate. One thing often overlooked when using software to provide resilience is that firewalls are traditionally areas where bottlenecks occur due to the process needed to inspect and enforce the policies. Adding additional overheads to the device to maintain state tables, share load information, and redirect traffic to the correct nominated firewall impacts the very performance that you are trying to increase. There will always be a place for this type of deployment, but what should be weighed is the cost of implementing this software versus the cost of implementing content switches, which allow for not only firewall load balancing but dependent on the content switch used can also provide value added features such as server load balancing, WCR, and other popular applications.

Using Content Switches

Content switches provide the most effective method to deploy comprehensive security while still ensuring excellent security. With the majority of content switch manufacturers, firewall load balancing requires the use of a clean and dirty switch placed on either side of the firewalls. This can be a single switch on either side or in pairs as we shown in Figure 9–1.

The reason for this is that maintaining state through the firewalls is critical. As discussed earlier, a stateful firewall needs to see the entire session to ensure that it is valid. Therefore, by providing a content switch at the top and bottom of the firewalls creating what is often called a firewall load balancing

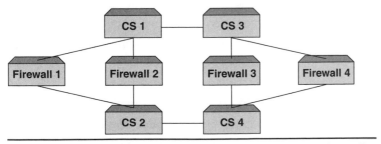

Figure 9–1   Clean and dirty side switches needed for firewall load balancing to maintain session state.

sandwich, the switches can ensure that the traffic is sent into the network via one firewall and the return path is sent out through the same firewall, thus achieving statefulness.

Achieving this is relatively simple, and each content switch manufacturer has their own method by which to accomplish this, but the basic concept is very similar. The need to have a preconfigured path is essential.

Creating the Paths

Different content switch manufacturers can support different numbers of firewalls that can be load balanced within a firewall load balancing sandwich. This can vary from a maximum of 16 up to 256. While we need at least two to make effective use of load balancing, the number that you want to use is relative to the requirements of your network. Regardless of how many we want to load balance, one thing will always be the same—how do we ensure traffic flows through a particular firewall? We have to create a path that the content switch understands.

One method is to configure a path by detailing every IP interface that the traffic will pass through, be they on the ingress or egress of a device, and then configure the switch to forward the packets from a session through that path—similar to "connect the dots." Likewise, the bottom switch will obviously need to have the same path configured to maintain a stateful session. This is a fairly effective method allowing multiple firewalls to be configured. However, it doesn't scale well when using content switches and VRRP in providing resilience.

The other process, which allows for multiple content switches on the clean and dirty side, is to use the interfaces on the clean and dirty switches as the end points of the paths. Configuring these interfaces as real servers allows the content switch to health check these servers ensuring that the path is active and usable. The other reason is that by using load balancing techniques within the configuration, the ability to dynamically change the path based on a link, firewall, or switch failure is achieved. However, there is still an amount of static configuration that is needed in order to get this process to operate efficiently. First, a routing table needs to be defined from the perspective of the content switch. This needs to have all the routes from the clean to the dirty side configured. For each firewall, there needs to be at least two routes configured, so the more firewalls within the sandwich, the more routes need to be configured. Once these routes have been configured, the health check is run through the different firewalls, thus ensuring that they are active and passing data. Figure 9–2 shows how we would set up interfaces as real servers and how the content switches see the different paths.

Let's look at the paths through the firewall from the viewpoint of content switch 1.

Traffic will flow from Real 1 (R1) Interface 1 (IF1) through Firewall 1 (IF2) to content switch 2 to R1 (IF1). Alternatively, should this link fail or the firewall fail, then traffic from this switch will flow from R2 (IF2) via Firewall 2 (IF2) and through to content switch 2 to R2 (IF2). The same method would be used from content switch 3. The reverse is true from content switches 2 and 4. As another level of redundancy should a content switch fail, the real servers are backed up by the real servers on the secondary content switch. In other words, R1 and R2 are backed up by R3 and R4. This provides a very resilient and dynamic configuration.

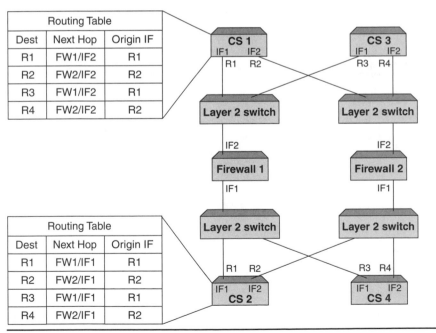

Figure 9–2   Creating paths for firewall load balancing to ensure that the traffic flow is stateful from the clean to dirty side, and vice versa.

This method allows for multiple firewalls to be deployed, as additional firewalls can be added to the configuration at a later date. All that is required is that additional paths for the new firewalls need to be added to the configuration. It provides the ability to scale to many firewalls while still maintaining just two content switches (or four if resilience is required).

This example used Layer 2 switches, but that is not necessary, as we will see later in this chapter.

Health Checking Firewalls

The key feature of firewall load balancing is the content switch's ability to health check through the firewall. This ensures that not only is the interface active, but the actual firewall is passing traffic. Typically, ICMP (Internet Control Message Protocol) is used, but often HTTP is preferred by the security administrators. The reason for this is that ICMP is often seen as stateless and not something that a security administrator would necessarily allow through the firewall due to its perceived vulnerability. Regardless as to which health check is used, it is important to ensure that a policy allowing the health check between all interfaces is configured with the initiating interfaces (or real servers) being the source IP address. The policy only needs to allow data between the clean and dirty side of the firewall sandwich and can be tightened as SIP, DIP, and protocol type are known, and can therefore totally eradicate any security threat.

Traffic Flow through a Firewall Load Balanced Sandwich

Redirection is what makes firewall load balancing work. It is the feature, discussed in Chapter 7, *Persistence, Security, and the Internet*, that allows us to load balance multiple firewalls. By creating filters that use the redirection function, we can redirect traffic through any firewall and still maintain state. We will of course have had to configure the paths prior to this, as it is this information that the content switch uses when making the load balancing decision. Figure 9–3 illustrates this.

1. Traffic enters the dirty side content switch and hits the redirection filter. The SIP and DIP are used to determine a value. The algorithm used to create this value is similar to that discussed in Chapter 5, *Basic Server*

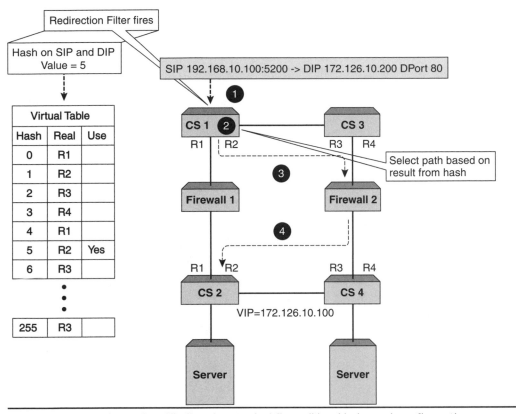

Figure 9–3   Inbound traffic flow in a typical firewall load balanced configuration showing how the path is selected.

Load Balancing. This value is then associated to a real server on the clean side of the sandwich. The real server that is selected for that particular SIP/DIP combination will always be the same due to the algorithm.

2. As the content switch knows about the real servers but only has one pre-configured route to it, it will select that route and forward the packet to the next hop. In this case, that is the firewall.

3. The firewall receives this packet still with the original SIP and DIP intact and makes a decision based on its policy whether to allow or deny the packet. On validation, it will then forward the packet to the destination address via traditional routing. In this case, it is the VRRP master that will forward on the packet.

4. All subsequent packets are routed through, and as the content switch is state aware, the session table has been updated with which real server has been selected, thus ensuring that the firewall load balancing is performed as quickly as possible

It is important to understand that this DIP could be any address anywhere within the network. It could be another router or appliance or even another firewall. Most probably it would be a VIP for some load-balanced service. On high-end content switches, this could be configured on the clean side switches. It should be pointed out here that not all content switch manufacturers can support multiple applications on their devices, so additional hardware may be required to allow for server load balancing. While this is not ideal and increases network complexity, this is a limitation of software. Therefore, when deploying firewall load balancing and server load balancing, make sure that the content switch can support both simultaneously if required.

The return traffic flow is illustrated in Figure 9–4.

1. Returning traffic enters the clean side content switch and hits the redirection filter. At this stage, the SIP and DIP have now been reversed. As we use both the SIP and DIP it is important that the algorithm used to create this value will yield the same result when the two addresses are interchanged. If this were not the case, then firewall load balancing would not work. This value will be the same as that on the inbound session, thus selecting the same real server. The content switch will update its session table for all subsequent packets within that session.

2. As the content switch knows about the real server but only has one route to it, it will select that route and forward the packet to the next hop. In this case, that is the firewall. As can be seen, it is critical that the return path is configured through the same firewall for the corresponding real server.

3. The firewall receives this packet with the SIP and DIP intact. It checks its session table and based on the validity forwards the packet to the next hop. In this case, the dirty side content switches. They in turn will forward them on to the correct next hop. In this case, the VRRP master will forward on the packet to the correct next hop.

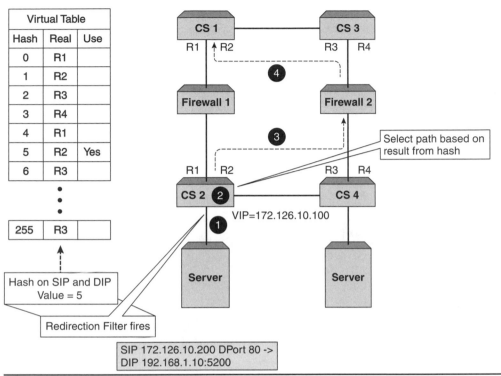

Figure 9–4   Outbound traffic flow in a typical firewall load balanced configuration.

One thing to remember when understanding traffic flow is that the dirty side switches do not actually send the data to the clean side interface (or real server). They merely use this as a mechanism to create a load balanced scenario, and it is this that allows multiple firewalls to be configured. Once the data arrives at the selected firewall, it will be handled by that firewall and routed or denied based on the policy. The firewall will not send it on to the real servers unless the DIP is for that server. This would obviously be the case for the health checks.

NATing Firewalls

NATing firewalls create all sorts of issues when performing firewall load balancing. The majority of early content switch designs preferred not to use NAT on load-balanced firewalls. The reason for this is that the load balancing metric used to determine the route uses both SIP and DIP. For ingress traffic, the

SIP/DIP hash will create one value and the packet will be routed through the selected firewall. This firewall then NATs the SIP, DIP, or both and routes the packet onward. On the return, the content switch performs the hash based on SIP/DIP. Unfortunately, these addresses have not been NATed back to the original so the value could potentially provide a different value to that of the ingress packet. The route selected will be through another firewall and this firewall will drop the session due to no corresponding entry in its state table. As is plain to see in Figure 9–5, NAT causes the firewall load-balancing sandwich to break. Fortunately, some content switch manufacturers have realized the necessity of NATing firewalls and have created a method by which to overcome this limitation.

The method by which this is achieved is configuring firewall load balancing as per normal on the dirty side switches. On the clean side switches,

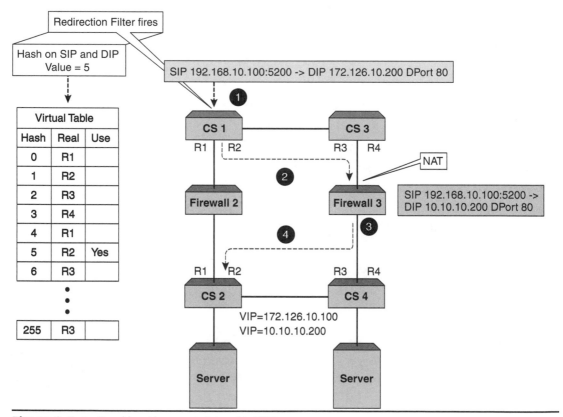

Figure 9–5. a Breaking the sandwich with NAT.

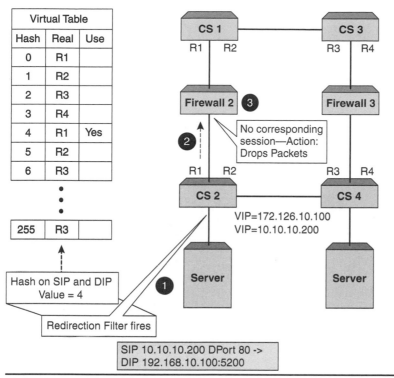

Virtual Table		
Hash	Real	Use
0	R1	
1	R2	
2	R3	
3	R4	
4	R1	Yes
5	R2	
6	R3	
• • •		
255	R3	

Hash on SIP and DIP
Value = 4

Redirection Filter fires

SIP 10.10.10.200 DPort 80 ->
DIP 192.168.10.100:5200

CS 1 — CS 3
R1 R2   R3 R4

Firewall 2 ③   Firewall 3

② No corresponding
session—Action:
Drops Packets

R1 R2   R3 R4
CS 2 — CS 4
VIP=172.126.10.100
VIP=10.10.10.200

Server ①   Server

Figure 9–5.b   Breaking the sandwich with NAT.

configure the switch to record the source MAC address in addition to all other session information. This feature is typically a single configuration statement. What this does is allow the clean content switch to document the source MAC of all traffic that ingresses the switch from the firewall. As it is the firewall that has routed the traffic, the SMAC will be that of the firewall. On the return path, the content switch will look up the session entry in its session table, see that there is a MAC address associated with it, and substitute the destination MAC address with the recorded SMAC. Layer 2 processing will then forward the packet to the correct firewall. This is illustrated in Figure 9–6.

This ingenious method is often called *MAC address persistency* and allows network administrators to use content switches when NAT or proxy type devices are used that rely on IP addresses to ensure that traffic is passed back to them. MAC address persistency can be used with a multitude of different applications and is not just associated with firewall load balancing.

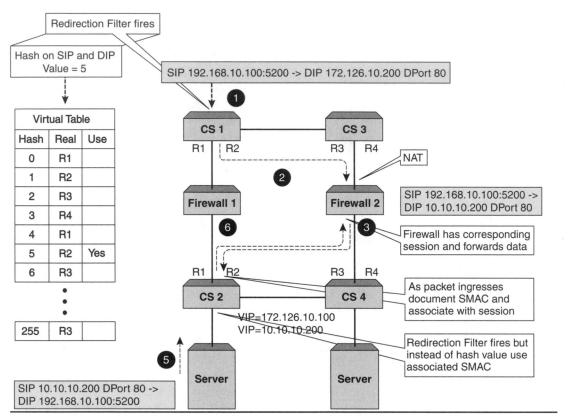

Figure 9–6   MAC address persistence shows how to overcome NATing firewalls for inbound and outbound traffic.

Policy-Based Firewall Load Balancing

Probably the most important reason why we load balance firewalls is to provide performance. While resilience is key as well, it is the performance increase that network administrators are looking for. One of the other benefits that can be achieved when deploying firewall load balancing is to make use of the intelligence within the content switch and provide a policy-based, load balanced solution. This is not a requirement for firewall load balancing, but one that is an added bonus. It should be pointed out that this feature is not common among all content switch manufacturers, so if this is something you require, ensure that the content switch you deploy can support this.

Policy-based firewall load balancing allows the network administrator the ability to create a set of rules that can be deployed on the content switches, ensuring that certain traffic types traverse certain firewalls. Figure 9–7 illustrates this.

This is done using redirection filters. By creating a redirection filter for HTTP, FTP, SMTP, and so forth, it can in turn be associated with different groups of firewalls. This gives a very granular level of control and allows firewalls to be configured for specific purposes. For example, all firewalls could be configured to allow inbound and outbound HTTP, but only a select few could be configured for FTP and SMTP. Whatever the requirement is, this feature can add a level of management and control of firewalls not anticipated. Organizations could allow a certain department to manage its own pair of firewalls and only allow traffic for that department's network to be load balanced through that pair of firewalls. Whatever the application, the ability to intelligently manage the session is key and it is this intelligence that makes up the fundamental architecture of content switches.

Topology Examples

Firewall load balancing brings with it its fair share of design and deployment models. For us to cover them would require a book in its own right, but we will

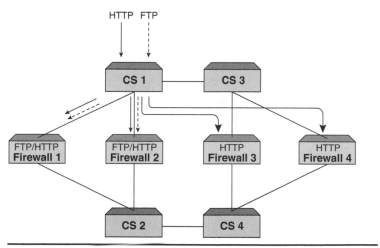

Figure 9–7   Policy-based firewall load balancing showing different firewalls handling different traffic types.

briefly describe some of the most common types, showing briefly the advantages and disadvantages of each

Multisubnet Implementations

Creating subnets between the content switches and the firewalls allows an easy-to-understand and easy-to-deploy configuration. This not only assists with troubleshooting, but also makes deploying further firewalls very simple. The reason for this is that each link between the content switch and the firewall is its own subnet. Static routes need to be configured on each content switch for each route, which will allow the health checks to function. Figure 9–8 shows a four-subnet design.

One key advantage of using subnets is that it can allow for comprehensive security. The reason for this is that the subnets do not have to be in public address space. The firewall is still totally accessible and it is the content switches that ensure that the traffic reaches the firewall. The only reason you would not have private address space is if the firewall needed to be managed over a public network or if NAT to a public address was required. If this is a requirement, then only the dirty side subnets need to be public; the clean side can remain in private address space.

One of the requirements for firewall load balancing is the need for subnets, and if these subnets need to be public, then the more firewalls that are added, the more valuable IP addresses are required to achieve this. To overcome this, some content switch manufacturers allow for a two-subnet firewall load balancing sandwich. This unique approach requires that multiple interfaces are configured on the content switches, but these interfaces need to be within the same subnet. Most Layer

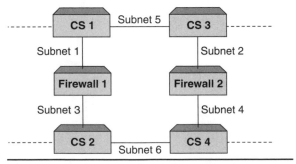

Figure 9–8   Four subnet firewall load balancing design.

3 devices will not allow this. Dependent on the content switch deployed, the ability to create an interface within a subnet is achieved by ensuring that all additional interfaces created use a /32 mask. This means that a switch could have the following interfaces as illustrated in Figure 9–9.

If a two-subnet design is required, you need to ensure that the content switch used can support this type of configuration.

Using Layer 2 Switches to Increase Flexibility

All of the diagrams shown in this chapter depict a pair of content switches on the clean and dirty side of the firewalls. The reason for this is that by deploying a pair and running VRRP, a truly resilient network can be achieved. If more than one firewall is required, then typically the organization deploying them is serious about resilience, and it makes sense to provide resilience in the content switches as well.

One of the reasons why we have not included Layer 2 switches in the design is because they are typically not needed. Providing these switches can increase site flexibility and provide good points for monitoring and troubleshooting. It must be remembered that when layer 2 switches are deployed, STP is often

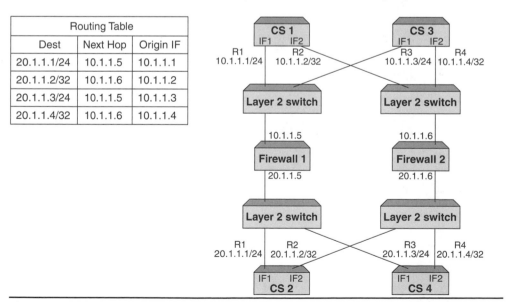

Routing Table		
Dest	Next Hop	Origin IF
20.1.1.1/24	10.1.1.5	10.1.1.1
20.1.1.2/32	10.1.1.6	10.1.1.2
20.1.1.3/24	10.1.1.5	10.1.1.3
20.1.1.4/32	10.1.1.6	10.1.1.4

Figure 9–9   Two subnet firewall load balancing design allows consolidation of IP address space.

configured. To increase the fail-over times, STP should not be active, and care should be taken to ensure that STP is not included in your design.

Using Layer 2 switches allows for a single content switch to fail and still allow for both firewalls to be active, or for a firewall to fail and have both content switches active. Moreover, if we had an uneven number of firewalls configured as per Figure 9–10 without Layer 2 switches, we can see that a failure of content switch could affect 66 percent of the site. Layer 2 switches would minimize this as illustrated.

As some content switches allow for multiple services to be configured simultaneously, Layer 2 switches allow for these additional appliances to be added with minimal impact to the content switches and maximum effect to the network. In addition, as content switch technology is more costly than Layer 2 devices, it is not always a requirement that servers, caches, SSL offload devices, and so forth need to be directly connected to the content switch. Deploying Layer 2 devices can decrease costs as well as increase resilience and functionality.

Layer 2 Firewalls

Load balancing Layer 2, or transparent bridge mode firewalls, are a challenge in their own right, but can be very effective in not only providing excellent performance but also increasing security. The reason they are more difficult to configure

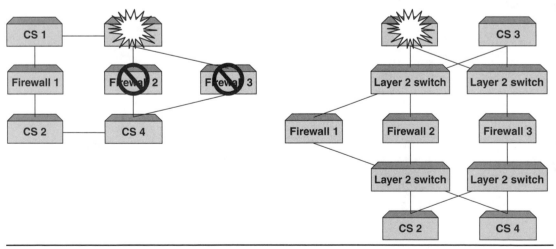

Figure 9–10   Uneven firewall availability in a content switch failure scenario with and without Layer 2 switches.

is that the static routes are to the opposite side content switch and not via the firewall, as the firewall is not part of the next hop as is the case with routing firewalls.

While the configuration may be more complex, Layer 2 firewalls also bring with them different deployment issues. The most common is the inability to perform NAT functions. This inadequacy is not a reason to not deploy them, just something to be aware of. NAT can be configured on another layer of firewalls or in the router, or content switch dependent on what is required. Layer 2 firewalls offer high performance and are often the firewall of choice when protecting time-sensitive applications such as streaming media or VoIP. However, with the advent of multigigabit firewalls with very low latency (often in the microsecond range), this requirement is not as critical. Much of the market for these firewalls is in areas where network redesign is an issue or where firewalls need to be as undetectable as possible.

Layering Firewalls for Greater Security

While load-balancing firewalls is a very common practice in today's society and is deemed an adequate level of protection, there are some occasions when the need to add addition layers of security is paramount. This is often found in financial or government installations, but is obviously not restricted to these organizations. What layering provides is a double layer, where if the outer firewalls are breached there is still adequate protection on the internal layer(s). We can see in Figure 9–11 how this is implemented.

This has different complications, but in our example, the second layer provides protection of the "crown jewels"—the database. This model is often implemented to allow developers and server administrator's access to the site, but still ensure that security of the main data vault is not breached. Some implementations may just be two layers of load balanced firewalls directly on top of each other, as is shown in Figure 9–12, while some will allow for server load balancing and other services such as SSL acceleration or WCR.

Often, the thinking behind a layered firewall approach is to use two different firewall manufactures for each layer so that if a security hole is exposed in one operating system, the whole site is not immediately vulnerable. This is an excellent method for protecting a site but is only for those with large budgets and an absolute desire for bulletproof security.

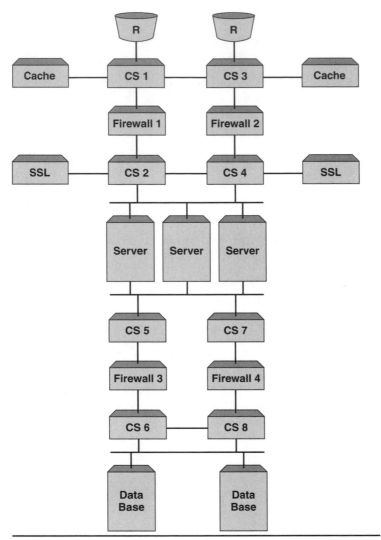

Figure 9–11   A layered firewall load balancing sandwich providing additional protection.

This kind of design also brings with it a more complex and difficult to troubleshoot environment. Care should be taken when designing or scoping this type of installation, and a comprehensive understanding of firewall load balancing is essential to the end user. In addition, understanding the constraints and flexibility of the proposed content switches is also key, as all content switches are not created equal when it comes to firewall load balancing.

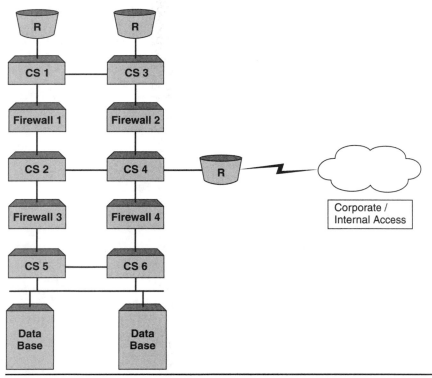

Figure 9–12   Two-tier firewall load balanced sandwich.

Using the Content Switch for Additional Protection

Content switches can offer additional protection to sites should this be desired. While most leading switches run Layer 4 processing in the ASIC, it makes sense to use the intelligence and speed of these devices to further increase packet inspection. By creating deny filters for all unwanted sessions based on TCP port, source or destination IP address, or whatever criteria is required, these switches can halt sessions destined for the internal network. This not only decreases the overhead that is placed on firewalls using traditional software that require CPU cycles to run, but also improves site performance as a whole. As security administrators need to be aware of all types of attacks and threats to their site, deploying filters in the content switches will not appear in the firewall logs. To overcome this, it is very easy to create a syslog server or some logging mechanism to catch all breaches of the configured filters or access control lists on the content switch in order to determine the types of attacks or threats that are occurring.

It should be pointed out that content switches, while excellent at providing security if required, are not firewalls. Their function is to intelligently manage sessions, but above all, their main function is to forward traffic as quickly as possible. Therefore, using a content switch is excellent for additional protection, but it should never be the only protection. Firewalls are the devices specifically designed for this.

Adding Demilitarized Zones (DMZs)

The need for secure zones or DMZs is normally dependent on business requirements or even security regulations within an organization. DMZs allow organizations to protect services and data from both internal and external access. The reason why this is so popular is that often information you want accessed by external users, while you want it protected, you do not want it in your internal network. This would be too big a security risk. DMZs offer the perfect solution for this and allow both internal and external protection.

While this works perfectly and solves security issues, it adds a bit more complexity to our firewall load balancing design. The more DMZs that are added, the more paths need to be created to ensure traffic flow. Achieving this can be quite involved and needs a clear head to ensure that the design functions.

The need to communicate between DMZs is often a requirement. To achieve this, the packet needs to traverse the firewall to ensure that the correct security policy is invoked. If you are using a tagged VLAN to provide differentiation between the subnets, it is important to ensure that the firewall selected can receive a packet on an interface and route it back out the same interface while still validating the security policy. This can be a limitation on some firewalls. This concept, using DMZs and tagging is shown in Figure 9–13.

As we discussed earlier in this chapter, creating the path is paramount in ensuring that firewall load balancing works, and while each vendor has their own method the bottom line is the same—a misconfigured path will break your solution.

Using the same method we used earlier for creating paths will add additional real servers (associated with IP interfaces) for every DMZ added. While this is fine, it can become very complex very quickly. This is not a reason to shy away from using multiple DMZs, but rather a reminder to ensure that there is a thorough understanding of the design. If we look at Figure 9–14 we can see that adding multiple

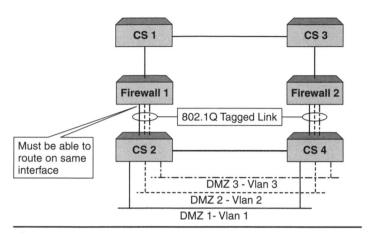

Figure 9–13   VLAN tagging and DMZs.

DMZs has increased the potential paths, and the need to create redirection filters forwarding traffic to the correct DMZ is paramount. Typically, in a straight through design, redirection filters used the "any any" policy. In other words, redirect all inbound traffic to the firewalls and let them do the routing. Likewise for traffic exiting the network. By now we are sure you have figured out that the redirection filter is not dependent on the end servers, but purely a mechanism by which to send traffic into a firewall with its SIP and DIP intact. So, by creating multiple DMZs, it would actually make no difference what the end point of the redirection filter is, but rather that the redirection filter forced the traffic to a firewall. The firewall will ensure that the traffic is routed to the correct destination. However, dependent on content switch used, health checks also rely on filters, so ensuring that all real servers are checked and available is a necessity for paths to

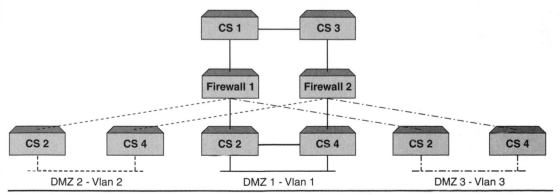

Figure 9–14   Multiple DMZs.

operate. Ensuring filters are created to "steer" traffic to the other content switches will ensure that the health checks are performed correctly and that the network is available for use.

DMZs do not have to be implemented using additional content switches, but this is often used to provide resilience. It is often simpler to design and deploy and makes troubleshooting that much easier. In addition, dependent on the firewall used, this can be an absolute necessity, as routing through the same interface is not always supported. Using multiple content switches will depend entirely on your configuration.

VPN and MAC Persistence

VPNs are at the forefront of any security deployment these days, and most organizations realize the benefit this technology brings. Not only does it allow remote, secure access into your organization over a public network, but also it drastically reduces costs of having to support leased lines or dedicated dial-up links. When providing business-to-business type transactions, a VPN allows for rapid deployment and ease of management. As VPNs gain in popularity and importance, so to does the need to scale the solution as well as provide resilience. This is particularly important when performing transactions and business-related functions. Just like firewalls, load-balancing VPNs is a perfect solution that provides performance and resilience, but it too brings certain challenges. To understand these, it is important that we see how VPN data and addressing differs from that of traditional data.

VPN in Action

A VPN is a connection between two devices that is often referred to as a *tunnel*. This tunnel allows encrypted data to be sent from any public network, and due to the encryption mechanisms used, ensures that the sensitive or important data is secure. There are proprietary methods as well as standards that dictate the method by which to encrypt and transmit data over a VPN. For the purpose of this section, we will assume that a VPN will encrypt your data and forward it to the correct destination. We will also assume that it will use a specific VPN address for the user and connect to the specified VPN termination point. Both the original SIP and DIP are encrypted within the VPN encapsulated packet.

Typically, a VPN will consist of a central VPN or termination point, which is typically the head office, and then remote sites or tele-workers connect to the VPN from many different locations over a public network, which is usually the Internet. This connectivity and encryption is detailed in Figure 9–15.

What VPNs allow us to do is set up a link that to the outside world looks like it is from a user to the VPN termination point. While this is exactly what the encapsulated packet looks like, the real destination address is encrypted within the data portion of the packet. It is the VPN termination point that first allows the session to be set up and then decrypts the data portion, strips off the encapsulation, and forwards the packet to the correct destination. Obviously, a VPN is a stateful device, as it will need to see the return packet, tie it to the incoming session, and perform encryption and encapsulation before routing the packet back to the source.

Load Balancing VPNs

Setting this up is identical to configuring firewall load balancing. We need to create paths for the traffic to flow through and for the stateful VPN devices to function correctly, and this is where the first problem arises. VPNs will not allow a path to be created through for unencrypted data. In other words, the dirty side switches cannot health check through to the clean side without breaking every rule in the security book. To allow a path for health checking, a nonsecure path for unencrypted traffic needs to be created. This goes against what we are trying to achieve with a VPN,

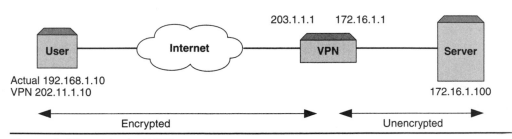

SIP	DIP	Encrypted Data	
		SIP	DIP
202.11.1.10	203.1.1.1	192.168.1.10	172.16.1.100

Figure 9–15   A typical VPN.

which is to allow encrypted traffic to a known termination point but hide our inside network. The only solution available is for the clean side content switch to perform its health check to the clean side interface of the VPN device, and the dirty side content switch to the dirty side VPN interface. This does not allow for automatic failover in the event of the clean side interface going down, for example. The dirty side will still be happily checking its interface and will be forwarding traffic to that interface, oblivious of the fact that there is no onward connection. This unfortunately is what will happen even without a content switch. It needs to be pointed out here that while a content switch does not offer the same form of resilience as it does with firewall load balancing, it provides other beneficial features such as increased throughput and the ability to perform policy-based VPNs. Now that we understand the limitations of VPN load balancing, we are faced with another problem.

The issue that we have is that when the packet ingresses the dirty side switches it will have a SIP of the user and a DIP of the VPN termination point, or what is often referred to as the *cluster IP address*. Using our redirection filters, we will select a real server (based on the SIP/DIP hash) to send the traffic toward and this will ensure that the VPN (configured in our path) receives the packet. So far, so good. The VPN device accepts the packet, decrypts it, and then forwards it to the correct device based on the actual IP address, which was encrypted in the data portion of the encapsulated frame. Again, no problems.

A large problem is looming on the return packet. It now has the original SIP as the DIP and the original DIP as the SIP. It ingresses the clean side switch and the redirection filter will select a real server based on SIP/DIP hash. As these are totally different from the initial ingress SIP and DIP, a new or different value will be calculated, thus potentially forwarding the packet through the incorrect VPN device. With no state information, the VPN will discard the packet and the session will time out. This process is detailed in Figure 9–16.

Fixing this is relatively easy, and as was discussed in other chapters, content switch manufacturers have realized that sometimes creating stateful flows with changing Layer 3 information is not feasible. Using trusty Layer 2 information can easily fix this. By recording the original flow's SMAC address on the clean side switch, this allows the return packets to be sent directly to that DMAC address, thus associating the session to the correct VPN device. This can be easily seen in Figure 9–17.

This method works perfectly, and by using content switches on both the clean and dirty side, sessions will flow through the correct device. Load balancing

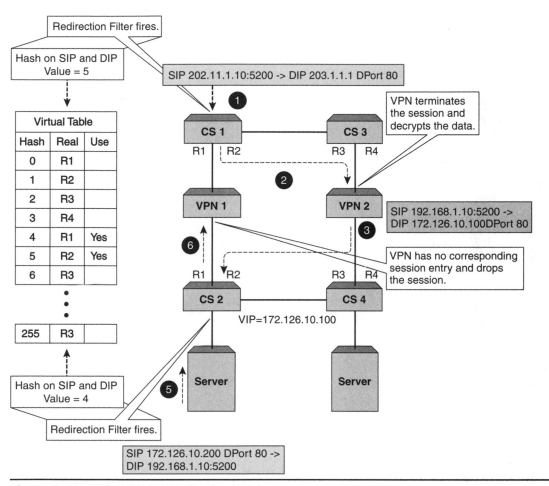

Figure 9–16   Why VPN load balancing breaks.

multiple VPNs is as easy as it is with firewalls if you remember that end-to-end health checks cannot be configured. Other than that, the same topology and design procedures and constraints apply, with the only difference being that VPNs need to handle encrypted packets.

Failure Scenarios

In nearly all of the designs we have produced and most of the installations we have done, the use of two dirty and two clean side content switches has been recommended. While this may make the salesperson happy, it will also make the network administrator happy. If you are going to the trouble of providing

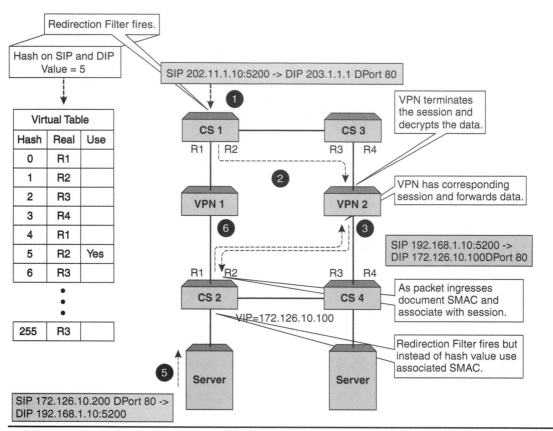

Figure 9–17   VPN and MAC address persistence.

two or more firewalls for resilience and performance, then it makes sense to ensure that there is no single point of failure in the design.

VRRP and Tracking

VRRP provides the most cost-effective and efficient mechanism in providing resilience on the content switches. What is required, however, is that any failure of any device should not bring the network down. VRRP allows for a failure of a device to not adversely impact performance. However, when using content switches, the need to ensure that the sessions flow through the same switch is important based on the fact that it is a session-aware switch. Therefore, while we build redundancy into our networks and a single link failure will not bring the network down, sometimes we can have an asymmetric flow of sessions. In a content switch, this is acceptable, but often the need to ensure that a switch will perform both ingress and egress forwarding is important.

Tracking allows this to happen. Tracking is a mechanism that actively changes the priorities of the VRRP instances. This allows all traffic for that VRRP instance to traverse a single switch. This ensures that troubleshooting, logging, and performance are increased, as link flapping or a random irregular connection does not cause the switches to continually swap priorities. If we look at Figure 9–18, we can see that a failure of a link will force the flow of traffic across the interswitch link. With tracking enabled, this failure would have caused all traffic for that VRRP instance to traverse a single switch.

Setting tracking is specific to each design, as there are different parameters that can be tracked, from Physical layer failures to Layer 4 failures. The only real way to test any installation is to actively test what occurs on a failure of each device, and then document and monitor the outcome. By doing this, the best method of tracking can be configured for that particular design.

Summary

Firewall load balancing is a very exciting part of content networking and one that allows network administrators to scale the firewall layer of the network. As technology evolves, firewalls are becoming an integral part of almost all organizations, as security is high on everyone's agenda. The traditional bottlenecks associated with firewalls are slowly being removed either by using firewall load balancing or as manufacturers produce ASIC-based high-speed firewalls. Regardless of how these firewalls evolve, we will most certainly still have a requirement to create a truly resilient, high-speed design that will require load balancing of some sort, be it external to the device or integrated within the

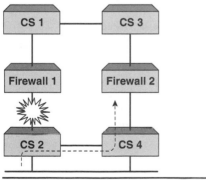

Figure 9–18   VRRP and tracking.

device itself. Understanding how to configure this as well as the traffic flow will certainly assist in designing and troubleshooting these networks in the future.

Case Study: Firewall and VPN Load Balancing

With network access increasing and the need to provide a truly global operation, Foocorp, Inc. has decided to increase security as well as access speeds by deploying firewall load balancing.

This will allow Foocorp the following advantages:

- Increase network and site performance
- Maximize capital expenditure by utilizing expensive redundant hardware
- Allow for policy-based firewall load balancing, ensuring that departments can contribute to the costs of deploying redundant security or not
- Increase resilience and availability for remote workers

Deploying Firewall and VPN Load Balancing

Firewall and VPN load balancing can be a complex configuration and often relies on planning of the deployment prior to installation. While complex, it is a logical operation and it is important that these following steps are covered:

1. Understand what type of firewall is being used (proxy, Layer 2, or Layer 3) as this helps with understanding the packet flow.
2. Find out if NAT is required on the firewall.
3. Based on available IP address subnets, decide which type of topology will be used.
4. Check network speeds and duplex types with the security administrator and ensure that you configure the firewalls and content switches accordingly.
5. Make sure the firewalls have routes to the internal networks.
6. Allow a policy on the firewall to allow the health checks through.
7. Ensure that the traffic flows through the correct firewall for both inbound and outbound sessions.
8. Test the setup by failing the content switches and firewalls, ensuring that connectivity is maintained.

We can see how this has been achieved by Foocorp in Figure 9–19.

By deploying firewall load balancing, Foocorp has been able to achieve the following:

- Increased network and site performance
- Dedicate certain firewalls for certain applications and departments
- Provide a scalable security solution
- Provide rapid fail-over in the event of a network failure

Firewall load balancing is a very cost-effective solution for maximizing all available firewalls regardless of manufacturer.

Foocorp has now deployed a comprehensive security network that allows for a very scalable, flexible, and resilient network. Any future additions or applications can be seamlessly accommodated.

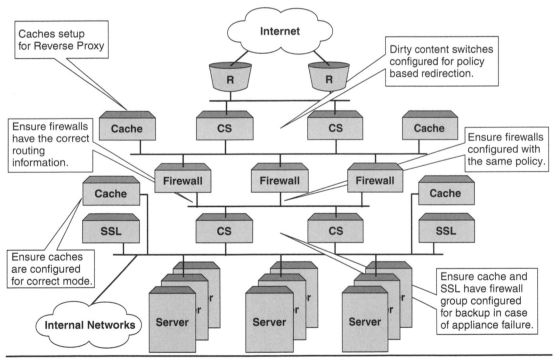

Figure 9–19   Foocorp, Inc. using WCR.

10

The Architecture of a Content Switch

Like any networking hardware deployed today, the underlying architecture of the device is often the differentiator when it comes to performance and functionality. Network administrators are determined to ensure that the devices installed are capable of delivering the functionality required today, and have the ability to provide new and enhanced features and functions planned for future release—in some cases, features not yet developed at the time of deployment. With network hardware having a typical life span of between three and five years, the requirement to ensure that the devices have some headroom for future application support is often a necessity.

It should be remembered that all content switches are not created equal, and while many have new and different features, it is important to understand how these will be implemented within your organization. With content switching making use of more information than traditional network devices, the traditional rules and criteria associated with device evaluation are no longer valid.

In this chapter, we will look at the difference between Layer 2 and Layer 3 switches and examine the additional requirements needed by a content switch in order for it to perform satisfactorily.

Typical Layer 2 and Layer 3 Architecture Considerations

When we look at the performance and functionality of Layer 2 switches, we immediately need to understand what the throughput is, how many MAC addresses are supported, is STP support included, is it nonblocking, and so forth. Anything less than wire speed throughput is typically deemed not acceptable in a Layer 2 device. Likewise, the lack of STP support or the inability to auto detect and negotiate link speed would be seen as insufficient.

In a Layer 3 environment, we see the basic Layer 2 functionality as a given and the ability to support multiple routing and routed protocols as an absolute must. With routing now being performed in the switching plane, the ability to forward infinitely more data has become a reality. While there will always be a place for the router, the days of collapsed backbones in the LAN environment are long gone. Layer 3 switching is seen as the norm, and as technology progresses, this too will become dated.

During the evolutionary process our requirements and acceptance of minimum functionality change with it. Just as it is currently the norm for most people to have a mobile phone, this was not the case 10 years ago. Mobile phones were seen as expensive luxury items that very few had or could afford. Today, Layer 2 and Layer 3 switches are the norm, and we expect nothing less from our network manufacturers. All switches need to have a comprehensive feature set that will typically run at very fast speeds. In addition, management of these devices must be simple and cost effective. With the maturity of the technology allowing for large-scale deployment, we are now able to move further up the OSI reference model without worrying whether the basics will function or be available.

Why Content Switching Is Different

Content switching is often referred to as Layer 4 through 7 switching. In short, that is exactly what it is. It has moved up the OSI reference model and is now associated with the Transport layer and above. These switches are sometimes called Layer 4 switches or even session switches.

Without doubt, content switches need to be able to perform the traditional functionality associated with Layer 2 and Layer 3 switches; without this, they would be seen as inadequate. However, we must not forget that these devices are not meant to perform Layer 2 and 3 tasks specifically, but rather look at higher layer information.

Content switching differs from traditional switching in many ways. It is important for network administrators to understand this when troubleshooting a problem, as this will allow them to easily locate the issue.

Packets vs. Sessions

Traditional networking devices typically make decisions based on frames in the case of Layer 2 devices, or packets in the case of Layer 3 devices. Layer 2 switches read the destination MAC address, look up the port associated with the destination address, and forward the packet as quickly as possible. A Layer 3 device needs to inspect a little further in to the packet and will need to see the destination network address, or IP address, in order for a forwarding decision to be made. Typically, no change to the addresses, or any other portion of the packet/frame, is made (obviously, cyclic redundancy checks and destination DMAC excluded). With both Layer 2 and Layer 3 devices, each individual packet is inspected and handled as a unique entity.

This is fundamentally different with content switches. While they obviously understand frames and packets and forward them as any Layer 2 and Layer 3 device would, they base decisions made on sessions. Each session is handled as a unique entity but is usually made up of many different frames/packets. By understanding sessions, content switches can then forward sessions to specific servers or manipulate each frame within a session. The session is the key to content switching, and this technology is often referred to as *session switching*. TCP sessions are discussed in detail in Chapter 3, *Understanding Application Layer Protocols*.

Breaking the Rules

One thing that needs to be understood up front is that content switching breaks traditional Layer 2 and Layer 3 rules—if this is all you remember, then that is a good start. By "breaking the rules," we mean that content switches actually have the ability to manipulate the packets on their way through the device. It is this functionality that allows content switches to be so versatile, and these benefits are discussed in much more detail in later chapters. Let's take a quick look at the basics.

In any content switch, the ability to perform the network address translation between the VIP we have attached to and the backend server address is key. This needs to be seamless and invisible to the user. This is normal in some devices (e.g., firewalls), but the content switch also needs to be able to change the TCP destination port to the required TCP port on the server. Moreover, the content switch also needs to be able to handle application redirection. This is when the switch receives a packet destined for a specific address and instead of forwarding it via the traditional route, it has to be able to redirect the a packet to another device by only changing the destination MAC address.

While all of this seems fairly simple, it is important that we understand that this is often happening at high speed, and the content switch is making intelligent decisions not just for a single service but for many different services and applications. While this may sound straightforward now, it will be of paramount importance when troubleshooting and testing a content switching design that needs to interact with other traditional Layer 2 and Layer 3 devices.

What Makes a Good Content Switch?

As stated earlier, not all content switches are created equal. In this section, we will try to determine the architectural features and functionality that differentiate one switch from another. Most content switch manufacturers are able to provide basic functionality, but we will see that session handling and content inspection depth are key areas. We would like to point out here that each content switch has its merits, and while each can handle content switching in general, it is up to the individual to ensure that the content switch selected has the architecture, performance, and functionality to provide the required services for a particular network design.

Session Setup vs. Simultaneous Sessions

Now that we understand the importance of sessions within content switches and how they handle and manipulate them, we can now see why session setup is more important than sessions supported.

Most traffic sent across content switches is HTTP. This is because content switching was traditionally focused in the dotcom world and was usually used to load balance Web sites. While this is still the case, the versatility of content switches has ensured that they are used in many other applications as well. HTPP, although sent across a connection-oriented protocol such as TCP, is almost a connectionless protocol. Each object retrieved for a Web page or similar is seen as a TCP session. Therefore, the switch needs to set up the session, serve the object, and tear down the session again. With many Web pages having 80 plus objects per page, you can see that many sessions will need to be set up and torn down by the switch. With HHTP 1.1 this is not as common. However, with that kind of requirement, a content switch needs to be able to handle busy networks and content sites.

Having a low session setup rate can impact the performance of a network and severely delay user response times. Some content switch manufacturers promote simultaneous session support as the key area in order to mask their inefficiencies in the session setup arena.

Let's look at an example. In Table 10–1, we can see that while content switch manufacturer A only supports 500,000 simultaneous sessions, it can set up and tear down 300,000 per second. Content switch manufacturer B can support 2,000,000 simultaneous sessions but can only set up 10,000 per second.

Table 10–1   Session per Second vs. Simultaneous Sessions

	MANUFACTURER A	MANUFACTURER B
Maximum simultaneous sessions supported	500,000	2,000,000
Maximum sessions setups per second	300,000	10,000
Time taken to set up 300,000 sessions	1 second	30 seconds

As can be seen, the ability to set up and tear down sessions is far more important than maximum simultaneous sessions. While we are not saying that a small amount of simultaneous sessions is satisfactory, it is important to consider the application being used and the delay incurred by slow session setup. In a typical browser environment, a user will open four TCP sessions to retrieve content. As can be deduced, the low-end or slower content switches will require a larger session capacity in order to let the users complete their request before moving on to the next user. Delay can be a huge issue in any server farm environment, and this delay comes to the forefront when we begin to actually inspect the content within the data.

Layer 4–7 Handling

Content switches can typically function extremely well when using Layer 4 information to make load balancing decisions. The reason for this is that the Layer 4 information is at a known point within the data packet and will never change. The source IP address, destination IP address, and source and destination TCP ports will allow x bits from the front of the Ethernet packet because they are resident in the IP and TCP headers and will never move—just the values will be different. It is therefore easy to develop ASICs to inspect those headers by counting x bits and scanning 4 bytes, in the case of an IP address. Once the necessary information is found, the switch can then make a load balancing decision. This is why Layer 4 switching is becoming readily available, as this functionality can be done in hardware because the data that is required is constant.

This changes, however, as we look at different applications and as we move up in to the upper layers of the OSI reference model. What happens when data manipulation is required in the case of streaming media or FTP load balancing? Often, addresses embedded within the data portion of the frame need to be manipulated (typically to the VIP of the site) for load balancing to take place. This type of functionality requires both brains and brawn. It is here that content switches begin to differ.

The minute we cannot predict the information required, or need to delay the session to see what application or content is being requested, is when the content switch needs to stand up and be counted. It is the content switch that has to manage these sessions; it is the content switch that needs to scan the packet looking for the character, or sequence of characters configured. These tasks will traditionally put a huge overhead on any device. Again, these tasks and requests are session driven, so now it becomes imperative that a content switch set these sessions up quickly, scan or manipulate the required information, and then send it on to the selected backend server. Session setup again takes precedence over maximum sessions supported, as the need to get the information from the user, send it to the server, and then forward the response is key to the whole user experience. A slow network will not have many users, and if it does, it is unlikely that they are enjoying the experience.

Different Approaches

When building a content switch there are typically two approaches: design one from the ground up, or use existing PC and network processors on which to base the platform. Let's look at the earlier methods of content switch design, before network processors came to the forefront.

Some of the early content switches were basically PCs with some form of operating system, usually an open source operating system (OS), and had multiple NICs installed. These devices would manipulate data in the application running on top of the OS, and many manufacturers had initial success with this approach because load balancing requirements were typically at Layer 4 only, high-speed links were rare, and content switching was still in its infancy.

As content switching became more important and more widely spread, PC-based architectures were often left wanting when processor-intensive tasks and application support were required.

Other manufacturers built their content switches from the ground up using purpose built ASICs and proprietary operating systems. This is obviously a much more expensive (and in the early days could be conceived as a more risky) approach, but one that if it worked allowed for large differentiation. Some manufacturers tried this and failed, and others succeeded and forged the way in content switching. Let's now look at PC-based, or central CPU-based, content switches versus ASIC-based content switches.

PC Architectures

Using a central processor to run intensive tasks brings with it the primary limitation of not having the ability to scale as we add multiple services and tasks to the device. Most content switches today have the ability to perform the following tasks:

- Server load balancing of any TCP or UDP port
- Global server load balancing
- Firewall load balancing
- Web cache redirection
- Application redirection
- SSL offload

- VPN load balancing
- WAN link load balancing
- Streaming media load balancing and cache redirection
- Intrusion Detection System (IDS) load balancing
- Layer 7 load balancing
- Wireless application load balancing for mobile services

While this list is not exhaustive, we can see that many applications can be configured within the content networking arena. The major issue with all central CPU-based designs is that the more applications that are enabled on a content switch, the more overhead is placed on that single, central CPU. Moreover, we should also remember that content switches are session-based switches; in other words, they are interested in sessions, not each and every packet. They need to maintain session information and group hundreds of packets as a single session. This may not make a difference in low usage sites, but will be an issue in large, heavily accessed sites. Let's also not forget that as we start to look at Layer 7 information, which has no fixed start and end point, the overhead placed on a single CPU is immense.

Another design issue often overlooked is the throughput of the bus between the ingress and egress ports and the CPU. With many-gigabit ports all receiving traffic, it is imperative that the CPU can service these requests as quickly as possible. Having a bus that can service a PCI-based CPU is okay in a computer, but with gigabit ports the bus (and CPU) need to be able to handle the aggregate throughput of the switches ports. The inability to do this limits the performance of PC-based designs.

To overcome this, PC- or central CPU-based designs try to offload as much processing of Layer 2 and Layer 3 to the hardware on the ports themselves. This can relieve the CPU from having to perform all tasks, although the initial decisions still need to be handled by the central CPU. This then allows the CPU to perform the Layer 4 through 7 tasks, which as we have discussed are far more processor intensive. Regardless of how the tasks are distributed, the content switch is only as fast as the CPU. The more sessions it needs to manage or the more applications that are configured, the more processing it requires, and it will obviously reach a saturation point. It is here that distributed architectures add value to the content switching arena. We should point out that with the increase in processing power and the ability to run multiple CPUs in a single device, the bottleneck is shifting. However, running this type of PC-based architecture still has potential for performance degradation. Most manufacturers are moving away from PC-based architectures, but this can be and often is a long and hard road to travel.

ASIC-Based Architectures

ASICs have traditionally been associated with high-speed performance, and that is typically what content switch manufacturers have managed to achieve when using this technology. By designing ASICs to perform the traditional Layer 2 and 3 functionality and the layer 4 functions leaving the intense Layer 7 applications to use software. By only having to use software for Layer 7 based functions, performance, session setup, and so forth can be maintained as additional users or applications are activated.

Obviously, by using ASICs, the need to ensure that the code is correct is crucial, and the need to be able to make changes to allow for new features is a necessity. What typically happens is that the majority of Layer 4 functions are programmed into the ASIC, and as new features are added or designed, the ASIC is either rewritten (if using programmable ASICs) or these features are offloaded or handled by software running on the content switch. This method enables the switch to cater to and grow with new features. Then, as most ASICs are respun every two years or so, these well-known and used Layer 4 and even Layer 7 functions and features can be programmed into the new ASIC.

This method is obviously more costly and can be fraught with difficulties if the ASIC is not well designed. Without a doubt, some startup companies using ASIC-based technologies have not managed to complete their projects because of unforeseen errors and design problems, and have subsequently been forced to shut their doors. Others have made it, but too late, and have not been able to capitalize on the market momentum and have also had to close. Others were first to market, had excellent ASIC design, and are market leaders.

Like all things in technology, changing designs and concepts will mean that manufacturers will shift from one technology to the next. Those manufacturers who embrace the next wave of hardware will be able to change with the times, offering top quality services and features regardless of hardware.

Where To Next?

With the advance in technology, network processors (NPs) have begun to be a very cost-effective option for many content switch manufacturers, and we are seeing the deployment of this technology in many content switches today. Some manufacturers have used these since the outset and have benefited from the cost effectiveness as well as the performance.

The reason for this is that NPs are much cheaper than ASIC-based technology, and are easier to work with because they are off-the-shelf hardware that can be easily programmed. In addition, as processor technology improves, NPs can be easily ported to new platforms. Moreover, performance is not such a huge issue as it was in the pioneering days of content switching due to huge leaps in processor design.

By using NPs, we will start to see the playing field begin to level, and it is then that features and functions will become the differentiator when comparing switch to switch. Although NPs might make life easier for the manufacturer, it is still a long, hard road to getting NPs to work. However, when they do, the ease with which manufacturers can change design and create different form factors for their switches will enable them to extend and grow their market share.

Associated Hardware

As content switching has exploded and organizations have begun to deploy applications to increase and streamline their business, the emergence of dedicated appliances to assist with some of the heavy processing has become popular. The reason why these appliances are gaining popularity is that they are designed specifically to deal with a certain application, thereby increasing the performance and manageability. This allows network administrators to deploy content switching as the central point or hub of the network, and hang these dedicated appliances off as "spokes" to increase application and network performance.

The first and probably most used appliance is the Web cache. This increases network performance by storing heavily accessed data local to the user. By using the content switch to redirect all cacheable content to the cache, the network and content can be optimized.

Offloading heavy processing tasks such as SSL from processor bound servers onto dedicated appliances such as an SSL offload appliance ensures that servers are free to perform the tasks for which they are designed.

Most manufacturers provide these appliances as part of their content switching portfolio, but in truth, any SSL offload appliance or cache will typically work with any manufacturer's content switch. There are many benefits to providing dedicated appliances for specific applications, foremost being the ability to totally dedicate all resources and processing power to increasing the speed of the associated application. Dependent on your requirements and network usage, this approach might be better for you and your organization.

Other manufacturers offer an all-in-one solution where they include all these applications within a single box. Obviously, this is easy to manage and also allows customers to turn on and off the applications they require without purchasing or installing new equipment. The downside to this is that scalability will be decreased and, if using a central CPU, performance will undoubtedly decrease as you begin to activate more applications. In addition, a failure of the SSL module, for example, could also impact the content switching and caching services as well.

Whatever your requirements, it is always important to plan and understand not only your initial network requirements, but also your expected future growth. Based on these investigations, only then can you truly make a decision on which type of content switch and associated hardware you require.

Summary

We are sure that as content switching continues to gain in popularity, it will become that commodity item that many believe it will be in the future. What we tried to present here is a high-level generic overview of content switches today and how they differ. Deploying content switching in your organization is an important part of your network design, and it is key that you understand what each content manufacturer brings to the table. As we have seen, not all switches are created equal from a hardware and performance perspective, and we need to separate the software features from the hardware when making a decision. Whatever your decision may be, there is a content switch that will meet your requirements.

Index